W0016780

Janet
I hope you enjoy
Those stories!

RON'S RAMBLINGS

Characters, Critters and Us Cantankerous Rednecks

Ron Garwood

Ron's Ramblings

Characters, Critters and Us Cantankerous Rednecks

©2020 Ron Garwood

print ISBN: 978-1-09833-564-9
ebook ISBN: 978-1-09833-565-6

RON'S RAMBLINGS

Characters, Critters and Us Cantankerous Rednecks

A local Montana history story
(or some stories of local history as told by)

Ronald Garwood

This picture, which I used for the cover of my book since it is one of my favorite views, shows my irrigation pump on the Missouri River, looking upstream toward Pickthorn and Nelson dredges, with the south bench in silhouette behind. I am not sure what year I took this picture anymore, but it has always been one of my favorites.

CONTENTS

INTRODUCTION

(and so it begins)

"any winter day that the sun shines and the wind doesn't blow,
is a nice winter day!"
-Marion Garwood

I live in Valley County, Montana which lies between the Canadian border on its north and the Missouri River on its south, approximately 120 miles west of the North Dakota border, just to give my readers some idea of the location of the place that I call home. This is not the Montana of the mountains and glaciers and rushing white capped rivers, but the Other Montana, the Montana of the prairies and gentle rolling hills and lazy rivers. Valley County is divided by one of those lazy rivers, the Milk River, and it winds its way across the county, from west to east. Valley County is just over five thousand square miles in area, which makes it approximately four times the size of the state of Rhode Island and approximately the same size as the state of Connecticut. When it comes to population, most places have us beat.

Valley County is north of the Missouri River and McCone County lies south of the Missouri river, and even though I do not live in McCone County, from my house I can see the McCone County Blue Hills across the Missouri River. I lease pasture for my cows from the state of Montana that borders the Missouri River. The eastern fence line of this school section pasture goes to the river and from this location, McCone County is only ninety yards to the south.

There are numerous individuals, characters, rednecks, culprits and cowboys that have made an impact, one way or another to the history of this river area. Some are still living on their farms and ranches at this time, and some are not! Are we going to live the rest of our lives without knowing about some of their stories? I would like to share some of those stories with you!

I love history and I profess that I know but a little bit of our history here. These are tales of some of the characters of the area and their stories; sometimes cute and laughable stories, sometimes more serious stories. Some of these people in these stories are about characters that I have known and will be remembered by me for many years. A few of these stories are about people I have never met but they live on in stories that have been told about them from reputable people that I know. This story is also about some of the pioneers and their ancestors that continue to eke out a life here in this beautiful, but sometimes unforgivable Montana countryside and the people who have called it their own for a time. Their stories should not be forgotten, and I will try to the best of my knowledge to share these stories by putting them in print.

Many of these folks are still living here on their land and some of them have gone on to a better and more heavenly place. At least, I hope they have! We should remember and honor them for what they have done to make this Missouri River Valley and Montana a better place. I feel most of these people are all interesting characters, but I'll let you be the judge for yourself! I feel that they are all fine people and they have made a difference to the area. The people that I consider to be poor Samaritans won't be mentioned here.

I hope you enjoy these stories of life on the Missouri River, also known to locals as the Big Muddy! The Missouri River was once hoped to be part of the fabled Northwest Passage, which was hoped to be an all water route from the Atlantic Ocean to the Pacific Ocean, but the Northwest Passage turned out to be a dream and not a reality. However, the river was still incredibly important and did turn out to be a major travel way to the interior of the Northern Great Plains. To get to the interior, you could walk, ride horses and travel by wagon, but it was slow and there was no road system. The fastest and easiest way to travel was first by canoes and pole boats, and then later by steamboat travel. This was the easiest way to access the interior until the building of the railroads and finally the highway system. I hope you enjoy these following stories, some of which may have been stretched a little! I hope you enjoy reading the history about some of our interesting rednecks and characters!

I started writing this collection of stories in the winter of 2010-11, but I did not get very far into my stories. The next winter, 2011-12, a winter that was much milder in weather than the previous year, was when I was able to put the majority of my thoughts into words. Additional stories and extra thoughts have been added on during 2012 (and 2013), and even now, several years later. Forgive me in my writing, if it seems that I have jumped from year to year, as I probably have indeed done just that. Forgive if my stories seem to overlap or repeat on some points; this is one of the reasons I call these "my ramblings". Ha!

As I look outside my window, I remember what my Grandfather Garwood said about it being a nice winter day. He said that any winter day that the sun shines and the wind does not blow, it is a nice winter day! On this day in 2011, even though it is -15F degrees below zero here on February 2nd , it isn't too bad outside because the sun is shining and it is calm. Apparently, the groundhog in Pennsylvania did not see his shadow today so they say that spring should not be any more than six weeks away. However, we can see the sun and therefore our shadow, so I am afraid it could be a little longer till we see bare ground. Any way those of us that live in Northeastern Montana are ready for spring. With all the rain we had last summer, we put up more hay than on a normal year. It turns out that is a good thing because this has been a long and cold winter, and we are feeding more hay than in a normal winter. Many people say to me that we live in paradise!! Well so far in the winter of 2010-2011, we have set a new winter snowfall record of 108 inches of snow, and even with that extreme weather, it still feels like paradise to me.

A Little Introduction to Myself

I was born on a cold night-or so my mother told me-on December 4, 1945 in Glasgow, Montana. My parents were Edgar and Theona (Toni)Moum Garwood, who named me Ronald Allen. Eventually, two sisters joined our family, Karen Arlene Stearns, who is two years younger than myself, and Diane Colleen Forbes came along a dozen years after I was born. I graduated in 1964 from Nashua High School. In the fall of 1964, I enrolled in Montana State College at Bozeman Montana. I attended two quarters in the first year and came home for spring quarter to help with the farming. In 1965, I again attended two quarters at MSC and spring quarter in Havre, taking welding, weed identification and basic mechanics courses. I wanted to be closer to home to help with calving and seeding wheat. I enlisted into the Montana National Guard in the spring of 1966. I decided that I was tired of schooling and decided that farming didn't sound so bad, so I said to heck with college. I did take agriculture courses when I did attend Bozeman, so I did learn about farming while in college but I was ready to return to the farm that I loved so much.

I was helping Dad and Grandpa farm our irrigated and dryland farm where my grandparents had homesteaded in the early 20's combined with land he and Grandma had purchased. To their original homestead, they had added five times their original acreage from Ira Evans and Grace Schick. At that time, they were running a 12 to a 15 cow dairy which they eventually sold in 1936. My grandparents sold the dairy business but not the farm. It was "the dirty thirties" and it was hard to make a living as a farmer so they took their son Edgar back east to Ohio, near Dayton, where my grandfather had been raised, and they purchased a small farm. They also had some fear of the Fort Peck dam failing as their farm was several miles below Fort Peck Dam, and at that time there was a lot of uncertainty to the integrity of the great earthen structure. My father and Grandma returned to Montana from Ohio in the early 1940s to put the crop in as it had started raining some, and they thought it was worth trying to make a go in Montana again. At this time Grandpa had a good job in Dayton so he stayed in Ohio. Grandma and Dad would return to Lewisburg during the wintertime. My father married Theona Moum in early 1945 but he was inducted into the army and grandpa Marion had to come back to Montana and run the farm. After Dad was released from the service, he bought the Sandy place in about 1957, Mattingly place 1962 the Musgrove place in 1964. Dad sold the Sandy place, now the Glenn and Steffanie Meier farm, and traded for the Merrick/Pointer place in 1978. I helped Dad clear about 40 acres of cottonwood trees and brush on the Musgrove place and we also dozed down cross irrigation ditches as Dad felt we had enough irrigated land to take care of on the home place.

In the summer of 1969, I started farming the Crow Place which was owned by Leo, Lyman and Bill Pattison for a two-thirds crop share and the Pattison family retained one third of the crop. There was about 160 acres of irrigated land on the Pattison place, so it kept me busy farming this property and helping Dad farm his land. I worked for him for the use of some of his equipment. I flood irrigated this land from the Missouri River using the 600 International tractor of Dads, running a pump with a long flat belt. I used this irrigation set up for a couple of years until we got electricity at the pump site and then I used an electric motor which was more efficient.

Also, in 1969, I met and married Patricia Ann Wesen, who changed my life with her faith in God! We were eventually blessed with three beautiful children, Stacy, Seth and Shawn, who all live in the area near us! Patty and I were married on September 13, 1969 and we bought a small house trailer and moved it on to the Mattingly place to start our life here in this beautiful river bottom. Soon after we were married, we bought land near Tiger Butte, the Walt Pederbecki place, which consisted of some outbuildings and grazing property, that we purchased from John Jakanoski. Dad continued to farm the place where our trailer was located until we bought this Mattingly farm from him with money made when we sold the Tiger Butte/Pederbecki place. We sold that property, which we had owned for six years and run our cattle on, to Ross Dorr. We built a new house in 1978 on the Mattingly property and immediately went into debt, and still are!

I was burned in a propane fire, which damaged my hands and face, in the fall of 1979. I spent 45 days in the Deaconess Hospital in Glasgow recovering from some third degree burns. I am so lucky that we had Blue Cross/Blue Shield insurance that covered most of my expenses. The burns scarred me but didn't stop me from being a husband, father and a farmer! The use of my left hand has limited me in doing some things such as typing but I get by with the use of a couple of fingers and my thumbs. I thank God that I survived this event to live a full life!

Patty and I have raised three children in this house and Patty still reminds me of the snow storm that was going on when we moved from our old trailer to our new house. I have always been inpatient when I want to get something done and I guess I didn't want to wait for spring! Ha! Stacy, Seth and Shawn still work and live in Valley County. When we sold the Tiger Butte property, we had to sell about 30 head of cows as this property was used for grazing for them during the summer. We have gone from 55 head of cows that I artificially bred for several years down to about 25 head, and now to 15. There are also two horses who are owned by my daughter Stacy taking up my best corral and barn space. I still farm full time and I have also leased the Ohlson farm for 23 years until the spring of the year 2020! I am also currently farming my fathers irrigated farm with the help of Seth.

Patty and I have made a great life on this Missouri River bottomland seven miles south of Nashua, Montana. Patty's parents were Clayton and Pearl (Zamotsny) Wesen, and when I married her, I married into a great family. Patty and I have three children and all are still living in Valley County. Stacy Dawn is our eldest and is a registered nurse at Francis Mahon Deaconess Hospital in Glasgow, the same place all our children were born and where I spent my ICU time after the fire. She has Bachelor Degrees in history and nursing. Seth Allen is our second child and he attended college at MSU Northern in Havre, worked for Town and Country furniture in Glasgow for years but has now joined me working on the farm. Shawn Michael us our youngest son, is a delight to everyone who knows him. He works at Milk River Activity Center and lives in an apartment at Transitional Living Complex in Glasgow.

Besides running the farm, Patty and I have had a US Postal rural contract for forty years total, in which Patty drove most of the time as I was busy farming, calving out my cows and feeding the cows hay. She thought it would be better to drive the route and I could be on call to come get her if she had trouble, or at least that's how I remember it. Our route came within two miles of our house so she could stop at the house to get another vehicle if she needed to. After forty years, we decided not to bid the route for another four years to deliver the mail south of Nashua. We do miss the mail patrons on the route that we have gotten to be friends with though, but we don't miss having to carry the mail through some of the terrible weather that eastern Montana can throw at us.

In the winter of 2010-2011 we had 108 inches of snow to deal with and a lot of wind which would get so bad that she couldn't see the roads. At times she would have to stop for a while or turn around and retrace her tracks. I think she only got stuck one time when she didn't make the turn and I pulled her out with my four wheeled drive tractor. One day it stormed so bad she couldn't make it the eight miles to the post office because until the county and state roads were snow plowed out, we were homebound. Her route was sixty miles long and she drove it six days a week. In past years when she would get stuck the patrons would watch out for her and get her out so she could finish delivering the mail. One time she got stuck and I couldn't get her out with my four wheel drive pickup so we finished the route together in my pickup. The next day we drove to her car in my tractor to get it out and had been pulled back up on the road. What a mystery! We found out that Russ Gilbertson had pulled it out when he was driving by to feed his cows. She has enjoyed not driving the route but she misses her patrons, great people like Russ, and many others, who will help you out in times of need.

We are both of retirement age but we are both very active workers and basically we both have good health. Patty has been a tireless worker since we got married. Besides driving the mail route for forty years in some extremely bad Montana winters, she has been a beautician, a storekeeper, and she is still bartending part time at Vicks Bar in Nashua. I am so lucky to have a great wife and our children that live close by.

I am currently farming with the help of Seth and I enjoy farming very much and one of my goals is to get out of debt, although I may have to sell the cows or some property to make that happen! This was one of my fathers' goals too and he did get out of debt with help from all of us in the Garwood family helping him. My father passed away quietly in his house south of Nashua in the fall of 2016. We miss him very much as he was a great father, respected by many people and a great role model for all of us that knew him. He is with my Mother in heaven as she passed away in their house in 2007. They were great role models for all of us that knew him. The farm and house has been a great gathering spot for friends and family over the years and we hope it always will be. There is a great view from that front porch!

Besides being a farmer and rancher, I always seem to stay busy. I am very active in the community and I have been on many community boards and chairing many of them. In the past some of these organizations were: Nashua Jaycees, Valley Resource Council, Nashua Lutheran Council Board, Nashua School Board-five years as chairman, Community Development VP with the Montana Jaycees, District Director-United States Jaycees, and Lower Missouri River Council VP. I am currently on The Valley County Conservation Board as a supervisor and past chairman, director on The Missouri River Council of The Conservation Districts, CMR NWS Community Working Group and I am currently on the Valley County Tax

Appeal Board. I guess I am a meeting person who feels that we need to be active in our local affairs even though it is hard to be a full time farmer and be active in so many boards and councils, I still try to go to as many meetings as I feel that I have time for.

I am an extremely active rifle and bow hunter. I really enjoy gopher, elk and whitetail deer hunting. I also do some fishing and trapping, but my farming and cattle interests take most of my time. I really enjoy archery elk hunting in the Missouri Breaks but our whitetail numbers are down from EHD disease from the last two years, so I might not be hunting much this fall. I had tried for over 25 years to get an either sex elk rifle permit without success so I started applying for the either sex archery elk permit in which I can hunt bull elk with a bow for about four out of five years. I have been extremely lucky to have drawn a Montana bighorn sheep permit in 1972 and a Shiras moose permit in 1991. I was able to fill both of those tags with a ram and a bull. I really enjoy my hunting here in Montana. I was able to take my first Merriams tom turkey in the spring of 2012. I have been hunting big game in Montana since 1957 and I have been bow hunting since 1966. I really enjoy hunting and I probably will hunt here on my farm until I am unable to.

As mentioned, I have been on many local civic boards over the years and I am currently a supervisor for the Valley County Conservation District Board and have been on this board since 2001. I am still a full time farmer, but I admit, that I am slowing down and I am not getting nearly as much done in a year as I used too!!! I love hunting, but am not as active as when I was younger and had more drive! A couple years ago I became a FWP's Citizen Advisory Council (CAC) member for region six, to add to the many organizations I have belonged to. I guess I am just a hopeless meeting goer, but I feel I am doing a lot of good for my community, and my family!

I really love hearing about the local history, visiting with people and I would like to keep some of these local history stories alive. Therefore, I wrote this book of stories along with some help from other writers! I thank

James Kurz , who I met along the Missouri river; I told him he should write a book, and he later asked me to write a chapter of the history of the area which he put into the very book that I encouraged him to write, which is called *We Were on The Missouri 2005*. I also thank Stacy, who is the editor of this book of stories, without her help this book wouldn't be happening!

I would like to thank all of the people that have helped me with these great stories of characters, pioneers, cowboys and rednecks who lived in this area in the early years. I have enjoyed interviewing these Montanans and I loved hearing their stories from the past. Thanks to everyone who helped share photographs and their wonder full stories with me for this collection. I apologize that in the editing process that there might not be space in this book for every story but I might have enough material for another book, so who knows what the future has in store? As my grandfather always said when he thanked someone, "much obliged". I would also like to say thanks to all the characters in this story that I never have met in person but just heard tales about, and I hope they don't mind I am sharing their stories. Thanks to you all!!!!

I hope that everyone who reads this collection of stories about our family, friends, neighbors and acquaintances, enjoy them as much as I have enjoyed keeping them alive for everyone to read. Along with my own stories, I have asked a few people to share a few of their own stories, related to family history or colorful characters. I am thankful to my friends for sharing.

Sincerely
Ron Garwood

Patty and I at our wedding in 1969, taken at the First Lutheran Church in Glasgow.

My family celebrating my Dad's 90th birthday. Seth, myself, and Patty in the back,
Shawn, Dad and Stacy in the front.

THE MISSOURI
AND THE MILK

(where the two rivers meet)

"the water of this river posseses a piculiar whiteness, being about the colour of tea with the admixture of a tablespoonful of milk"
– Lewis and Clark Journals, May 8, 1805

"I wonder what this country looked like when a hundred thousand buffalo crossed the Missouri River?"
-Jack Nickels

The Missouri River

The Missouri River is the longest river in the lower forty-eight states. It is a tremendous flow of water that is comprised of hundreds of creeks, streams, and rivers. These waterways are started by springs in mountains and high areas of the plains and fed by winter snowpack run-off. These flow mostly in an eastward direction, to join the Mississippi River, which then flows southerly to empty into the Gulf of Mexico.

The Missouri is formed by the Madison, Jefferson and Gallatin Rivers in Western Montana near Three Forks. The confluence of the river was discovered by the Lewis and Clark Expedition when they explored the Missouri River traveling northwest-ward, starting near St. Louis. The expedition named these three rivers that form the Missouri River after then President Thomas Jefferson, Secretary of State James Madison and Treasury Secretary Albert Gallatin. They were sent on an expedition by President Thomas Jefferson to hopefully find an all water route to the Pacific Ocean. This did not pan out as they encountered the Rocky Mountains, which was, and still is, a formidable barrier to the Pacific Ocean. They followed the Missouri River system as far as they could, before finally determining it was not the "North West Passage" that they were hoping for. Continuing to move westward, they crossed overland through the mountains with horses they obtained from the Nez Perce Indians until they came to the Columbia River system which they then followed to the Pacific Ocean.

I am lucky that I live on a farm where my house is a mile from the Missouri river. I am so fortunate to have been raised nearby here on my parents' farm, where my grandparents started farming in this countryside with a 40 acre homestead. My grandparents proved up on the land to get a Homestead Patent. They received their Homestead Patent, which was signed by Calvin Coolidge, in 1926. This original family homestead is one and a half miles from my house.

Even though at this time I do not own one acre of land that touches the Missouri river, I maintain one pump site for irrigating my crops of alfalfa, wheat, barley, peas and lentils, which I rotate on my farm. My property is about a quarter of a mile from the Missouri at three locations, but as it does not touch the Missouri, I have an easement for a ditch and pump site to irrigate my property. I lease eighty acres of state land for grazing and use some grazing from my sister Diane, and her husband Scott Forbes, for trade for his use of some of my equipment. I maintain three fences that extend into the river which the high water and winter ice is hard on. Farming and ranching is a great lifestyle, but some years it is a struggle to make ends meet. We have had good years and bad years, and even though the bad seem to outnumber the good, we persevere. Some years I have a tendency to make it rough on myself by over-spending on the budget.

But looking out my front window and seeing the cottonwood bottomlands and Tower Hill, makes it all worthwhile. Tower Hill (or Signal Hill, as it is sometimes called) (or sometimes known by locals as TV Tower hill) is part of the Blue Hills, as they were known by the early day pioneers of the area. This tall hill is about three miles south and across the Missouri river from my farm. Tower Hill is accessible by a gravel road (Tower Hill Road) which is east of Fort Peck Dam on the south side of the hills, and has many translator towers on it, hence its nickname. These translators can be seen for many miles. My father, Edgar Garwood, was one of the original members of the Valley County TV District, along with Les Pippin, Ron Wallem and a few others. These men were instrumental in bringing TV to our area and the primary translator was located on this hill. I remember playing on the sandstone ridges nearby while my dad worked on the translator towers and buildings. Ron Wallem would always warn me about rattlesnakes that were in the area. From here we could look across the river and see our farm. From this peak, you can see for many miles along the Missouri River, the Milk River and the huge expanse of Fort Peck Lake.

The Missouri River makes a half circle bend around my farm and is about one mile away from my house on the west, south and easterly directions. My father and Rufus Anderson, a "next door" neighbor, bought a right-of-way for an irrigation ditch and road from Homer Peters. This right-of-way is ½ mile long and one hundred feet wide and goes to the Missouri River. They built up a pump site to irrigate with. They bought the land in 1949 and started pumping in the spring of 1950. Our families have been continuously irrigating since then, with the exception one year (2011), due to the flooding of the pump site. Flooding, or high water on the Missouri was caused by water releases from the spillway from excessive runoff from the mountains that filled Fort Peck Reservoir. At the time of the purchase of the right-of-way, this was the first I remember being on the Missouri river, and I was 4 years old. We went there often during that irrigation season to check on the pumps and for many more years after. The water in the river is clear and cold; it comes from the bottom of Fort Peck Lake, flows through the powerhouses and back into the Missouri. I have always enjoyed irrigating from this section of river.

The Milk River

From up on Tower Hill you can see the crooked Milk River for miles and miles, the same today as when William Clark used this hill to survey the landscape. He could see that the Milk River snaked and meandered through pretty flat countryside and twisted in such a manner that he felt it unlikely this was the route to the west that the expedition was searching for. From Tower Hill, Clark could also see the direction that the Missouri River was heading toward, most of which is now covered up by Fort Peck Reservoir, lying in a south-westerly direction from Tower Hill. Clark could also see smoke from Indian campfire from an area now called Porcupine Creek near the present town of Nashua. Nashua is an Indian word meaning "meeting of the waters".

The Milk River gets it start in the mountains east of Glacier National Park in Montana near Browning. It flows northward and into Alberta, Canada for about 100 miles and then it flows back into the United States west of Havre, Montana. In 1964 when I first went up to visit the Musgroves, we went through a small town named Milk River, Alberta. It was not until that time that I realized that the Milk River that runs near our farm, flows eastward in southern Alberta, and then back into Montana. It flows into the Missouri River less than a mile downriver from the Fort Peck Spillway, which is just across the river from my homeplace today. The confluence of the Milk is just a mile east of my house on the north bank of the Missouri River.

Many small tributaries from Alberta, Saskatchewan and Montana flow into the Milk River watershed. The Saint Mary River is also part of the hydrology of the Milk River. The Saint Mary River originates in

Western Montana and it flows into Canada eventually flowing into the South Saskatchewan River and eventually into Hudson Bay. The Unites States, in order to utilize its share of the Saint Mary River system, needed a diversion canal to divert water into the Milk River. Between 1906 and 1911, the Saint Mary Canal was constructed with two long siphons that carry water from the river and into a canal that feeds into the north fork of the Milk River. This siphon/canal system supplies water during the irrigation season to provide water for irrigators along the Milk River. This system that diverts water from the Saint Mary River into the Milk River is very important for the economy of the irrigators along the Milk River system. This water in the Milk River is also important for the survival of the pallid sturgeon, which is a listed endangered species. This co-operation between Canada and the US helps to provide extra water for both countries along the Milk River.

The Milk River is famous for its distinctive color, as highlighted in the quote that starts this section. The water is a greyish-brownish-white color that the Lewis and Clark expedition felt looked like a teaspoon of milk in a cup of tea. This led to the name of the river. The unusual appearance of the water results from clay and silt that is suspended in the water.

This river also floods some years, mostly in the spring, related to either snow melt in its tributaries, runoff from the mountains or ice jams in its twisting, snake-like path. Flooding can occur later in the year, also, usually related to high and sudden rain falls. I can remember when the Milk River had high water three times in one year. I also can remember walking across the gravel bed of the river near Nashua and the flow of the river had stopped many years ago in one our past drought periods!

The Lewis and Clark Expedition

On May 8th of 1805, William Clark and Meriwether Lewis, of The Lewis and Clark Expedition arrived at a river that came into the Missouri from the north. Clark explored the south bank of the Missouri, while Lewis explored the north bank. Clark climbed the lookout hill which he referred to as Observation Point (which is commonly referred to as Tower Hill) south of the Missouri River, which lies opposite of the murky river coming into the Missouri from the north. Meriwether Lewis was on the north side of the river at the confluence of these two rivers, and he paddled up this new river to the north. This river was what the Mandan and Hidatsa's Indians called "the river that scolds all others". The men on the expedition thought the river looked like a cup of tea with a tablespoon of milk in it, therefore Lewis and Clark named this river the Milk River. This river has a grayish, brown color and it flows into the Missouri River about one and a half miles to the east of my house. The Milk River holds that unusual color on the north side of the Missouri for a couple miles downstream during heavy spring flows. This can be seen from Observation Point (Tower Hill), on the south side of the Missouri.

Lewis paddled up the Milk River for several miles and determined, due to its numerous bends, that it was not the "North West Passage" they were searching for. They gave up on this river and returned to the rest of the party on the Missouri. They "nooned" it at the confluence of the Milk and the Missouri and later that day continued upriver for a few miles until they camped for the night. From his observation on the hill, Clark could see a fork off the Milk River, which had a lot of trees on it, that came into the Milk River from the north. He had considered that this river might extend the United States border further north into Canadian territory. They determined that this river, which was later named Porcupine Creek, did not go far enough north to extend our northern boundary with Canada. The confluence of the Milk River has changed since then, so I really do not know exactly where it was at that time, possibly as much as a mile more east than it is now.

Their campsite the night of May 8th was within a few of miles of my sisters' property on the north side of the Missouri river. This is in the area that Lewis and Clark saw the first "moos'" deer on the expedition. Their campsite that night might be where the Corps of Engineers dredged sand out of the river for the Fort Peck Dam. These areas are now known to locals as the Dredge Cuts.

In 1806, on the return trip from the west coast, Lewis and Clark divided their expedition in western Montana in order to explore more territory on the journey home. William Clark, Sacagawea, her infant son Pompei, and a few others had returned eastward by floating down the Yellowstone River in southern Montana. Meriwether Lewis moved east, first by horse to reach the Marias River (which the previous year they had named Maria's River), and later by boat as he floated down the Marias into the Missouri, where he passed the confluence of the Milk and Missouri about August 12, 1806. He met up with Clark, who was waiting for him near the Yellowstone confluence with the Missouri in North Dakota. This area was named Camp Union, (later known as Fort Union) at the confluence of these two great rivers, as well as for the rejoining of the expedition.

A picture of Tower Hill, looking south, from my property on the north side of the Missouri. My daughters' horses are grazing in the foreground.

Another view of Tower Hill from my farmyard, with the fog and sunlight showing the hills in silhouette.

PIONEERING
(the good old days)

"I come from pioneer stock, developers of the West, people who went into the wilderness and set up a home with nothing but a pair of oxen"
-Joni Mitchell

"To hell with the rich people, us poor folk will survive."
-Loren Musgrove

My family root's in Valley County
Marion and Gertrude (Bailey) Garwood

I would like to start this section by writing about my Grandparents on my father's side of the family, Marion Garwood and Gertrude Bailey Garwood. The life they lived and the stories they told are some of my first memories of pioneers.

Grandpa was born in Dayton, Ohio in 1899. He was raised in Dayton and his dad, Harry Henry Garwood, also known as H.H., operated a streetcar in Dayton, and they lived on a small farm near Pyrmont, which lies between Dayton and Lewisburg. H.H. Garwood was also a bit famous for making his own special salve to treat minor ailments, and my Dad still has a couple tins of his grandfathers' famous salve. I do not remember Grandpa Marion telling a lot about the stories of his boyhood days, but he shared a few. One story that he told me was when he was a youngster walking down the street with his father, my great grandpa, in downtown Dayton and he was told that walked by the Wright brothers bicycle shop. I think this was after their flight at Kitty Hawk, N.C. so they were already famous. It is just amazing to me that he was alive and by their shop during that historic time period. Maybe they even made the plans for their plane that very bicycle shop.

Grandpa's father was Harry Henry was married to Ida B Mills and they had five children, sons Amber, Rollie and my grandfather Marion, and a daughter's Elsie and Farest. I don't know much about Ida, but she was born in Pyrmont, Ohio.

Grandpa's father lived on a farm nearby at Pyrmont, Ohio, and I believe Grandpa's brother, Rollie, had a farm there, also. This maybe was on that same farm, but I am not sure. Grandpa had one other brother, Amber 'Pops' Garwood, who was a used car salesman and sold Grandpa and Grandma the car that they used to come to Montana on their honeymoon in 1920. Amber later moved to Montana and lived pretty near his brother, at least by Montana standards, about 40 miles away. Grandpa had a sister called Farest and her husband was Blair Stevenson, who also moved to Montana after my grandparents had put down roots here, and they lived near Oswego, and then later south of Nashua.

My Grandma Gertrude was from Jackson County, Kentucky, near Gray Hawk. She had been married when she was quite young and lost her husband in WWI. I believe his last name was Rice. She later met and married Grandpa Marion in 1920. On their honeymoon they were driving a Maxwell car that they bought from Grandpa's brother Amber. They worked their way westward on a wheat threshing crew and eventually worked their way to Montana to visit Grandma's Uncle Frank and Aunt Lucy Bales.

The Bales had a farm and ranch near the main road north of the Missouri River, near the Lismus ferry which crossed from there to the south side of the river. This area was known as Second Point to locals. They farmed near the river and also operated a highway house, a bed and breakfast, which was made of logs. They had built up their business to be quite profitable for the times. If only the Bales and the other pioneers on the Missouri upriver of the proposed Fort Peck Dam would have known what was coming for them!! When the dam was completed, it flooded the Bales out, as well as hundreds of others. It was 1933 that the Corps of Engineers started the process to build the Fort Peck Dam, so several years after my family first moved to this area.

In 1920 while Grandpa Marion and Grandma Gertrude were here on their honeymoon, they put money down to a person whose name has been forgotten, on a forty-acre homestead property. This property is south of Nashua and about a mile north the mouth of Milk River. This area at the confluence of the Milk and Missouri, often called "the mouth" or "the point" was where we often in later years fished on Homer Peters land. After the down payment, they then went back east to Ohio for the winter. The next year they came back to Valley County, Montana with their new baby, Edgar, who is my father, to finish out their three-year homestead agreement and start a new life here in Montana.

My grandfather Garwood and I were very close and we had a lot in common. He was only 47 years older than me and we both liked farm animals so, when I was about 12 years old, we went into the pig business together. From his small farm in Lewisburg, Ohio, he brought back some Hampshire piglets in the back of his '51 Chevy truck, which had an enclosed and covered rack on it. One year when I was in 4H I took some pigs to the Valley county fair and I brought home the Grand Champion Ribbon for a boar that we had raised from that registered Hampshire from Ohio. That ribbon, which was stored in an old chest of drawers, was later lost in a fire on our property. That fire was in the fall of 1979, and from November and into December, I spent 45 days in the hospital during hunting season! After about five years in the hog business, we sold the hogs and bought some beef cows and I still have cows that have derived from that Black Angus beef breed stock. In 1969 we bought a registered Hereford bull from the Beery Ranch at Vida and from that combination, we ended up with black baldy cows which, in my opinion, are about the best cross for a beef cow.

I hunted with Grandpa Marion until he died in 1987 and I still have his .300 Savage model 99 lever action which I cherish. I still use it for hunting some years and I took my first moose with it in Canada. I do not use it much now as I want to protect it because it is a family heirloom. He also taught me how to trap and bought me my first traps. I still remember our first trapped beautiful red fox on the hill above Dad's bins about a half of a mile from Dad's house. That was in 1962. I also caught my first bobcat down by the river and I still can walk to within one hundred feet of where I caught that cat today. What an exciting day it was when I brought that cat home to show Grandpa.

I loved my Grandparents dearly and still miss my grandpa's humor and sayings. He was an old horseman that struggled to use the modern mechanical horse "tractors". He used baling wire a lot for repairs. I still use wire and duct tape for repairs. I do not know how I could farm without those items. I am a lot like him, I think!

The move from Ohio out west to Montana

Marion and Gertrude returned to Montana in the spring 1921, along with newly born son Edgar Garwood, to prove up on their 40 acre homestead. They decided it was not enough land to make a living on, so the following year they purchased 120 more acres that bordered them from Grace Schick, daughter of Bill Schick. The 40 acre homestead was isolated and the purchase of this property gave them access to a county road. My grandparents had a difficult neighbor who lived to the east of their original 40 acre homestead. This man always carried a double barreled shotgun and he would walk the boundary line between them and was not a very good neighbor. Dad thinks that this neighbor was hoping they would quit their homestead so he could maybe get it. This man had left Kentucky, changed his last name and Dad said the neighbor never went outside after dark. This neighbor happened to be a shirt-tail relative of my Grandma Gertrude, as he was married to her aunt.

Sometime after my grandparents proved up on the 40 acre homestead, they decided to move the small house they lived in, which was made of cottonwood logs, to the Grace Schick farm location. They got a neighbor to help, placed the log house on skids, and together with two teams of horses they pulled it about ½ mile west. This new location had good water for their livestock. This is where my fathers house and farm buildings are currently located and where I was raised. There was a hill behind the house and several coulees to explore and play in. Their farm then had about 40 acres above the house on a hill where there was no good way to access that feild. When the present county road was built many years later, they needed dirt fill for the road. Dad talked the county crews into getting the dirt from up and over the hill near where his bins are now, so he could access the upper field so he could farm it.

Grandma Gertrude always had chickens that she raised and she sold eggs to people in Nashua. She also had turkeys that were herded around to forage and to control grasshoppers and crickets around the farm. They also purchased and operated a dairy and delivered milk and cream to Nashua. The cream was taken to the Great Northern Railroad depot in Nashua. It was hard work milking up to 15 cows and delivering it 6 miles (by road) into Nashua. The milk cooling shed was about 100 feet from the cotton wood log barn that they milked in. That barn is not there anymore. The cooling shed is still standing and the concrete holding tank is still in good shape. They would have to fill the tank with cold well water to cool the milk down so it would keep cool until it was sold. They used a lot of the milk bi-products to feed hogs and they always had corn to feed their cows and calves. I do not think they ever had sheep but I do not know for sure. Grandpa had an old corn binder he would use in the 50's and would stack the corn bundles in stooks (bundles of corn) and leave them in the field to dry. Later in the fall we would bring in the bundles to the barn and shell the corn for the hogs and milk cows and stack the corn fodder for winter feeding. I still have that corn binder out by my barn!

One story my grandpa told, several times over, was that he had hurt his back somehow. There were not any doctors here to help his back. They decided he would have to go back east to see a doctor. Grandma and Edgar would stay here to take care of the livestock, but grandpa decided that he would have to cut some wood to last them till he returned. After a couple of days of sawing and chopping wood, his back got better and the pain went away. I always remembered this and when I have back problems, I take some aspirin for the pain and I go for long walks up and down hills to hunt or check my fences. Sometimes I cut some wood like grandpa did and most times this solves my back problems. I went to a doctor for back pain one time and the x-ray cost was over a hundred dollars. Since then I decided I would get my back in by myself. I have been fortunate to learn many things from my Grandpa's experiences.

My grandparents spoiled me pretty bad for my hunting and fishing habit; a habit that I loved as a young person and still do. During the tough life when they lived here, they had to live off the land as much as they could. Grandma Gertrude came from the hills of Kentucky as a youngster, where they also survived on wild game. If I went out hunting for rabbit, pheasant, grouse, Hungarian partridges, ducks and geese, she would help me clean everything I brought home to her. Except for deer. During the fall hunting season, when I was younger, Grandpa would help me skin my deer. I loved hunting and my grandpa would help with the skinning and cutting the meat. There were times when I would ride my bike back from the point on the river with up two stringers of catfish, sauger, drum and other fish. Grandma Gertrude always helped clean the fish, would cook the fish and wild game and it always tasted great. She was a super hard worker for a small woman.

When my parents got married and started having children, my grandparents built a small house about 150 yards from the farmhouse, and moved into that home, leaving the main house for us. It was nice having them so close to us. On some mornings my sister Karen and I would walk across the dry slough to their place for breakfast when we did not have school. If it was too muddy, we could walk around the road, which was only a little over a quarter of a mile around, to eat pancakes with them. She would make them in the shape of an animal or whatever we wanted her to create. They always tasted better that way and she was always baking so it always smelled good when we got to their house. Such great memories!

Cutting ice from the river for summer use

During the winter all the neighbors would get together during nicer weather to cut ice with special long one-handled saws. This was dangerous work so people worked together for safety. The ice was stored in underground "ice houses" that usually had a door that faced to the north so when you opened the door to get ice out during the summer it would not let the sun light in. They usually packed the ice in wood shavings from cutting wood for their stoves. They also used wheat straw to help insulate the ice from melting during the summer. They usually cut ice from the Milk River as it usually froze more evenly and hard. Ice from the Missouri was dangerous as it froze uneven and had thin ice in places. Before the Fort Peck Dam was built, the Missouri used to freeze over near here, but after the dam was built, the Missouri no longer froze, at least for several miles downstream.

The pioneers at that time did everything by hand, cutting wood, pumping water and farming with horses. Grandpa started with one team of horses and later broke another team so he could use one team in the morning and the other in the afternoon. He would break a young bronc by having the young horse along side a trained and gentle horse, until it was broke to work.

Grandpa said that in the evenings, when he was taking off the harnesses, and feeding and watering the horses, the mosquitoes were so bad on the horses that when he was ready to come in the house at night, he would run around the house to get them off of him. He would also be hollering to grandma to get ready to open the door to try to keep them out of the house. Ha! I have also done this to keep them out my pickup after changing the irrigation tubes in the early morning or around dark. I have great respect for my grandparents, parents and all the other pioneers, for the hard work they did just to survive and settle this land. We have it so much better than them, it is hard to imagine what they went through back there in what was supposedly "the good old days".

During the winter when they had to deliver milk and eggs to customers in Nashua, my grandpa fixed the sleigh so it was enclosed and he made a stove out of an old rusted out milk can with a stove pipe out the top. Ash was better firewood than cottonwood, and would last longer before going out or having to add more wood as frequently. I do not have much ash around, but have lots of cottonwood, so I burn it more often.

My dad went to school in Nashua and either rode a horse or walked, or sometimes in the winter he would cross country ski to town. Dad's horse was called Tony. Once in a while Tony would buck Dad off as he did not like crossing the old Milk River Bridge on the South side of Nashua. That bridge has since been torn down. If Tony got loose, he would head home and Dad would always find him waiting at the gate on the hill above Grandpa's house. Sometimes Grandma would come in with the milk and meet Dad after school near the Milk River bridge on the south side of town and then he helped to deliver milk and eggs, and when they were done delivering, they could go home to the farm together. Dad said at times during the winter the stove would not keep quite warm enough in the sleigh and some of the bottles of milk that were away from the stove would start to freeze. The cardboard in the glass bottles would get pushed up by the freezing milk in a curve. Dad would eat this frozen milk and he compared it to milk shakes of today and said it was quite a treat.

Jack Nickels was a classmate of Dad's, and he remembers that Dad at times would drive an old Model T pickup with chains on the rear wheels to school. Dad was a pretty good mechanic and Grandpa was not. Dad learned mostly by experience and from talking to his Great Uncle Ben Stenbakken in Nashua. Ben was my Mother's Uncle. One time when grandpa was on his way home from town, he got the pickup stuck crossing the coulee a mile northwest of the house. It was after a rain and while trying to get it unstuck, he broke the differential or axle in the rear end of the car. He walked home and later when it had dried some, they used a team of horses to pull the pickup home. They pushed it under a lean-to roof attached to the house. Dad was probably about 12 at the time and he borrowed tools from Bernard "Ben" Stenbakken, and Dad took the differential apart himself and got the new parts from Uncle Ben's garage. He then put the parts in and tried it out but he had put the part in backwards. Therefore, when he tried to back out of the garage, the pickup tried to go out the front!! He had to take the differential apart again and turn the ring and pinion around so it would drive in the right direction. This time it worked and this is how he learned from trial and error to become a pretty good farm mechanic. After he got grandpa's pickup fixed, he got to use this Model T pickup to go to school some. Jack Nickels remembers Dad driving to school in that old Model T when he was in the eighth grade, but Dad remembers more about riding his horse, Tony, or cross-country skiing to school during the winter.

Sometimes he would spend the week at the Bollinger's place, to make it easier to get to school. Grandma Gertrude would sometimes cook and clean for them and she would also work part time at the Nashua Post Office. As I said, she was a hard worker and people did what they had to do to make ends meet, just like we do today.

Playing baseball on the Nashua team

Grandpa was a very good athlete and was an amateur boxer back in Ohio. Dad said he was pretty quick to fight and could handle himself really well. He was in several fights and I do not know if he ever got beat, at least Grandpa never admitted it to me if he did. He loved to play baseball and Nashua usually had a good team. Most communities had teams at that time.

Grandpa was a pitcher and had a great fast ball and curve ball. One year a semi pro baseball team was traveling around the country playing teams and looking for good players. They played Nashua with grandpa pitching. I guess the semi pro team got shut out by him and they asked him to join them. He was tempted! But grandma got the last word in when she told him that "we have a farm to run here". He showed me how to throw a curve ball, but I ended up playing shortstop in little league. Charles Brocksmith Sr. was the manager of the team and Grandpa had a lot of respect for him. I talked to Charlie Sr. one time about 30 years ago or so, and he told me that Grandpa was a very good hardball pitcher.

Charles Brocksmith Sr. was a banker and his parents were one of the first families in the area. His mothers' family, the Sargent's, founded the town of Nashua. Grandpa and Charlie were good friends from the past. Grandpa and I wanted to get some beef cows and we did not have the money to purchase them. Charlie was the President of the First Security Bank in Glasgow, Montana. We needed a loan. Grandpa said to me, "I guess I need to go see Charlie again, with my hat in my hands". The two of us went into the bank together in about 1963 to talk to Charlie. That was my first experience to the world of banking. We got enough money at that time to buy some bred cows, and later on, we bought a bull.

Grandpa played the guitar and mandolin

Grandpa also loved music and played the mandolin and guitar. His brother Amber and brother-in-law Blair Stevens played banjo and drums so they started a band. They played for several years together and cut some records. I remember seeing some of these. They were 78's and just for the families to enjoy. They played at the barn that the Markle family now has restored at the old Anderson place, which was later farmed by Ivan Miller. This place had a barn on a high hill overlooking the Missouri River. In 2009 the Markle family had a barn dance where the public was invited. There was a large turnout, and everyone had a great time. There was a large concrete slab that was used for dancing outside on warm evenings.

Grandpa played the mandolin most of the time, but I never heard him play with a band. He would practice and I would listen to him. One day, when I was younger and he was getting pretty old, we were hooking up his Fordson tractor to a rake. We were trying to hook up the power take off and it came apart and dropped on his left fingers, breaking one really bad. So bad that the bone was showing. He had not taken off the removable drawbar on the three-point hitch and he had his hand between the drawbar and drive shaft. This turned out to be one of the main fingers he used to press the strings between the frets to play his mandolin. This really bothered him as he knew then that he would not be able to play for a while. I am not sure if he ever played well after his finger healed up. I always think about what happened when I hook up the power take off on his old 1953 Ford tractor that I have now and still use. I watch where my fingers are when hooking it up! Sometimes we learn from these bad experiences.

The homestead is proved up

In 1926 my grandparents got a document called a patent from Washington D.C., signed by Calvin Coolidge, that said they had proved up on the homestead and it was theirs. Many homesteaders sold the land after they had proved up on the patents and went elsewhere as the life was so much harder than they expected. But many stayed on, including my grandparents. The government would only let a person homestead once in a lifetime. If you homesteaded once you could not again unless a person changed his name and got away with it. In the river bottom, the most you could file on was 160 acres. In the hills you could file on 320 acres but there was not much for water there unless you found a deep well. Most homesteaders hauled water. There was a short period of time that a couple could homestead on 640 acres if in strictly grazing country. In 1932, Grandma and Grandpa bought another 160 acres, the Ira Evans place, which bordered their land to the South. It was close to the Missouri river but not on the river. When they were running the dairy, they needed a lot of water, hay ground and grazing.

Grandpa was missing the ends of a couple of fingers from getting them caught in chains of old machinery (or an auger?) He had one finger that looked pretty fair but was missing about half of an inch of finger and the fingernail came out of the center about where the bone was. He would whittle on it with his knife to keep it from getting too long. I have a finger about like his, but mine was from a propane fire in 1979. I have to trim the stub of the fingernail the same way he did. Grandpa was always strumming his fingers on the table and would walk his fingers towards our hands when we were young. It was a good game he played with us! My children remember him doing that to them, also. He was a fun Grandpa to be around. I think that when he did that with his fingers, we were kind of intimidated by his hands, especially with that one stub of a finger that looked like a short bone sticking out. He was always joking when he did it and us kids enjoyed his playful nature.

The coming of The Fort Peck Dam

President Franklin Delano Roosevelt signed a presidential order authorizing the Public Works Administration Project for the Missouri River Dam project at Fort Peck. This project would put a dam across the Missouri River and would put thousands of people to work! This was during the great depression, during the dry and dirty thirties! People left their farms, ranches and towns in Montana to find work at Fort Peck.

In 1933 a government man in a new Plymouth pickup drove into the yard to talk to my grandparents. Dad said he was really impressed with this pickup as it was so shiny and Dad had not seen anything like it at the time. They were told the Corps of Engineers were going to build a dam upriver and they needed a 100 foot right away through Grandpa's place for a railroad line that would run from Wiota, which is east of Nashua, crossing the Milk River and then to the Fort Peck Dam site. This provided work for neighboring farmers on the Fort Peck Project. All of the trees and brush had to be cleared from the right-of-way for the railroad. The contractor could not use dirt from alongside of the track for railroad bed. They purchased dirt from the hills nearby to build up the track bed from about four feet to over ten feet in some low places. Three-foot diameter culverts were put under the fill at all low spots and creek crossings. Dad said that large loud trucks were used to move the dirt from the hills to the track beds.

Jack Nickels said there was a wagon trail that meandered up Milk River Coulee and over to the other side of the hills. This is on the south side of the Missouri. The homesteaders used this trail to get out of the river bottom. This is the same coulee that the Fort Peck Spillway was eventually built in. There were also some reports of a ferry on the Missouri, which was used by people to cross the Missouri River to go to Nashua or Glasgow. We have decent roads now, but back in those days, travel could be a struggle.

Jack Nickels said that he had talked to the contractor foreman of the railroad about food for the workers. He was in school but he had a large flock of turkeys like most farmers did, as they kept the grasshoppers down from all around the farm. Jack said he made a deal with this foreman to deliver dressed turkeys to him for a good price. Most of the farmers sold dressed turkeys to the railroaders if they could get a good price for them. My grandmother raised and sold turkeys to them and to others in town. I have seen a picture of my grandmother and Edgar, my Dad, herding turkeys around and watching for predators. I have also seen a picture of my grandfather hauling clean snow to the house in a metal tub. This made soft water when melted was excellent for washing clothes.

Dad remembers when the trucks started hauling out dirt from the spillway, which was south of the Missouri River, but the trucks were loud enough to hear from the farm. The workers used the same large trucks with oversize tires and no mufflers that they used to build the railroad line. They hauled dirt out of Milk River Coulee to make the spillway. The dirt was hauled to the west of the spillway. From the south side of the river you can see two distinct layers of dirt that was laid there. The first layer was by the trucks in the 1930's. The second layer was from later years and was laid on top of the first layer. This dirt came from dirt that caved into the spillway. These clay, bentonite and adobe soils were deposited here in these hills from the last ice age and are very unstable. This is why the Missouri River changed course here next to these hills! This soil and its instability also lead to the Slide of the Dam in 1938.

Harold Moecker worked on the dam at different jobs. He was working in one of these dump trucks moving dirt to the area west of the spillway. He respected his motors and he did not like to run them at high RPMs so he was taking it easy with the motor and he killed the engine. It was cold and they could not get the engine restarted so the foreman drove up and fired him on the spot!! I knew Harold and he was a good man and a good mechanic. Harold got a job later with Rufus Anderson building the Administration Building up on the hill in the town of Fort Peck.

Dad tells me a story about Harold. Harold's wife Celia was a real church goer and Harold was not. He had a patch of weeds called Canada thistle on a little field on his farm, which was about four miles from Dads house, just southeast of Nashua. The idea is to not let the Canada thistle ever grow out of the ground to replenish its root reserves and if the thistle does not see the sun for a long period of time it will die! This is a really tough Montana noxious weed. Harold decided to summer fallow the patch all summer to get a good kill on the weed. His plan was to till the patch every Sunday so he would not forget and miss working the ground. He did this all summer long and he killed out the Canada thistle in one year. Dad says he thinks that Harold did it also to get out of going to church! Sounds like my Dad, who was also always working on Sundays!!

Celia and my mother went to church most Sundays together. Amarlys Moecker, Harold and Celia's daughter, married Victor Weinmeister, and they lived on the old Tom and Doris Anderson place, about a mile and a half east of my parent's home place. They built a large blue Harvestore silo that still is a landmark here on this river bottom. Vic and Amarlys had 5 children, who are Duane, Randy, Cindy, Mary Lou and Gene. These kids were all good athletes at Nashua High School. After Celia's daughter Amarlys passed away, my mother began taking Celia to church each Sunday. They were good friends and neighbors and attended the First Lutheran Church in Nashua. Celia was the woman that told mom that the early homesteaders called the hills east of Fort Peck the Blue Hills, probably called that because of the noticeable blue clay that forms these hills.

Amarlys bought the Higgins place, which was just east of the Moecker farm, when she was a teenager with help of her father, Harold. The Higgins house was two stories, and stood for many years, but finally fell down in a storm in the summer of 2011. It was a bare single walled house with a nice set of steps that led upstairs. It stood on the hill looking north toward the Milk River and Nashua.

Fort Peck was a government town and was designed by the Corps to house workers and project managers. While the town was being built, the workers lived in tents, and constructed barracks at first and later houses. In 1934 work was started on the Administration Building and four hundred houses were built for families to live in. These workers also constructed a Recreation Hall, a theater, a bowling alley, a post office, shopping center, fire hall and school. The Fort Peck Hotel was built for visiting dignitaries and is still in use today. The Rec Hall is still standing and is used by people in the Fort Peck community, and the Fort Peck theatre is also still in use, with the theatre used for impressive and well attended theater projects every summer. The Ad Building, the Rec Hall, the Hotel and the Theatre are all buildings on the national register of historic places.

There were many boom towns that sprang up like wild flowers after a good spring rain. These towns were needed to provide services for the growing workforce at Fort Peck. Ernie Pile once wrote that Wheeler was the wildest town in the USA!! I wish that I could have been alive to see the boomtowns and the Fort Peck dam during its Hey Day! At the time of its construction, Fort Peck was the largest earth filled dam in the world, and still remains one of the largest. It still fits criteria for being the largest hydraulic earth fill dam in the world. The construction process of building this hydraulic filled masterpiece is amazing. It just boggles the mind when you see pictures of the railroad tracks, dredges, barges, and miles of dredge pipe across land and river, booster pumps, electrical wire to run the dredge pumps, the high voltage power lines from Great Falls and all of the boom towns surrounding the project. The enormity of it all in the 1930's is almost too hard to believe!

The town of Fort Peck was given up by the Corps of Engineers and is now incorporated. The town of Fort Peck is still a neat place to live and visit, and the area in and around Fort Peck still has homes being built. Some of them are huge homes!!! The mayor in 2012 was John Jones, who is a retired teacher and former football coach at Nashua High School.

I still remember going to picture shows at the theatre with my mom and neighbor kids. It was always neat to sit up in the balcony. The Fort Peck Theatre still has great plays during the summer months in this beautiful old building. It is always well attended and there are some concerts there also. I also can remember the drug store across from the theatre where you could get soft drinks and ice cream. What I can really remember is that Fort Peck had all paved streets and how clean and green it was there!

I also remember going to the swimming pool down by the river and I remember going to Kiwanis Park to picnic under the cottonwoods. It was and still is the place to go to recreate in this area! I can still remember going to the old Buckhorn Bar when there were the inlaid silver dollars under glass on the bar. I think the bar was bartended by Roy Christensen at the time. I have a photograph of a painting by Pat Musgrove Vossler of her father, Loren Musgrove and a man who looks like Brownie Doke. Pat painted this painting while looking at the picture that was taken many years ago in Wheeler! It is hard to believe that there were over 15,000 people living in this small area during the 30's!!

Missouri River Farm Life During the Dam Days

The Feds paid Grandpa and Grandma $10 an acre for 5 acres and told them they would get the land back when the government was through with it. This was for the railroad right-of-way. The railroad took five acres from them with a fence on each side of the tracks and two crossings in that half a mile. This split up the farm and made it hard to farm and herd cows back and forth, with gates to open and close each time they had to pass through. The Corps started clearing brush along the railroad right-of-way and grandpa got some work and was paid for clearing brush and trees with his team. He worked most of the winter until it was time to start seeding crops.

The railroad, including the bridge across the Milk River, was finished in 1934, which was less than a year after starting it. Most of the rock from the snake pit quarry near Harlem, steel, gravel from Cole Ponds and some lumber for the building of Fort Peck and the dam, all came in by rail across grandpa and grandmas place. Dad said there would be days that several trains came through in a day. Most of the lumber for building the barges and boats came from the large amount of trees in the area of the dam; they were built there, at what was called the Fort Peck Boat Yard. That is why they termed the barges the Fort Peck Navy! At first the trains that came through were Great Northern trains. Later on, the trains were down sized and were Corps of Engineer trains.

When I was a youngster, I remember seeing the yellow engine pulling cars once a day, sometimes it was only a few cars, and sometimes it was several. This was during a period of time when the second powerhouse was being built in the late 1950's. The track was only about 300 hundred yards from my parent's house, and at times we would put a couple of pennies on the rail and go down later to find the flattened-out copper. When the second powerhouse was finished around about 1960 the Corps decided to eliminate the railroad.

In 1962 they started to tear down the bridge across the Milk River and take the rails off the track. They took the best wooden ties but let the adjoining landowners take the remaining ties so the Corps would not have to. These were still some great ties that were in pretty good condition. Grandpa, Dad and I spent a lot of time removing them from the railroad right away to our farm and stacking them so they would weather well and be able to dry out after a rain or during winter snow periods. We had some stacked at Grandpas place and also here on my home place, which we had just acquired in 1962. We used the best treated ties to build the barn that is built back into the side of the hill at grandpa's farm.

When the railroad was all taken out, the Corps forgot about their promise to give the land back to the landowners, like they said they would do when they had taken or purchased it from them in 1933. My Dad and our neighbors had to fight hard to get it back and had to pay $70 an acre in about 1970 to purchase it after receiving $10 an acre in 1933. My Grandpa was really happy to have it back in our name. This railway had split his farm in half for many years. This was at a time when they were running up to a fifteen-cow dairy. They had to trail the cows back and forth over the crossings while opening and closing two gates each trip. I remember that grandpa said when we got the right of way back, "It's about time we got it back, but I wish they would have taken the fill dirt back where they got it from". This fill dirt came from the hillside on grandpa's place. We have had to move the dirt back to our roads and to low places, so that we could farm it again. It has been a never-ending project to move this fill out and we are not quite done to this day.

My grandfather lived about 10 miles from the project and it would have been almost too far to drive back and forth from the farm if he worked there as he was running a 12-15 cow dairy! I think that grandpa and dad had some resentment for the project because the railroad split the small farm in half. I also think they had worries about living just below this dam, with water over their heads, and maybe had a thing to do with the family leaving for Ohio for a few years! Later, when grandpa got a good job in Dayton building and firing machine guns, it gave them enough money to move back to the farm. They finally moved back to Montana for good in the early forties, after it started raining again.

The building of Fort Peck Dam was one of President Roosevelt's plans to help get the nation out of the recession. It put a lot of people to work and the building of the Fort Peck Dam allowed thousands of people that worked on the dam to make a good living. The dam was started in 1933 and was finished in 1940. In 1938, the slide of the dam into the lake area caused the Corps of Engineers to have to find more dredge sand for the dam. This good sand and topsoil was found five miles away from the dam site. The Nelson Dredge and Pickthorn Dredge areas provided the soil to be pumped up on the dam to finish it. The Corps of Engineers are going to have a 75 anniversary of the Fort Peck Dam the summer of 2012!

One of Grandpas' neighbors, Riley Peters, worked for grandpa some, putting up hay for his dairy cows and work horses. He sold his homestead to Abe Peters, his father, and went to work on The Fort Peck Project as an operator on the swing bridge near Park Grove. This bridge pivoted to allow the Dredge boats and tugboats to go back and forth from the main river to the first, second and third dredges. The third dredge could be what is now known to locals as the Trout Pond. The swing bridge would move back into a position to allow trains and vehicles to pass through from Park Grove to Fort Peck. This bridge was taken out in 1939 and was just east of the current bridge at Park Grove.

Riley Peters was one of the operators that worked on the swing bridge. His homestead was just east of my farm. Some of the homestead buildings still remain but are not in very good shape. Riley moved on after the Fort Peck Project was completed and my grandfather said he never seen him again. Riley was younger than grandpa, and he worked for grandpa at times. Grandpa liked Riley and he was a friend.

Riley and many others like him sold their homesteads during the building of the dam and moved on to work on other Corps projects. Most of these people made more money working for the Corps of Engineers than they ever would have on their small farms, so they moved on to a better life for their families!

Building of the Barn into the Hillside

Dad, Grandpa and I built this barn in 1962 and it was well built with a metal roof and still stands well. It is very warm during the winter and stays cool during hot weather. The first floor was built back into the hill and we hauled out the dirt with an International McCormick M and loaded it into a scraper pulled by an International 600 that we could spread out on low spots of the lower fields. The same dirt was also used to make ditches for irrigating and to build a dike below the barn which keeps water that runs from the hills west of the barn from flooding the lower fields. My Dad used this outfit to level all his fields on his own, after he had the first thirty acres leveled by Mr. Hansen. We used the best ties that were given to us from the railroad to line the barn to keep the hillside from caving in. We poured a concrete floor and Grandpa Marion built the stalls and gates, which were great to keep livestock in during inclement weather. He was a great gate builder and always used bolts and not nails. I am still using some of the gates he built fifty years ago, some of which have been outside for many years and have weathered the test of time. The alfalfa hay was baled in small square bales, as we still do. The bales were stacked by hand in the barn, sometimes during very hot weather. The bales were to be fed to the cows and pigs in the cold weather months when there was deep snow and no grazing available to the livestock. We ground up our own raised oats, corn and barley, which was stored in a wooden bin upstairs in the barn. It always stayed warmer in the bottom of the barn as it was below ground level. It also stayed cooler there in the hot summer months.

Grandpa liked to have a field of corn as he was from Ohio, where they raised corn and soybeans. He had a corn binder that he brought here from Ohio that would tie two strings around about thirty stalks and we could drop off several bundles at one time by releasing them with a foot lever. Next, we would set all of these bundles and lean them against each other until we had a stook. These were comprised of about twenty bundles and then we would put twine around them so they would stand upright in the field until they had dried out. It was always neat to see a field full of stooked corn stalks in the late fall when the orange harvest moon was coming up over the horizon. Our old corn binder was pulled by our 1956 Ford tractor until the early 60's and before that, it was pulled by horses. The binder is out along the fence line but the wood is in rotten condition and presently would not be in field condition. I have never seen another one like it here, but there were a lot of small grain binders in this part of the country. A month or so later when the fodder was dry, we would pull a stone boat, which was made of two logs for runners and boards cross ways on them, to bring in the corn harvest. These stone boats or wagons were used to bring the corn to the barn by pulling with horses or with a tractor. The ears of corn were removed from the stalks and run through a hand-operated separator to remove the shelled corn from the cob. In the real old days, the ear of corn was picked off the stalk and thrown into a wagon to be brought to the bin or barn. Next, we ground up the corn grain to feed to the pigs and then the stalks and leaves we fed to the cows. This is how we always put up our corn.

There was a small bin upstairs with a wooden chute with a control lever to allow the ground grain to be controlled manually and to come down a chute into a bucket to be fed to the livestock in the lower room. That way you did not have to go up and down the stairs to bucket the grain down to the animals. There was a sliding board on the bottom of the chute to control the amount of ground grain you needed in the bucket. There was also an opening in the upstairs floor so we could drop small bales of hay to the alley way downstairs. This had a removable lid which you could walk on it when it was not being used.

My grandpa was an excellent wood worker and spent many a rainy day and evening building the stalls and gates in the bottom floor. There is an alley way down the center of the bottom floor, with feeders on each side to hold hay and grain for the cows. A person can walk lengthways through the barn without ever having to go in with the cows. There are also two large swinging doors on each end of the south of the barn which had small windows for light, as well as interior gates that could remain closed while the doors were opened to let in light and fresh air.

Later, when I moved the livestock operation to the Mattingly place, which was better for calving, we used the barn to park machinery. To this day, we still park machinery and automobiles in that barn. There is a large rolling door on the top floor at ground level that we can drive our small tractors in and we also store some machinery in there. We have a small grain cleaner where we can clean alfalfa seed or grain. It is just a great all-around barn!! The sides and the roof are lined with corrugated steel that has held up very well after all these years. We finished building the barn in 1963 and we had a barn dance where some neighbors came over for a great community party. It was Grandpa's idea to have a barn dance like he used to play for in the 20's and 30's, "the good old days", as he called them.

The dismantling of the McNeil Bridge House and moving it to present site for the house

When my grandparents purchased the Grace Schick place, they needed more room to live in and there was not a lot of cottonwood on their property for more logs. Deciding they needed a bigger house, they used timbers that were purchased from Rusty McNeil, who had originally "liberated" the timbers from the railroad, possibly without permission. Family story is that Rusty McNeil used the "liberated" timbers that were originally part of a railroad bridge to build himself a home. We are not sure where this bridge was located, but a new bridge was built and the old bridge was dismantled and the timbers were left at the site, being unused. Rumor has it that Mr. McNeil may have gotten in some trouble for this project. When grandpa purchased the timbers from Rusty, he got permission from the railroad to use them. He dismantled them from Rusty's house, marked each timber, and moved them one at a time for the two-mile trip to the farmyard, where he then put the house back together. The timbers were numbered and put together just as they were at McNeil's place. This has turned out to be a very stable and well insulated home. The timbers were 10 by 12 inches and assorted lengths, the longest being about 10 feet in length. You can still see the original exposed timbers from the front porch.

A few years later Grandpa pulled in another homestead house from the Evans place after he had purchased that property. He then split that house into two halves, lengthwise. He put one half on the back of the bridge timber house and attached the other half to the front. The back section became a bedroom and the kitchen. The front became a full length screened in porch that our family, relatives and friends have enjoyed immensely for many years. My father slept there when he was a youngster and I slept or camped out there during some summer nights. My parents have lived in this house since 1945. My dad has always kept this house up and added a bathroom with running water in 1957. Since then he has added an extra two bedrooms, a large family room and an attached garage. There is a lot of history to how this house was all put together and became a great home.

Kasten/Mattingly/Garwood Place

My grandpa Marion told me that he had farmed the Dave Kasten Place, later known as the Gene Mattingly place, in the past. This is the place that Patty and I have lived on since we were married in September 1969, which we purchased from my parents after we sold the Tiger Butte pasture. Grandpa Marion raised hay here back in the 30's for his dairy and stock cows. I have found horseshoes in the fields here and I wonder if they came from his work horses. At that time his brother, Amber and Amber's son Arthur, lived in the homestead house here. I was reminded of this from Art Garwood when he came down to visit one time when he was getting on in years. I could see he was very moved when he went into the old house, which is now my trappers shed. We looked around in there for a while and when he left, he thanked me, saying, "Seeing this house has done my heart good". Art had spent a lot of years in Wolf Point and then moved, first to Great Falls, and later to Havre where he ran the Gold and Silver Shop at the mall there. He spent a lot of time panning for gold and gems. He wrote an article about the old town of Dearborn in western Montana. Art has passed now and was a first cousin and very close to my dad, Edgar. Karen and I would visit Art, Betty and their son Bob, and one time we spent a few days panning for gold. We did not find any gold that time, but Bob told me he did on other occasions. I always had great times hunting and fishing with Bob and we sometimes found some small gemstones. Bob and I were as close as Dad and Art were, as friends and cousins.

Selling The Garwood Dairy

In 1936, after several dry years, Grandpa had to start feeding his cows green tumbleweed thistles and also put these up for hay when nothing else would grow. The drought was so bad that my Grandparents and Dad sold the dairy and cows to a neighbor, John E. Paul. He lived about two miles west of their place. With the money they made from selling the dairy, which included the dairy cows and dairy equipment, not to be confused with the actual farmland, Grandpa went back to Ohio and bought 120 acres of land near Lewisburg, which is northeast of Dayton. His brother Raleigh lived nearby, and years later bought part of that Ohio farmland. Grandpa's plan was to farm this property and go back to the farm in Montana when the drought ended. Grandpa got a job in Dayton at Frigidaire, building appliances. When the United States was getting into WWII the factory where Grandpa worked started building arms for the armed services. Later on, one of his jobs was to fire every machine gun that they put out to see if it operated properly. I was always fascinated by him being able to mow down targets with a .30 caliber or a .50 caliber machinegun for a job. It was his job to test these guns! It was no wonder why he enjoyed his job so well!! Years later when I was in the National Guard, I was able to have fun like he did firing .30 and .50 calibers machine guns. I always enjoyed hearing his stories. Grandpa was quite a storyteller, especially to someone like me who always enjoyed hearing about history of the area. I just wished I was able to record his stories as I have been able to do with my dad.

When it started raining again in Montana, probably in the early 40's, Grandma and Dad would come out in the spring to put the crop in and then go back to Ohio. They would return to Montana in the fall to harvest the crop, if there was one. They eventually started getting some crops to harvest. When my dad was called into the service, Grandpa quit his job in Dayton and farmed in Montana until Dad returned home. When my Dad was discharged, no one knew that he was headed home. A neighbor and good friend, George Raymond "Punk" Nicol was in Grandpa's yard working on a piece of equipment. Grandpa and Punk looked up to see a man walking down the hill toward the house and Punk said to Grandpa, "Well, look Marion! There comes Eddie", and that was my Dad returning from military service. My Dad had gotten off the train in Nashua and walked home. My dad has been on the farm here ever since.

My Grandpa was a tobacco chewer and always used Days-work tobacco. He had it with him all the time. I snuck some from him one time and never tried it again. It was terrible tasting stuff. One thing I noticed is that he never swallowed, but spit the juice out quite frequently. One time he coughed and swallowed when he had a chew in his mouth and I seen him turn a greenish-purple and almost thought he was going to croak. It was a good thing that he had coffee to clear things out. The great grandkids always remember him with chewing tobacco for himself and black licorice for them.

When we were out fencing it was hard work and we always had a few mosquitoes buzz bombing us. Sometimes we had some bug kind of repellant but not all of the time. Grandpa had a bald head in later years and if a "skeeter" got him on the top of the head through his cap he would holler, "that one must have had a beak an inch long." It was just an expression, but he used it quite a bit of the time.

Grandpa Marion got me started drinking coffee. At the time when I first tried it, I thought it was bitter. We would take a break from fixing fence and have a coffee break. What a great idea it was, to take time out from working by having some coffee!! Now that I think about it, I know why a lot of work does not get done on time. I really enjoy my Java, but I do not take time to stop into the coffee shops but carry a go cup with me most every place I go. My thermos is along with me too! I probably drink a couple of pots a day, but it is still better than 4 or 5 pops like I used to. Grandpa used to carry some cold coffee with him in a tin can with a cover in the old days when he was burning brush and clearing land to farm. He would warm up the coffee in the tin can over a fire and pour him a cup when he needed a break! I am a lot like him.

Grandpa and Grandma would go back to their small farm in Ohio most every winter in their old Chevy truck with their chickens in the back. They sold eggs in the Lewisburg and Dayton areas. They always brought something back to Montana if they could afford it. They would go to Wright Pattison Field near Dayton as others in the area would. The Air Force had a dumping ground there where much of their unusable material was left for people to reuse after The Great Depression. I wish there was a place that people could leave some of the usable stuff that they do not have room for so other people could make use of it. We should be recycling more, as we are in a mini depression now. My Grandparents would bring bought and recycled items back to Montana.

In the years my Grandparents traveled to and from Ohio, they brought back many items for the farm. Over the years these items include two Shetland ponies, Silver and Paint, some pigs, a 53 Ford tractor with front end loader (which I have now), a Minneapolis Moline manure spreader, numerous three-point implements, and always brought lumber for building purposes. Grandpa was always going to auction sales to visit with friends and he bought a lot of machinery at sale prices. I am a lot like him!!

They brought back all of the lumber that was used for a small house that Grandpa constructed for my Grandparents to live in, as Mom and Dad were living in the house on the farm. They built it in a grove of cottonwood trees about 300 yards south of the bridge timber house, but still near the barn and chicken coop. They used the same well as the folks did and there is plenty of water for both houses. My Grandma did not have indoor plumbing until she was over 70 years old. That was when they bought a lot with a trailer on it in Apache Junction, Arizona. A few years later they bought and set up a trailer near their small wooden house and this trailer had running water in it. She was one tough pioneer lady and was only about 5 foot tall. She did not drink much water and Dad said sometimes he remembered that she would only take a damp and wet her mouth.

One time, Grandma was watching Karen and I outside of the house. I was about 10 and Karen was 8 and I do not remember what I was doing but it kind of got her upset. I guess I was not listening to her very well. I guess I kind of have a mind of my own and a stubborn side! I cannot remember what I did but she lost her temper. For some reason she had a broom and I think she got so mad I thought she was going to whomp me with it! In the yard at Dad's place there was an old auger. I ran around the auger once or twice trying to get away and then I starting climbing the auger to get up away from the broom. Then she really got mad thinking that I might get dirty or greasy from the auger. Imagine that!! I finally got up high enough that I was out of broom range! All I know was I was not coming down until I was safe! She finally settled down and coaxed me down somehow. I did learn not to make her mad enough to lose her temper with me and in the future I was not so stubborn around her. I guess I am lucky that I have lived as long as I have!!

Another time I remember was when Grandma and I were out behind the barn gathering up some kindling for her cook stove. She always cooked with a wood burning stove so she needed lots of kindling for getting the fire going in the stove. While we were gathering wood, we stumbled on to a 4-foot long bull snake. She did not like snakes and I kind of do. She hit it a few times and it was writhing around and I reached down and picked up the snake and started playing with it. It wrapped around my arm and then I got a hold of it behind the head like they show you on the outdoor shows. She was not very happy with me! I felt that I had control of it and it could not bite me. She finally made me put the snake down and she shook her head in disgust with me. I think she hollered at me, "put that thing down".

Irrigating the Wheat and Alfalfa Fields with Cold Missouri River Water

Grandpa owned irrigated land that was eventually leveled with a slight slope down grade from the main ditch. Most of this was leveled by my father, Edgar Garwood. In later years, when Dad was running the place, Grandpa Marian often helped with the irrigation. He liked to irrigate while he was taking care of the fences and cows. Grandpa would irrigate at night as well as during the day and was usually tired a lot. Irrigated fields are divided into checks, ours are between fifty and one hundred feet wide, and the checks are created by raised rows of dirt, called dikes. His method involved lying down in the next check, beside the dike, near the end of the field. He would fall asleep with his arm across the dike to let him know when the water was near the end of the check so he could change the irrigation tubes and put the water into the next check. I have tried his technique for irrigating my own fields but the mosquitoes always get the best of me and I go elsewhere and do something else until I can make my irrigation change. Grandpa was out of some pretty tough stock!

It seems like we do not have as many mosquitoes as we used to as we are more aware of how to keep them from hatching in stale water and maturing. Also, it seems like with the help of bug repellants, we can put up with them more than we used too. I maybe only use bug repellent a couple times a year for mosquitoes, but black gnats are something else. They get under your glasses, cap and in your ears, and you get welts from them. When they are bad and there is not any breeze to keep them off, you have to get inside, have a head net or use repellent. It has been over 30 years since Grandpa left this world but I miss him still. I am so fortunate that I was able to spend so much time with him, as well as with my father.

When we are irrigating with this cold water I often wonder if it sets the crop back some from stress. I know that the farmers that get water from the Milk River say that the warm water might be better for the crop. Who really knows? Maybe the cold water might even be better for the crop if it is stressed from drought? All I know is that I enjoy irrigating, like my grandpa did. It makes the crops grow if we have not had recent rains. It is enjoyable to be able to irrigate but it is hard work keeping the ditches clean for water to pass through. The cleaner the ditch is, the lower the water level and there is less seepage from the ditch. One good thing with the cold water, is that the cold water in the ditches makes a good place to hide a barley pop or two to have in the evening!

The Montana farm while the family was in Ohio

There was a neighbor that lived to the north of the farm named Charlie Johnson. He was a WWI vet who had been gassed in the war and left with a stutter from his war injuries. He was always a good neighbor. He had a homestead shack above the hill behind Grandpa's farm. The main county road came down the hill through the yard and then south toward the river. After Grandpa and Grandma sold the dairy and went back to Ohio for a while, Charlie Johnson and Rawhide Johnson, no relation to each other, stayed at the farm to watch over it. Charlie's shack was not much to speak of and Rawhide had lost his farm to the spillway project and needed a place to stay. They both agreed to stay on the farm and look after the place.

Charlie had an old McCormick Deering tractor that he farmed with. I am not sure if he had a car but I remember him driving around in that tractor. The tractor had steel wheels with steel cleats on it, and he drove in the borrow pit because of this. There was not any paint on it, but it seemed to run good. Old Charlie must have been a pretty good mechanic and he cared about that tractor. One spring when my Dad and my Grandparents came back from Ohio, they did not see the tractor around. Grandpa found out that it was in his log milking barn. Charlie could not get the tractor into the barn, as the tractor was too tall for the doorway. Instead of taking the overhead exhaust pipe and muffler off, he chipped the concrete floor of the barn back enough to get it in through the swinging door and out of the weather. Grandpa was pretty upset with old Charlie but eventually took it in stride as he did not plan on starting up a dairy again. Whenever Grandpa told me that story about Charlie and his tractor he always shook his head in disgust!! We did use that old barn for livestock and we always milked a cow for fresh milk until I was almost out of high school.

I remember spending a lot of time in the barn with my old BB gun shooting mice that would come out from in between the logs in the walls. I was able to hone my shooting skills trying to eliminate those varmints. I later used a Remington bolt action .22 caliber to shoot gophers that made numerous holes and mounds in my Dad's fields. I also spent a lot of time in the winter shooting the numerous jack rabbits and I used Dad's 1951 Ford pickup to get around in. It was very good on the back country trails and it had two mounted spotlights, one on each side that could be operated from inside of the cab. Rabbit hunting was an after dark sport that many of us did to help pass the winter and we could make some money at it. A box of .22 caliber shells cost about one and a half cents apiece and we got about 0.35 to 0.50 cents for the rabbits. Later on, we could get 0.75 cents for them. Gas was about 0.25 to 0.30 cents a gallon. We usually could make money, but mostly it was fun.

Dad said one day after they had gotten to the farm from back east, probably around 1940, Rawhide was complaining about an upset stomach so he asked for grandma to make him some sagebrush tea. She took some sagebrush leaves, I guess, and made some tea out of the concoction. The next morning Dad woke up from sleeping in the porch, and saw Rawhide running around and hollering at his pigs as he tried to get them back in the pen. Dad thought the sagebrush tea trick had worked pretty good since the ole timer had acted like he was pretty sick the evening before. He said he cannot remember if he ever used it himself to know if it really worked or what it worked on. At that time the county road came down the hill and through the yard and Rawhide felt good enough to get his pigs out of the road, before someone drove by.

Day to day life on the Montana farm

The old log homestead shack was being used as a hog house in later years. When Dad told me it used to be the house they lived in at one time, I could hardly believe it. It stood solidly for years but the roof finally caved in. Some cabins have lasted longer than others. On a neighboring place about a mile away, there is an old homestead log cabin that was built with cottonwood logs and the walls are still standing. It is in the cottonwood trees so the wind cannot get to it but falling branches have been hard on the roof. A house goes to heck, after the roof gets bad and caves in. The cottonwood walls seemed to last longer if the logs were cut and allowed to dry out before being used. The homesteaders did not have the luxury of time then as they had to get a house ready before winter set in. Green logs will settle a lot if put in a house wall in that condition.

Cottonwood cannot be put in the ground as fence posts and be expected to last very long. In this bottom only badlands cedar, diamond willow (and maybe choke cherry) will make good fence posts. Diamond willow is a very strong, tough and good-looking wood that can be used for canes and a lot of other uses. The pinkish and pale-yellow wood is quite striking. Diamond Willow has gotten its name from the distinct look it has after small branches are removed from larger branches. When carved correctly, this leaves a pattern that has the shape of a diamond. It is a very unique look, but the tree is common around here. There are a lot of people that make canes from diamond willow. Jack Nickels has made a few and he says you have to cut it when it is green and not to big around or the cane will be too heavy. Ash is very strong and a heavy wood that makes good handles for axes and horizontal rail poles for corrals. It is probably the best firewood to be used in the stoves in this area.

Ted Steagall was another nearby neighbor on the farm. He had a house about halfway up the hill and about a mile west of Grandpas farm. Dad remembers riding horseback over to see him. He was a bachelor and had a one room homestead shack. Dad remembers that he had a bad habit of sticking a long piece of wood in the stove to keep it burning and push it in every once in a while so he would not have to cut it. Dad does not remember a lot about him, except that he was a loner. I guess his house burned down and he sold the place and went to the Kalispell area and they never heard from him again. My Dad thought his fireplace skills may have had a lot to do with his house fire. Steagall had a homestead patent on his property that I have a copy of.

A story Grandpa told me about, was one year they had a pretty poor crop year and did not have much money. I guess they did not have enough money to pay the property taxes on the farm. Grandpa liked to have a brew now and then, so he went to town and got into a small poker game. He said he got lucky and won enough to pay the taxes. I guess when he returned home Grandma was pretty "fit to be tied" with him, until he showed her the money. I can imagine her now and she probably would say, "Oh well", as it was one of her favorite sayings. I often have repeated her saying of "oh well", and Dave Renner, a good friend and classmate of mine, would remark to me, when I would say oh well, "that's a deep subject for a shallow mind"!!

Grandpa was a pretty good fisherman but did not seem to have a lot of time to go unless I wanted to go down to the point. This is what we called the point of land where the Milk River flowed into the Missouri. This was a great place to fish and was near our house. We caught channel cat, sauger and drum, and we threw away a lot of shiners, which are bony and almost impossible to eat, but we cut some of them up for bait. My other grandpa, my mothers' father, Adolph Moum would go fishing with me or with Grandpa Garwood. There were times we would bring home a lot of fish that we ate. Grandpa Marion did not like to eat fish very well but would have some at times. It seemed like anywhere on the Milk you could catch catfish but the Missouri was not a very good fishery except for some good deep holes. The current was almost too strong unless you threw spoons or spinners to get trout. The Mouth of the Milk was the best place to fish for years, but a couple of high water events eroded the outside bank and filled in the good fishing hole.

Edgar and Theona (Moum) Garwood

My parents were Edgar and Theona (Moum) Garwood. I am the oldest child and I have two younger sisters, Karen and Diane. I was the first born and Mom said it was very cold on that December day when they went to Glasgow, which is where I was born. At that time they lived in an apartment above Moms' uncle Ben Stenebakken's garage in Nashua, which was where my dad worked as a mechanic at that time. My Dad was an excellent mechanic and did his own mechanic work all the years that he farmed. Most of his work was done in a heated, 10x30 foot garage on the farm next to the house, and this garage is still standing. He has this old coal and wood stove in his house that once was in this garage. This stove has a double wall on it, so you cannot burn yourself by touching it. It is a very good wood stove but it does not have a very big door on it. The wood has to be cut just "right" to fit in the door. When dad was real young he burned his hand on an old single walled stove that would get very hot and he was never able to open his hand all the way open after that, but he has very good use with it and by looking at it you would not know it had been burned. He bought this old stove at an auction north of Nashua and he had it in his garage so he could heat it and be able to work on his vehicles during the cold winters, which can get very long here in eastern Montana. The northeastern part of Montana is more like western North Dakota weather and not as warm as the western and southern part of the state. In 1955 he built a larger shop to store more machinery in and could work on his tractors, as it had large doors. He was able to store his combine in it at that time, and still does.

Dad was scheduled to start school when he was 6 years old at the South Nashua School. The school was only one mile north of the farmhouse and it would have been very handy for him to have gone to school there. The teacher was Dessie Roberts and her father was Ed Roberts who lived on the school section land that I now lease as grazing for my cows. This is about a mile west of my current residence. He had lost the farm that he was living on and just squatted on the State land for several years. Dessie Roberts later married Gene Mattingly and they lived near the Missouri River until their retirement. Their old farmstead is the place that Patty and I now live on. We have raised all of our children (Stacy, Seth and Shawn) here. I believe it was homesteaded by Frank B. Kasten, and I have a copy of the homestead patent signed by Woodrow Wilson, the President at the time. It was later bought by Claude Mattingly, who was in WWI. Claude had homesteaded south of the Missouri in McCone County and then after the war he had purchased this farm just across the Missouri river in Valley County. My father bought the place from Gene and Dessie (Roberts) Mattingly in 1962 when Gene retired from the Army Corps of Engineers. Gene worked on the power lines out of Fort Peck Dam and he was the line boss before he retired. They did not have any children and after retirement, they moved to Truth or Consequences, New Mexico.

Dessie Roberts was a school teacher and taught at many schools including the South Nashua School and the Faranuf School, which is out by the Burke Ranch in southwest Valley County. When I started hunting out there, I remember asking permission from Don and his mother Myrtle Burke. Don later married Julie Gullickson and they had three kids, Keith, Kelly and Casey. Their children attended the Faranuf School near the ranch, until the school closed. Keith is ranching on the home place and Kelly has the Marcus Handley place. I have a copy of a picture from the Glasgow Courier when Dessie Roberts taught at the Faranuf School. In the picture was Dessie, along with students Don Burke, Myron Brown, Gordon Brown,

June Brown Castleberry, Jim Simon and Warren Brown. This picture was taken in 1930.

Anyway, back in 1927 the South Nashua Grade School was being taught by Dessie Roberts. This school house was less than a mile from Grandpa and Grandma's house. After the Watters family moved to a farm near the Galpin community, the Watters family attended the Galpin school. After that the South Nashua School was closed because there were not enough enrolled children to keep the school open. That summer before the school closed, Grandma took my father Edgar up to visit the South Nashua School and see Dessie. They figured that he would start school there in the fall. He would have liked to have gone to school there with Dessie as his teacher, and it would have been close. He ended up going to school in Nashua which was about 4 miles away across country. To get to school he rode a horse or cross country skied to school until eighth grade when he quit school, and sometimes he walked when his horse Tony bucked him off at the bridge! He quit school when my grandparents moved back to Ohio for a few years during the dirty thirties. Dad was not used to big schools, so he did not attend high school in Lewisburg, Ohio as he thought the school was almost as big as the town of Nashua. Dad was very good at math and electronics and quite smart even though he only went through the 8th grade.

In Ohio, and later in Michigan, he did mechanic work. For about a year, he worked construction on a bridge in Saginaw, Michigan, until he started coming back to Montana to farm during the summers after the dry years had started to pass. In the early forty's he was able to pay the back taxes on Grandpa's farm and the seed wheat loans. The thirties were tough times with the depression and dry times, and a lot of farms changed hands as they were up for taxes for whoever could pay them up. Grandpa's place was up for taxes for some time. Dad was able to pay up the taxes as Grandpa had maybe almost given up on the Montana farm and he had a good job in Dayton, Ohio. For a few years after that, Dad and Grandma farmed the land and he was able to make a living on it, while Grandpa worked in Ohio, both on the Lewisburg farm and at his plant job. Dad and Grandmother went back to Ohio those winters.

Dad met my mother after she moved here with her family. She first moved from Bottineau where she was born, and then Crosby, North Dakota with her parents, Adolph and Inga (Stenbakken) Moum, before coming to Nashua. They lived and farmed north of Nashua on the Ben Stenbakken place, who was Inga's brother, until he later sold the place. After that, they leased and ran a hotel in Nashua around 1940, and during that time, Grandpa Moum leased some land very near Nashua that he farmed. Later, Grandpa Moum worked as a laborer for the Great Northern Railroad and lived near the train depot in Nashua. Mom and Dad were married on February 7th of 1945. I was born December 4th of 1945 when Mom was 20 years old. She graduated from Nashua High School in 1944, and I in 1964, only twenty years apart. Mom worked at the hotel and Dad worked as a mechanic for Ben Stenbakken, my Mom's uncle, and they lived in a room above Uncle Ben's shop. After my Dad had come home after his time in the service, my parents had moved into Nashua, while my Grandparents still where running the farm.

Within the first year after I was born, my folks moved back out to the farm into the bridge timber house where they lived ever since. Until then, Dad would split his time and travel back and forth from Nashua to help on the farm and also work as a mechanic in Nashua. They have added many rooms to the main house over the years and a garage was built on, too. My Dad actually dug out a small basement by hand with the help of Grandpa and myself, probably in the late fifties. We had an elevator run by a small engine that we shoveled dirt into, which was then transferred up and into the 1951 Ford pickup. That pickup had a grain box and hoist on it so we could take it out and dump it where we needed some fill. We also had a 1938 Ford truck with a hoist that we also used. We also used both of these trucks to haul grain for the fall wheat harvest when they were not hauling dirt. After the dirt was taken out of the basement, we put screen on the walls and we put concrete grout in the screen and smoothed it out. This is referred to as screeding. We also put a concrete floor in the basement. On the east side of the basement is where we had the water line come into the house from the well, which is south of the house, below the hill, and was by Grandpa and Grandma's small house. We also had the water softener and water heater put in the basement. I had my room down there for several years as it was nice to have some privacy from the girls, and during the summer it was nice and cool down there. I really enjoyed living in the basement during my high school years and I did not mind at all that I had to walk outside the house to get to the basement. When I would come back from college it was nice to have my old room back. After a couple years of taking college agriculture classes at Montana State University in Bozeman, I joined the Army National Guard. I stayed in my basement room until I married Patty and we moved into a small trailer on the Mattingly place, which is approximately one and a half miles south of my parents' home place. This is the place where we still live at and where we raised our three children.

My sister Karen married Gary Stearns and had three children: Steven, Scott and Shari. Gary worked for Montana Power Company and they lived in Lewistown, Malta and now reside in Harlem. Karen was a beautician and later worked in a bank. For several years both Karen and Gary work at the Lumber Company in Harlem, but they are now retired.

After graduating from high school, my sister Diane was living in Apache Junction living with our grandparents, and helping take care of our grandmother, Gertrude Garwood. She met and married Scott Forbes. They summer in Montana and winter in Arizona. They have a different house now, but for many years lived in the trailer that Grandpa and Grandma had lived in. Scott is a real handyman and an especially fine steel worker. He has worked in a welding and fabrication shop for over 20 years. When he builds something from steel, he does a good job and when done it looks like it was professionally made. They still came to Montana for the summers and farmed with my Dad. Diane and Scott helped Dad with the gardening, which they all seemed to enjoy. Dad also kept about a half an acre of organic wheat that he uses to make my mothers' homemade whole wheat pancake recipe. They are (in my opinion) the best pancakes around and after Mom's passing, Dad learned to make them and he sometimes had two or maybe three breakfasts in a day. He enjoyed making them for himself and others. He was really proud of these pancakes! Dad has since passed on a couple of years ago, but until that time, he had homemade whole wheat pancakes every day!

In the fifties, Dad bought 320 acres of fairly sandy land, which was the old Marten Milstin place, about 7 miles west of their house, and that my folks owned for about 20 years. We referred to it as The Sandy Place, because of the soil consistency. This place is now the Glenn and Stephanie Meier ranch at the present time. When we started farming this highly erodible, sandy land we learned a lot about farming by using strips where we cropped the land every other year. We summer fallowed by controlling weeds and storing up moisture for the next crop year. Dad was a Valley Conservation District Supervisor then and learned a lot about how to eliminate erosion on this unstable, sandy soil structure. We found out how to summer fallow right after a rain and when we worked the ground then it would have small chunks of ground that would stick together and would crust over and harden to help prevent the soil blowing off from the wind. We just could not work it when it was dry or unless we had to control the weeds when they got taller and then maybe you could get away with it. At that time we did not have Glyphosate chemicals such as Roundup to spray the summer fallow which would kill every weed growing. This sandy land grew better barley than wheat as the wheat off this ground had low protein in the grain which made it not as profitable. Barley did not need high protein in it to be good for sale, so it was more profitable. This farm had a good sized cottonwood base hip roofed barn built by Martin Milstin, and it that had a nice loft with a rope in it where us kids could play in and swing on. My Dad did not have cows at this place, and as he did not live there the barn was not kept up and eventually the old barn came down in a bad storm. Charlie Johnson, who use to have a farm just north of Grandpa's farm, lived on the "Sandy Place" for a few years and his well loved 15-30 McCormick Deering tractor was pinned down for a while after the barn came down.

Charlie, who had helped keep the Montana farm running when my Grandparents went back to Ohio, had a homestead that bordered Grandpa's place to the north over the hill. Dad thought he had the place bought, as Dad already had money put down to buy the place. The realtor in charge of this transaction, an apparently sleazy realtor, came back the next day and said that someone had offered more for the land and that Dad could not afford to pay what the other person offered for it. This happened in the forties, and Dad was only about 20 then and did not know his rights and let the place go. A person learns from these kinds of stories. But even into his 90's, Dad still talked about how dumb it was for him to not get the land when he had placed a down payment on it!!

The Yager's lived on the south side of the Missouri river, right across and a little to the West. They live a little north of the old site of McCone City, which population wise, was one of the largest boom town during the building of the Dam. Many of the people who lived there worked on the spillway at Fort Peck Dam. John Yager had bought a tug boat from the Corps of Engineers but he had trouble with keeping the engine running. Dad was a very good mechanic and John contacted Dad and asked him to work on the engine and get it running. John was maybe using this tug boat to move barges around for people that had acquired them from the Corps. He would move them near the ranchers' place during high water so they could salvage the wood and the steel off of them. A lot of barns and other buildings here in this bottom are made from the decking off of these barges. The tug boat was south of the river and Dad was on the north side, and he had to get across the river to work on the boat. Dad decided to wade across the river with some tools to work on the engine. He had to walk back and forth some to find shallow water, but he made it across and got it running after a couple trips! The river must have been low at that time, because you certainly can't wade across it anymore.

John Yager had some farmland for a while on the north side of the river so Dad drove over to talk to him. John was still farming with horses at the time. Dad was only about 20 and John was getting pretty old. Dad was waiting for John at the end of the field. Dad noticed that Johns' corn rows were pretty crooked, but you have to remember he was seeding with a team of horses. When John had gotten up to Dad and after they told each other, "Hello!", Dad was giving him kind of a time about his crooked rows. John thought a little about this and told Dad. "Don't you know sonny, is that you can grow more corn in a crooked row, than you can in a straight one!!" Ha! I knew John's son Bud pretty well and we drank more than a few brews together before he passed away several years ago from heart problems. We were in the Nashua Sleighers snowmobile and sledding club for several years together and attended many functions together.

Buds wife, Virginia (Bellon) Yager and her son, Toby still operate the ranch right across the river to the west of my place. Even though our houses are only two miles apart, the river splits our farms and we live in two different counties. One night, Bud and Virginia babysat our daughter Stacy, when we went to a Jaycee and Jayceen function in Scobey, I believe. Bud said he remembered being woken up in the morning from some loud noises. Here he found her playing in the pots and pans in the kitchen! She was about two at the time and was having fun making noise with the utensils. Bud always told me that story when we met, as it was he remembered it well.

On that occasion, Patty and I stayed at the Meyer Mansion in Scobey. Many nights after attending a quarterly meeting in Scobey, many of the couples would stay overnight at Gary and Bonnie Meyer's house. It was the get together place after the club closed down and most of the couples would sleep on the carpet somewhere in the house rather than driving a hundred miles to home after drinking all evening. This happened many times after meetings in Scobey, so therefore their house was dubbed Meyer Mansion. We really thank Gary and Bonnie for supplying a bed and breakfast for many of us in the wild Jaycee days!! Those were such great times and Jaycees really helped me and many others to be better speakers and civil servants!

The Meyer's had three children Ron, Ken and Deana (now Ferestad). The Meyers moved to Fort Peck quite a few years ago so we see them fairly often.

Dads' very good friend George "Punk" Nicol, farmed land near the Sandy place as well as northwest of Dad's house. This worked out as they could help each other out if the other needed it. There was water and damp ground in the low spots; we farmed around the water holes and eventually kept working inward and we would get stuck often. The soil was light, sandy, and we always had a long cable on the tool bars that we used for pulling out the cultivator. If you got stuck and could not pull the cultivator anymore, we would get unhooked from it and get out to dry ground and then hook the cable in between, you could usually get it out by yourself. If you could not, you would have to go find a neighbor who was working in the area to help get you out so the work could get done. It happened to everyone at times, so we helped each other out and enjoyed the visits when we did get together. Sometimes while having a visit, we shot gophers.

There were hundreds of gophers around, which are now called Richardson ground squirrels. We spent a lot of time shooting them with a .22 rifle to try to control them as much possible. If you did not, they would eat your crop out 10 or 20 feet from each den. This was very enjoyable being able to carry a gun on the tractor to give us a break from the constant dust and we learned good shooting form from this practice. The gophers prefer the lightest soil possible to make their dens in. It was in this sandy soil that I first seen burrowing owls. They are small and eat gophers, mice and prairie dogs and they use gopher holes for protection and nesting. It was in this area also that I first seen badgers, otherwise known as "gopher chompers". Badgers will dig gopher holes out, even all winter long, which is part of their survival. They make large holes but they get a lot of gophers, so we did not mind so much.

Friends of mine, Melvin and Leroy Novak, said that their Dad Joe hated badgers so much he would chase them down with a 12 inch crescent wrench and when they turned to fight he would finish them off with the wrench. If you know how vicious they are and look, you would have to very brave to do this. I have trapped badgers and I always used a .22 to dispatch them and to use a crescent wrench is border line crazy in my book.

In the 70's sometime, Dad traded this Sandy Place for the Lee Merrick place, which Terry Pointer had owned for several years. This place is on the north side of the Missouri River and much closer to Dad's place than the Sandy place was, which made it easier to farm. This is where I now summer my cows and they have good water to drink and can cool off in the river. Dad had 32 acres of tilled ground and about 90 acres of brush and grass on that place. My sister Diane and her husband Scott own this place now.

Terry Pointer had a ranch in McCone County and would bring his cows here for the winter. In the spring he would move them back out into the hills where there was good summer grass. Terry and his family lived on this river ranch in a mobile trailer for a few years and were good neighbors. Their children Tom, Sean and Kathryn graduated from Nashua High School. There is land out south that was called Pointer place, as well, and is located east of the dry arm of Fort Peck Reservoir. There was a small community out there and some of their neighbors were Zack and Cecil Bennet, Loren and Bernice Musgrove, Kris Sorenson, Palmer Strand, Tom Pointer (Terry's father), George Boyum and a little further away the Bill Kirkland ranch. These places were on Spring Creek, Bobcat Creek and Bear Creek. Bernice Musgrove was a teacher and home schooled many of the kids out there.

My family got to know the Musgrove's real well as they moved down on the Missouri River bottom with their children Pat, Lee (Buck) and twins Karl and Karen. They moved to a place only three miles from Dad's and they become good friends with my sister Karen and I. We spent a lot of spare time together with the Musgrove's and have many stories that we can tell on each other. My Dad purchased their place the summer of 1964 so they could move to Fort St. John, British Columbia, Canada to start a new ranching life. Bob Strand and I went up to visit them in September of 1964 where we hunted and seen black bear, moose, deer and heard our first wolves howl. Since then I have been up to see them and have always enjoyed myself when we go up to visit. Loren and Bernice and their kids came down to visit many times also. When the Musgrove's were about ready to migrate to the Upper Cache Creek, which flows through their place into the Peace River, I got to meet Jack and Peggy Nickel at the Musgrove house as they were friends with the Musgrove's. Since then I have got to visit with Jack many times and I really enjoy his cowboy humor. He is a great man and now, at ninety-eight, he is still pretty spry and is an icon of an old time cowboy. His ranch is in McCone County, near the Missouri River. Peggy has been gone now for several years and Jack is now remarried to Pearl.

When I started to write this book, my Dad was about to turn 92 in April 23rd, 2013 and at that time was still is pretty spry, but he did use a cane some. He called his cane his best friend. He had chores every day, feeding and watering his and Diane's cats in the barn and his shop twice a day. He would open the doors in the morning and close the doors every evening so the wild critters could not get in. He also was still cutting some of his wood for the wood stove. Scott Forbes and I would bring in some longer lengths of wood and he cut them to the length that he wanted. He also got some wood from Rick and Silver Tihista, and Rick and his wife, Pat, would get hay from Dad for their horses and cows. He kept the chain on his chainsaw sharp with his angled hand file. Feeding the barn cats and keeping his house warm gave him a purpose and the will to get up every morning and get after it! Several years ago, Dad and I went over to the Nickels Ranch in McCone County to visit Jack and Pearl. Jack and Dad were classmates in school and they had a great time visiting about the old times. Dad has since passed but these two men are some of the great icons of the South Nashua country!

Plumbing and Pole-vaulting

The best year of my young life, 1957, was when I was 12 years old. I could hunt big game, we got running water in the house (so no more visits to the shack out back) and we got black and white TV. What a great year! The two "holer" toilet was about 100 feet behind the house and across a ditch. In the old days people would comment on the toilet as whether it was a one or a two "holer"!! At one time we had to cross to it on a plank but dad later put in a bridge over the ditch to get to the "shack out back", as we called it. The ditch was a real shallow but about ten-foot wide, and during snowy or icy conditions it was pretty tough to cross, especially when you really had to go to it in a hurry! This outhouse started leaning pretty bad a few years ago and after some heavy snows lay on, it finally fell flat to the ground. We did use it for emergencies for quite a few years and it served its purpose pretty well.

When I was about 10 years old, Karen and I were playing outside of the house and I got the idea that I could pole vault across the ditch. I am not sure what I used for a pole, but Karen watched me ungracefully soar about 3/4's of the way across. I landed backwards into the far bank side of the ditch. When I landed, I hurt my left arm. It was dislocated at the elbow and stuck out of the joint rather grossly. Mom was not very happy with me! We took the trip to Glasgow to see the doctor to get it put back in place. Maybe this is why I did not try pole vaulting in High School!

Stories as told by to me by my father, Edgar Garwood:

A story that my Dad tells is from about the last time he seen Simon Anderson. Simon was an older brother of our next door neighbor, Rufus Anderson. Simon was getting pretty old at the time of this story and he was maybe 20 years older than Dad. Dad maybe was still fixing radio and television sets at the time, as he traveled all over the county side. Many people still remember Dad for this service! Anyway, Simon told Dad that he could remember things that he did as a small kid, right down to the finest detail, "but what I did yesterday, just forget it!!" He would say this while lifting his arms up in the air with disgust! None of us are getting any younger and I think we all can relate to this story!

Dad tells a story from his youth when he had a pet skunk. The name of his skunk was Joe! He had the skunk for a few weeks with no trouble and he was getting quite fond of him. It seems he had not seen the skunk all day and he went up to the "shack out back" before he went into the house for night. When he came out of the toilet, he saw movement under a wooden grain bin nearby. The bin was built up on blocks so water could run under it and not get the grain wet as it was along the side of the hill and water ran here with it rained. Dad said that he looked under the building and he could see the skunk playing around under there. He crawled in a few feet and reached in and grabbed the skunk by the tail and started pulling it out. All of a sudden he got sprayed in the face!! He said he barely got out from under the shed before he ran out of air. When Dad tells the story he says, "it wasn't Joe!!" Dad said that was the last time he had a pet skunk!!

Another story Dad would tell was about how in the spring of 1936 after Marion Garwood said: "That's enough, we're quitting the dairy!", Grandpa Marion took the money from selling the dairy cows and equipment to John E. (Johnny) Paul and went on a trip to Ohio. He bought a 120-acre farm and a used Chevrolet car from his brother Amber, who was working as a used car salesman, and returned to Montana to move the family back to the Lewisburg, Ohio farm. He did not sell the Montana farm but let two bachelors, Rawhide Johnson and Charlie Johnson, (not related that I know of) watch the place for them. Dad had planned on starting high school in Lewisburg. In the fall on Dad's first day at high school when he went to Lewisburg he thought that the school was as big as the town of Nashua. This scared him so much that he never went back for the second day. He got a job at a gas station doing clean up and then pumping gas. Dad said at that time gas was .21 cents a gallon in the car. A patron wanted five gallons and he gave Dad a $5.00 bill. Dad did not figure the change right and gave the man back $4.95 in change. The man was a local man and said, "Sonny. You gave me back too much money." He then gave Dad back a dollar bill to put in the till. Dad did not say how long he worked at the gas filling station but he always remembered that mistake making change.

The next place Dad talks about working at is in Michigan. Dad's Grandparents on his Mother Gertrude's side of the family lived in Michigan, although they were from Kentucky originally. He had gone to visit his Grandparents and he found a job carrying hod up to brick layers with the C.B. Culbertson Company. He would carry the hod filled with bricks and supplies up ladders to a second floor and it was hard work, but he was a hard worker. When he went to get his first check the secretary asked what was his social security number? Dad then asked her what a social security number was? She told him he needed a number before Dad could be paid. Dad was only seventeen at the time and he told her he was eighteen and made up his birth date so he could get paid. He worked with this company on several jobs and finished the season working on the Saginaw River Bridge. The old decking were wood planks which were very slippery and there were a lot of accidents on this bridge. They replaced the facing of the bridge with metal that was narrowly spaced for better traction. This surface allowed rain to fall through to the river below. His foreman on these jobs liked Dad and he was told that if he came back he would be made a foreman as this man had been promoted up. Dad liked the work but he did not like the damp cold of the Michigan north country. He did not want the job of having to tell workers, many who were older than him and who had worked for this company for several years, how to do their jobs. He decided to come back to Montana to try to make the farm profitable. It was still the late Dirty Thirties and he would seed a crop and wait out the summer, if it did not rain he would go back to Ohio with Grandma Gertrude for the winter. Grandpa Marion had a good job with Frigidaire in Dayton, Ohio so he stayed there most of the year. The rains started coming in the early 1940's so Dad was able to make a living from the Montana farm that he still lived on until the day he died.

Adolph and Inga (Stenbakken) Moum

Adolph and Inga were my grandparents on my mother's side of the family. They met north of Nashua, Montana while crossing paths on a country road but spent their early married years in North Dakota, where most all of their children were born, ten girls and one boy. Their children were: Eleanor, Inez, Theona (who was my mother, who is mostly called Toni), Helen, Adolph (called Al), Florence, Donna, Gloria, Darlene, JoAnn and Sandra. They moved to Nashua, Montana in 1939 after having lived in and around both Bottineau and Crosby, North Dakota. Grandpa Moum had a brother that lived north of Nashua whose name was Alfred, but they moved here to help with the Stenbakken farmstead, which was Grandma Inga's family. This land was also northwest of Nashua. Erland Stenbakken, was married to Jorunn Madland and had sons Herman, Eivand, and Bernard, and daughters Annetta, Inga, Georgine and Mary. Erland and eldest son Herman filed homestead patents on adjoining quarter sections in 1908, starting the Stenbakken connection to Valley County.

This land eventually came to Bernard (Ben) Stenbakken, a younger son of Erland. Grandpa Moum farmed for Uncle Ben for some time as help was needed on the farm. A tornado destroyed that house and Ben later sold the farmland to Adolph Nybakken. The Moum's then moved to the Golphney Place, where their youngest daughter Sandra was born. The Moum family lived on this place, which was near the Porcupine Creek, and Mom always told stories about swimming in the creek. Eventually, they took over the rent of and operated a hotel in Nashua, and my Mother remembered that it was The Nashua Hotel. At the time the Moum family moved to Nashua, the Fort Peck Dam project was nearing completion.

Grandpa Moum later started to work for the Great Northern Railroad as a laborer. They lived in a small house along north side of the railroad tracks. It seemed to me that when we visited them it was interesting to watch the trains go by and watch the mail bag from Nashua be picked up by a man on the train with a hook without the train even slowing down. The train speeding by in Nashua was always exciting for a farm boy and it was much longer than the train that I was able to see that was going back and forth slowly from Wiota to powerhouse project on my Dad's farm. I cannot even imagine my grandparents and their children, living that close and getting any sleep with the tracks a hundred feet away. There was also a vehicle crossing about three hundred feet away from their house. The engineers of every train had to blow the whistle at every crossing and this one in Nashua was no exception. There was a larger house to the west of the Nashua Depot that was lived in by the depot master, and next door to that was the house my Grandpartents lived in. This was a neat, fairly large building that was busy with all kinds of deliveries going both directions. I remember going into the depot with Grandpa at times and it was an interesting building for this time period in Nashua. Later on, when the depot was not needed by the railroad, it was sold or given to the town of Nashua and is now the Senior Citizen Center. It was moved across the tracks to Front Street, on the south side of the tracks and off of the railroads property.

When I was young and I was still in school in the lower grades, I can remember at times walking over to see Grandma and visit her if Mom was coming in to get me after school. At the time I remember visiting my grandparents by the train station, I spent time with my Mom's siblings that still lived in Nashua. Ellie, the eldest of the Moum children, had moved to Seattle already. JoAnn had already graduated from high school and was going to college in Bozeman, Montana to be a nurse. Aunt Sandy was still in school in Nashua and Aunt Helen's daughter Beverly was living in Nashua with my Grandparents. The rest of the Moum siblings had started migrating to the west coast after completing school. About 1956 Grandpa and Grandma and the rest of the family still living in Nashua, with the exception of Mom and Inez, who had married and stayed in Valley County, moved out west to Seattle.

It was great having my grandparents living in a neat city like Seattle as it was such a great place to visit. There was so much to see, like the Government docks where ships of all kinds would go through from the Pacific Ocean to the inner ports on some lakes in the Seattle area. I liked going to the Woodland zoo with its many animals to see and it had a small railroad train to ride on.

I remember one time we were at the zoo. This small railroad train did not have any tops on its cars. I had ridden on it in the past and it just made a big oval loop all around the park. There was a big sprinkler that was going around and around and I got the idea, not my cousin Jim, to pull the sprinkler up next to the tracks. I pulled the sprinkler up close to a tree so the driver could not see it until the engine was right next to it. Jim and I waited a ways off behind a tree to see what might happen. I figured that the train would go through the spray and the people would get just a little wet. When the train came around the corner and got into the stream of water, the driver stopped, not knowing what to do. I think he was going to back up, but just sat there for a little while until he decided to continue forward and went through the sprinkler. I think the riders got a pretty good watering on a warm summer day!! We laughed some, then Jim said we better get out of here before we get caught and we ran to the other end of the park. If I remember right maybe Nancy and Karen were on the train or maybe not, as it has been a lot of years ago. Who knows; maybe they enjoyed it, but then maybe not!!

There were so many great places to eat on the sea shore and I learned how great fish and chips were. My cousins, Jim and Nancy, lived on Bainbridge Island and we would have to take the ferry over to see them. I have such great memories of staying there and fishing, rowing on a small boat with Jim, seeing trout in a small stream, catching and releasing crabs that were hiding under small rocks. I also remember eating blue berries off the bush and I loved watching ships go by. It was such a great place to vacation with my parents, even though my Dad had to stay at the farm at times. I still remember picking those big, black slugs off of the vegetables in the garden in Seattle. I still have a lot of cousins that still live there and also in the Portland area. I sure do not get back there as much as I would like to. When we went out there to visit, we often took the train, and in later years my Mom would pack up the grand-children and take the train out to Seattle to visit family. Stacy and Seth have found memories of their trip's with Grandma Toni.

Of my Mom's siblings, her sisters JoAnne and her husband Don Thuring, Darlene and Sandy still live in Seattle, as well as her only brother Al, and his wife Joyce, who currently live in Poulsbo, which is on Puget Sound. It's nice to have the family connection on the coast, although we do not make it out to visit nearly as much as we would like.

Eleanor, or Ellie as she was known, was the oldest of the Moum children, and she was the first, but not the last, of the Moum family that moved to the Seattle area. She married Navy man Arthur Ericson and they had two children, Jimmy and Nancy. She and her husband ran a smorgasbord and restaurant, and they visited Sweden and Norway a number of times. Ellie compiled a Moum family tree book with information dating back as far as 1766. This included information on her great, great, great, great grandmother who was born and raised in Ogndal, Norway, and traced the roots of her son Arent and his wife Sirie. The lineage traced through the time that Anton Moum immigrated to the United States. Ellie worked on this family tree project until her death in 1976.

Inez married Louie Maas and lived in Glasgow, which is about twenty-five miles from Dad's farm. He was a jeweler and worked for the St. Clair jewelry store in Glasgow. He liked to fish with Dad, and I remember fishing with them at the Pickthorn dredge cuts. He had a small boat and the old trailer is still on the farm. He had a heart problem and died when he was quite young. They had a girl, Bonnie, who is the oldest of my first cousins and was only about 12 at the time when her father Louie passed away. Karen and I spent a lot of time with Bonnie as we were the only cousins of the Moum family that lived here in Valley County. Mom and Inez were very close and got together often. Inez later married Myron Brown, and they lived in Glasgow for many years before moving out to Woodburn, Oregon sometime in the 80's.

Theona, the third eldest child, was my mother and was known as Toni to family and friends, although my Grandpa Marion Garwood always called her Theona, "because that was her name". Ha! She was born Bottineau

County North Dakota and she often talked about the beauty of the Peace Gardens in Bottineau. She graduated from Nashua and married my Dad, and lived the rest of her life in Valley County. She had three children, myself, Karen and Diane. She loved to cook and bake and always kept us well fed, and she enjoyed reading and watching television and listening to music. She also was a great letter writer and when she could, she enjoyed going to visit family and friends. In their later years, Mom and Dad spent several months a year in the warm climate of Arizona, and Mom was particularly fond of these trips south. Mom passed away at the family farm in 2006, and we all still miss her very much.

Helen was married to George Shaw in Seattle and lived in Kalispell, Montana, where George was from and owned a mine. They had four children, Danny, Jerry, Douglas and Beverly. Helen suffered from poor health and for some time, the youngest child Beverly lived with my Grandparents.

Al, (although his name is Adolph, no one ever calls him that), was the only boy of the Moum family. I can't imagine having that many sisters, but I think he was pretty spoiled by them all. Al married Joyce Hansen and they have three children, Alane, Adean and Alan. Al and Joyce lived and worked in the Seattle area, having a house on Puget Sound that was wonderful to visit, and now have a home in Poulsbo, Washington, which is on Liberty Bay. One way to get to their home is by Ferry boat, which is pretty neat. They have come to the farm to visit on many occasions over the years and are always welcome guests. They have also supplied a place to stay when their Montana relatives have come to the coast to visit. Uncle Al is famous in the family for calling on birthdays and singing Happy Birthday, and his love of conversation, which is a Moum trait! I always remember Uncle Al with a camera and taking many pictures. They make their home in the Seattle area but have done a lot of traveling all over the country visiting family and going to blue grass festivals.

Florence married Joe Corrado of Portland Oregon, which is where they lived and raised their children, Jodine, Joe, and Kari. Joe worked construction his whole life and was just a great guy to spend time around. I remember their house in Portland had a great view of the river, which I think was the Columbia River. Uncle Joe used to talk about swimming in the river as a youngster but talked about how polluted the river had become and how he would not dare swim in the river now, and that was probably over fifty years ago when he told me that. Florence often made trips back to Montana and would stay on the farm with my folks. My Mom sure enjoyed these visits from Flo, as we all did.

Donna lived in Seattle and had one son, Gregg. Donna also used to come out to visit almost every summer and always enjoyed the train ride out to Montana. She loved to sleep and drink coffee out on the screened front porch of Mom and Dad's farmhouse. Her son Gregg spent a couple summers on the farm helping Dad and me with some of the farm work. Donna always enjoyed being on the farm and Mom always enjoyed having her come to visit.

Gloria was never married but lived in Seattle and was close to family out there. Gloria used to make trips out to Montana, usually traveling with Donna on the train, and always seemed to enjoy her time on the Montana farm. She always seemed to have a cup of coffee handy and also enjoyed time on the front porch, just watching cars go by on the road and enjoying the scenery.

Darlene moved out to Seattle after high school and was married to Victor Spino. Uncle Vic was also a great guy and I loved to visit with him. He was proud of his Italian heritage. He was a great pool shooter and I could never beat him. Darlene and Vic had a great home in Seattle and raised three children, Michael, Michelle and Mark. Darlene was always very well dressed and very nice and had a wonderful smile, and she and Vic made occasional trips back to Montana to visit the town where she grew up and graduated high school from.

JoAnn was the youngest of the Moum children that graduated from high school in Nashua, and she has never missed coming back for an

All-School class reunion. She married Don Thuring, a really great guy, and they were blessed with three children, Britt, Bryan and Brenda. JoAnn was a nurse and Don worked for the Corps of Engineers. They are very active in their local church and have made many much appreciated trips to Montana to visit the farm. Stacy remembers making several trips out to Seattle, and Don and JoAnn always provided a welcome place to stay and a friendly face at the train station. They lived in Germany for several years with Don's job and now live back in the Seattle area. They have a second home at Ocean Shores and though I have never visited that home, I have seen many pictures and it looks like a beautiful place.

Sandra, or Sandy, as she is known, was the youngest of the Moum children and perhaps the only one who did not graduate from high school in Nashua. Sandy was married to Ray Nutt and lived in Sand Point Alaska, and had a daughter, Kandi. Sandy was later married to Earl Yarbor. She lived in Alaska for many years before moving back to the Seattle area, where she still lives today. Sandy was my aunt, but was only a few years older than me, so she sometimes feels more like a cousin than an aunt. Sandy is known for love of animals.

On my Mom's side of the family, I have plenty of cousins, but only a few are close to my age. Bonnie was around two years older than me, and then I was the second oldest cousin, Jim Ericson was third, Karen was the fourth and Nancy Ericson was next. We were older than the rest of the cousins, but we all got together often for family get-together's in Seattle or at Dad's farm. It seems like everyone enjoyed going to the farm.

My grandmother Inga passed away from cancer when I was only about 11 or 12 years old so I do not have a lot of memories about her, but she was a loving wife and mother who raised eleven children. When she moved to Seattle with Grandpa Moum, we did not get see them but about once a year. It was so sad that she died so young and a lot of her grandchildren did not get to know her.

Grandpa Moum would come out from Seattle after Grandma passed away to visit those of us that still were here in eastern Montana. He drove a black '51 or '52 Chevy that still sits gracefully in the sod on a hill above my parents' farm. This car is about a hundred yards from where a friend of mine, L.B., calls our "bone pile", which is where in the old days everyone discard their junk, and some used up treasures. Like the old saying goes, someone's junk is someone else's treasure!! Awhile back now I looked through Grandpa's car to see what I could find. I opened the trunk and looked in it. In the trunk was his old lunch box, and it reminded me of how Grandpa used that lunch box when he helped with irrigating and went fishing. Grandpa liked to fish and we would spend many hours fishing at "the point", which is at the mouth of the Milk River. Once when we were fishing together there, we seen a rattlesnake that was swimming across the Missouri River toward where we were fishing. Grandpa got a long stick and kept pushing the snake off shore until it went down stream toward the east side of the Milk River.

Another time I was fishing with both of my Grandpa's when one of them caught a huge long sturgeon back a little ways from where the murky water of the Milk River meets the clear, cold Missouri River. This species of fish was caught back in the 50's and lots of anglers used to catch them using earth worms for bait. From what I remember about that fish, that it was about five foot long. At that time, it was not an endangered species and we had several meals from it. We also caught a lot of sauger, channel cats, drum, suckers, carp and shiners (or goldeye's). These shiners were not very edible because of their many bones but they made great cut bait.

When Patty and I were married on September 13, 1969 we bought a medium sized trailer and moved it down on the Mattingly farm that Dad had bought in 1963. The next spring Grandpa Moum made the trip to Montana like he did most years to stay on the farm and help irrigate. He decided that we needed a good lawn around our trailer. I am not sure where he got the Kentucky bluegrass but it was a variety that did real well here in eastern Montana. He leveled the yard and tilled it to get rid of weeds and unwanted native grass. He seeded the grass and watered it daily and sometimes twice a day in hot weather. The lawn turned out great and after almost fifty years it is still a thick and beautiful stand of grass that does not need much care or water. The most care it needs is frequent mowing because it thrives so well. Grandpa Moum also planted Mom and Dads' lawn which has flourished for 60 years. It looks quite a bit like the grass he used at our place. Patty still talks about how hard he worked to plant, water and establish the lawn in our yard. We thank him yet again for our great lawn after living here for 49 years.

Grandpa Moum really liked to dance, even when he was in his 80's and up to his 90th birthday, he was quite agile for his age. He lived in a trailer house in Seattle by himself, but he was next door to my cousin Jim Ericson, who was very close to Grandpa and watched over him in his later years. When Grandpa passed away, I think he was just a few days short of his 94th birthday and he still had full head of thick gray hair. He was a very distinguished man who worked hard all of his life.

Amber Garwood, his son Arthur and grandson Bob; Farest Garwood and her husband Blair Stevens

My grandparents ended up moving to Montana from back east, and eventually another Garwood joined. My grandfather's brother was named Oral Amber, but I have only ever heard him called Amber, and his wife and their young son Arthur moved out to Montana, but I am not sure what year that might have been. They moved to Wolf Point, MT and the family operated a liquor store and later a grocery store until the late 1960's. Later, Arthur and his son Bob operated a gold and silver shop in the mall in Great Falls and later in Havre, Montana. Bob and his wife Theresa continued to live in Havre until their deaths a couple of years ago. Bob was a year younger than me and we used to spend a lot time fishing together, and sometimes hunting. Arthur was a man that was always looking for gold and silver. He had a small floating dredge on the Dearborn River. Karen and I stayed with them for a few days and found some small rubies or garnets, but no gold nuggets.

My Dad was an only child, so I did not have any first cousins on his side of the family. I have a 3rd cousin, Bob Garwood, who was a year younger then me and he lived in Wolf Point, which is about thirty-five miles away. Bob's father was Art, whom was my Dad's first cousin. Art was the son of Amber Garwood, my grandfather Marion's brother. Bob loved to fish and I kind of did too. Bob was crazy about fishing and he also enjoyed taping music on cassette tapes. We have fished all over the state together. He loved to start a campfire along the river or lake and fish all night long. He also liked to eat fish more than I did and he preferred catfish. I remember when Bob's family lived near Great Falls and our family came to visit. Art was an avid metal and gem hunter. He owned a small floating vacuum that they called a dredge that would suck sand from the bottom of streams and where we would pan and screen to maybe "get rich". It sure was exciting to be in them cold streams on warm days looking for gold. We did find some small garnets and other stones that were pinkish; I do not know where they got to now, but at the time I had one and Karen got to keep one.

My grandfather's sister Farest and her husband Blair Stevens also moved from Ohio and lived in Montana for several years. They operated a gas station and small store north of Oswego on old Highway 2 until the highway was moved north to the present location and away from their business. They eventually left Oswego, although I am not sure what year that might have been. After that, they moves south of Nashua and lived on the Musgove place, which my Dad bought in 1964. They were living on that place early in my marriage and Patty remembers that people would call our house to visit with them, and she would have to go down the road to get them and bring them back to our place for the phone call. They later moved to Arizona. Blair was a musician by trade and he, along with my Grandpa and Uncle Amber formed a band, played music here in Eastern Montana and even recorded several records for family entertainment.

Louis and Elvira (Osterberg) Wesen

Many fine, hard working people carved a life out of the Milk and Missouri River valleys. The Garwood's can trace their land back to homestead patents in eastern Montana, as well as the Wesens and Osterbergs, which are my wife Patty's relations.

Louis and Elvira Wesen were my wife's grandparents on her fathers' side of the family. I did not know Louis as he died before I married Patty, but I did know Elvira. I really respected "Grandma Wesen" as she was a pioneer homesteader who came to Montana and homesteaded west of Glasgow, Montana in 1909, when she was around 21 years old.

Elvira was born to John and Christine (Matsen) Osterberg in the Swedish community of Kensingston, Minnesota in 1888. The family had eventually settled in northern North Dakota, near Mohall. Elvira had first visited Glasgow in 1907 along with her sister Ester Osterberg, to visit their older brothers Edwin, who had homesteaded west of Glasgow, and Henry, who had homesteaded just north of Glasgow. The Homestead Act requirements had changed around that time, and Elvira was able to homestead 320 acres, instead of 160 acres. Her first homestead shack was about a mile west of her brother Edwin Osterberg's place, who had homesteaded near the Mahon-Hoyt reservoir seven miles west of the Glasgow Courthouse. Ester also had a homestead near Henry's place. So, several of the Osterberg siblings homesteaded in Valley County, including Edwin, Elvira, Henry and Ester. Their brother Johnny Osterberg also farmed in Valley County.

Louis Wesen was born September 13, 1886 to Claus and Anna (Oberg) Wesen in the Swedish community in Starbuck, Minnesota. Later the Wesen family moved to North Dakota where there was land available to be homesteaded. I have heard the name Tolley mentioned, which was near Mohall. The Wesens and Osterbergs knew each other from their time in North Dakota. Louis came to Montana in 1908 and homesteaded land on the north bench on Roosevelt Trail. He later sold his improvements to Syven Hanson or possibly a Breigenzer. He later worked for the Hauge Bakery and talks of "throwing" candy on a hook and pulling it. He went back to North Dakota after selling his land in Valley County, but I am not sure what year that was.

While proving up her homestead, Elvira worked for Dr. Hoyt two days a week washing clothes, cleaning and cooking for a dollar a day. She would also spend time with her sister, Ester Osterberg (later Mrs. Tom Nilson), who had homesteaded her own land northeast of Glasgow, by the Opheim turnoff. Elvira's homestead shack was a double wall 12 x12 with a rounded roof, which was nearly identical to her sister Ester's shack. They can be told apart in photo's only with a discerning eye. Elvira's restored homestead shack has been donated by the family and moved to the Valley County Pioneer Museum in Glasgow, Montana, and is on display to the public and is a great example of homestead homes. At some point after being used as a home, the building was used as a corn crib and granary. That's how pioneers did it, they used and reused and not much went to waste. There are many great family pictures of Elvira and Ester and their homestead "shack's", pictures that include brothers Edwin, Henry, and even a dog and a horse. At some point, Elvira went back to her North Dakota home at Mohall to help with threshing and renew her acquaintance with Louis Wesen.

Louis and Elvira were married December 6th, 1911 in Mohall, North Dakota. A son, Alton, was born the next year in Mohall. In the spring they returned to Montana to prove up on her homestead. Vera was born in 1914. They proved up on the Homestead August 27th, 1914 and the Homestead Patent was signed by then President Woodrow Wilson. However, later in 1914 Louis developed a leakage of the heart and Dr. Hoyt suggested that they move to better climate so they moved back to North Dakota. Hard to imagine the climate was that much different, or much better!! Louis worked on rented farms near Mohall for the next ten years. Five children were born in North Dakota: Clayton in 1916; Maurice in 1918; Paul in 1921; and the twins June and John, in1923.

At the end of November, 1924 the family headed back to Montana in a 1918 Model T Touring car with side curtains; they traveled the Roosevelt trail. The first night they stayed in a hotel in Williston. Elvira's brother, Bernard, visited them at the hotel that night as he was riding in the boxcar carrying their team of horses, furniture and other possessions. Somewhere around Frazer they broke a spindle on the front wheel and pulled the car to town with a truck to get parts. They left about dark for Glasgow and got lost a couple of times, eventually ending up at a gravel pit. Elvira was the navigator and thought the big dipper was in the northwest but it actually rotates around the North Star.

When they realized they were lost they found a nearby ranch house and they stayed that night there. The next morning they had realized they had been heading north towards Scobey. That day was December 1st, and they continued on toward Glasgow and when they arrived, they stopped at Elvira's brother Henry Osterberg's home to visit. Turns out that Henry is the grandfather of Isabell Hill Collins, who is a classmate of mine from the Nashua class of 1964. It seems like everyone knows everyone in these smaller communities. They then hauled their belongings from the railroad boxcar with their wagon and team to Edwin Osterberg's house to west of town. They lived with Elvira's brother Edwin in a house by the Mahon and Hoyt Reservoir. After moving back to the Glasgow area, three more children were born to Louis and Elvira, Forrest, in 1925, Rita in1931, and Myrna in 1935.

They broke up most of their land with six horses and a sulkey, which is a one bottom plow. In 1925, to go to school, the children walked to the Harebo place and rode the bus into Glasgow. For two years their bus driver was Carrie Milman, who lived at what is now the Don Jones place; this bus was pulled by a team of horses. In the winter the bus was a wide-runner sleigh and had a wood burning stove in the center for heat. It was an hour ride to the red school (the catholic church now), and later the South Side School and then the High School in 1928. In 1938, Louis Wesen drove the school bus, which had evolved to a truck with a bus on the back.

As the children grew up, they all had plenty of chores to do, from hauling water, chopping wood, chopping ice, to watering, milking and feeding the cows. Elvira baked bread every other day and there were always lots of dishes to do for a family of twelve. Clayton remembered washing clothes with a two cycle gas engine Maytag washing machine. It did not work very well and he ran the agitator some times by hand. "It was hard times", Elvira explained, "It was hard to send them all to school in clean, warm clothing; coats and shoes didn't grow on the farm." In those days you learned to use every piece of cloth for patches. One neighbor said she was a specialist at making something out of nothing!

The Wesen's can be very proud of their family. They had good work habits and were confirmed in the Lutheran faith. They were taught that voting was a privilege and decision making was important. Five of their six sons served their country in WWII, with one chosen to remain behind to help work the farm.

Lewis Alton, enlisted in Combat Engineers and served in the European theatre. He farmed Northwest of Glasgow on the Jensen Trail. He married Carolyn Rosin who was a school teacher at Glasgow. They had four daughters: Dorothy, Christine, Carol, and Louise. His wife Carolyn still lives on their farm place on Roosevelt Trail.

Vera married Vic Melanson in 1936 during the Fort Peck Dam days. They moved to Sundance, Wyoming. They had two sons Douglas and Don. Vera was secretary to the county extension agents and later married rancher, George Sommers in 1971 after the death of her first husband Vic.

Clayton joined the signal corps in February of 1942. He was stationed at White Horse, in the Yukon Territory and helped furnish communications on the Alacan Highway, which was in the planning stages of being built. He married Pearl Zamotsny in August 1944. They lived for a short time in their marriage in New Orleans, Lousiana, but then moved to Glasgow, where all of their children were born. Clayton is remembered for his green thumb and massive gardens he and Pearl grew over the years. He worked for Bob

Rundle for several years at Glasgow Electric in a shop on Front Street and eventually owned his own shop, Wesen's Radio and TV Service in the old Buttrey's store south of the Post Office in Glasgow. My children all got their first bicycles from Grandpa Claytons shop. They had four children: Evelyn, Patricia (she's mine!), Gary, and Beverly. Clayton passed away in 2005 and Pearl passed away in 2018.

Maurice was drafted and served in the 6th Infantry and served in the Phillipines and New Guinea. He graduated from the University of Montana with either a forestry or wildlife degree. He farmed the home place and later Alton's, after Alton's death. Maurice loved being a farmer and he loved to bowl. He married Lois Rice Hukill in September of 1971. They have two sons, Douglas Hukill and Mark Wesen.

Paul was a pilot and joined the Army Air Force when World War II started. He was in the Air Transport Service (transporting paratroopers) and he served in the African and European Theatres. He married Marjory Simundson in 1951. He graduated with a degree in Veterinary Science from Pullman, Washington and practiced in the Seattle area for many years. They had four children: Karen, Steven, Barbara, and Phillip.

John stayed and helped with the farming during WWII. He later attended Montana State University and married Delores Lee and they were married in Waseca, Minnesota. John farmed the home place for years and bought the Henderson, Miller and Harebo places, and his sons (and now grandsons) are part of the farm and ranch operation. They had six children: Curtis, Susan, Joyce, Donna, Mike, and Lisa. John passed away in 2013 but left behind a great legacy of agriculture in Valley County.

June went to Northwestern Business College in Spokane. She worked in Washington D.C. and Minneapolis. She married Roger Kimpton in Minneapolis and they moved to Seattle where she was a church secretary. They have four children: Alan, George, Nancy and Janet.

Forrest joined the Army Air Force in 1944 and went to Gunnery School. He graduated from Montana State College and worked for the

F.H.A. He married Mary Jo Gluckert and they lived in several towns in Montana during their marriage before her death in 1977. They had five children David, Dan, Mark, Diane and Tom.

Rita attended schools for the Deaf in Minneapolis and Great Falls. She married Walter Herbold in 1963. She worked for the Montana School for the Deaf and Blind. She was a great help to Johnny on the farm when she was younger. She could speak very little but was able to communicate well with sign language and her wonderful smile.

Myrna graduated in Nursing from Minot State College in 1956. She married Dave Bell in 1957. They lived in Worland and Sheridan, Wyoming and Dave worked for the phone company. They had four children, Barbara, Jeff, Mike and Cindy.

Through several generations, the Wesen and Garwood families still are involved in agriculture in Valley County and have flourished from the roots our pioneering loved ones have planted in this countryside.

Founding Root's in the Nashua Area

Charles C Sargent, Civil War veteran, Indian Interpreter and Scout and Founder of Nashua and the Brocksmith connection to Valley County

Charles C. Sargent was an early merchant and homesteader in this country-side and was the founder of the town of Nashua. Charles was born in 1946, in either Louisiana or Texas, to William and Phebe (Lee) Sargent, who were from Alabama and Mississippi, and who were migrating to Texas around the time Charles was born. William Sargent died and left Phebe in charge of their young children, as well as a Texas plantation and a number of slaves. She would eventually lose practically everything during the Civil War.

In spite of being born in the south, the sympathies of Charles C. Sargent were with the Union and he left home when he was only 15 years old and enlisted in a branch of the Union Army, the Arkansas Infantry. I had it relayed to me that Charles C. fought in several battles and was captured and was a prisoner-of-war for a short time. He was exchanged for other prisoners and finally made it back to his unit. He voted for Abraham Lincoln in 1864 and he was later discharged from the Union Army in 1865, at the end of the Civil War.

He then enlisted in the US Calvary and came to Montana soon after it was made a territory, as a soldier in Company C, 31st Us Infantry. He arrived at Fort Union, on the Missouri River, before 1866. The American Fur Company Post was then at Fort Union, on the Montana-North Dakota territory line. The company that he belonged to came up the Missouri River on a boat called the *Mary McDonald* to a location that would become known as Fort Buford, which is also on the Missouri River, after the Missouri and Yellowstone have joined. His first duties on arriving at his post were to help with the building of Fort Buford. Mr. Sargent helped cut the first timber used in the construction of the new fort and also helped dig the first grave at Fort Buford. Mr. Sargent served for three years in Company C.

After his discharge from the Army, Mr. Sargent became a civilian scout and served the government for five years. In this service his duties were to detect smugglers and illicit traders. He was a scout for the party that went up the Yellowstone River to Terry's Landing on a steamboat with supplies in search of General Custer's command, which was coming from Bismarck, North Dakota. The supply party met General Custer's party near Medora, where it joined the command of General Terry, and this combined command, with Mr. Sargent serving as scout moved on to the mouth of the Powder River. The forces of Custer and Terry would split, with Mr. Sargent moving on with Terry's force to the mouth of the Rosebud, and at this point Mr. Sargent returned to Fort Buford. General Custer's command would travel up the Powder to the countryside that his force would soon be annihilated in, known for many years as the Custer Massacre, but now more formally known as the Battle of the Little Big Horn. Mr. Sargent had remained with General Terry while his best friend, Charles Reynolds, remained with Custer's command and was killed in action under General Reno during The Battle of The Little Bighorn.

Mr. Sargent lived an adventurous life but did not tell his stories lightly. One story that was relayed to listeners actually involved a question in regards to unseasonably heavy snow storms. One experience he had was when he was carrying a dispatch from Fort Lincoln to General George Custer. A snow storm got so bad he and a Crow scout he was traveling with had to take cover in a coulee to wait out the severe weather. The weather had become so cold and he and the scout were so lightly dressed that he had jumped off his horse and was waving his arms and jumping in an attempt to stay warm and he was prepared to start a fire to keep warm, knowing that a fire might draw unwelcome attention and lead to their deaths. While gathering dry wood for a fire, he heard the faint sounds of a barking dog and upon investigating the area, he found General Custer's command in the next canyon. This was a late spring storm which occurred around the first of June in the badlands and took place near Sentinel Butte, North Dakota.

During the winter of 1876-77, Mr. Sargent left the government service as a scout and took up civil pursuits under Joe Leighton, and Indian trader and was sent to Wolf Point to build a store. After the store was completed and opened, Mr. Sargent was in charge of the operation of this store and also assisted in the building of a store in Poplar which was later opened by John Thompson and Company. It was around this time that Mr. Sargent, who was fluent in the Sioux language, became an agency interpreter at Wolf Point and later Poplar.

Following the completion of his work as an interpreter, Mr. Sargent engaged in hunting and trapping along the Missouri River and sold chopped wood to steamboats traveling on the river. He had different business opportunities over the years, including working in Wolf Point in the store of W.B. Shaw and also became a farm instructor to the Indian's at Box Elder, which at that time was a sub-agency to the agency at Poplar.

Around 1886, Mr. Sargent realized that with the construction of the James J. Hill Great Northern Railroad that was planned through this region, settlers would soon be coming in, and that if he desired to have his choice of a homestead, it was advisable to make an early selection. Sargent was advised of a division point that would be near the confluence of Porcupine Creek and the Milk River. He moved the family to the Nashua area and it was there that he squatted and homesteaded in this location. He took his claim at what would be the present site of Nashua. He built his first house on the bank of the Porcupine Creek, which would continue to become the site of his residence until he built the new Sargent house, a much larger home in 1920. For a number of years he engaged in ranching, although in 1888 he put in a stock of goods (for resale or trade) in the same log house he was using for postal purposes, as he had been appointed postmaster of Nashua the following fall.

Mr. Sargent was key in the founding of Nashua, Montana and getting the town a separate school district and was on the school board for many years. He took part in surveying the first road in Valley County and was instrumental in the building of churches, schools, bridges and roads, and he was one of the organizers of the First National Bank of Nashua. He reportedly felt that in doing so, he was rendering a service that was expected of any man who was being a good citizen. He donated lots of land for the building of public buildings in his community and the main road in Nashua still carries his name.

Mr. Sargent married Rose Ann Carey, a daughter of Bryan Carey, in Chicago, and his children were Mrs. Ralph Berger and Mrs. Rose Brocksmith, both of Nashua. Mr. Sargent insisted on being buried in the cemetery of the town they helped found and both he and Rose are buried on the hill in the Nashua Cemetery, overlooking the town they helped build. (Taken from: Nashua Community History 1897-1977 The Way it Was, A Bridge Between Then and Now" and Footprints in the Valley)

Charles C. Sargent's daughter Rose married Henry C. Brocksmith, a free-spirited rancher and cowboy type in 1901. Henry became a partner to his father in law on the ranch, and after their marriage, Rose and Henry worked long, hard hours on the ranch. Even though the work was hard, the couple enjoyed their life on the ranch and in time were blessed with children Charles Henry, Norman and Pheobe. Happiness and hardship seemed to be an everyday part of life for the Brocksmith family, but tragedy struck when Henry was killed in an accident in California, leaving Rose a widow with three small children to raise and a ranch to care for.

As reported by family, Rose Brocksmith endured a lot of hard work and many trying circumstances in order to keep them fed. To make ends meet, she took in washing and ironing, all done by hand on a washboard and with fire heated irons. Charles Henry and Norman had to keep plenty of wood cut to supply the fires. Despite years of back breaking work, Rose Brocksmith enjoyed excellent health and lived into her mid 90's.

Charles H. Brocksmith, who most in these parts know as C.H., which is how he will be referred to in his section, to make the Charles' in the family less confusing. C.H. grew up on a ranch and is noted to have his first horseback ride at 2 months of age, when his mother dressed him up and a family friend, Jack Teal took him for a ride round Nashua. C.H., as the eldest sibling of three, assumed a parental role in the family after his father's death, and he had many duties. He sawed wood for 5 cents a log, and those were big logs for the money, drove a horse driven hay baler for 50 cents a day, operated a trap line in the fall and spring on the Big Porcupine Creek, worked as a shoe shine boy in a Nashua barber shop for 15 cents a shine, helped with sheep shipping for the J.B. Long Company. He did all of this while as taking care of the family wood supplies and caring for the family's livestock operation.

C.H. and his brother Norman were the first graduating class from Nashua High School, and C.H. later graduated from the Pacific Coast School of Banking at the University of Washington in Seattle. He also pursued graduate study at the University of Montana in Missoula. His banking career started when he was 18 years old when he started working at the First National Bank of Nashua under the tutelage of E.T. Peterson. Banking was in his blood and it became his lifelong career, with ranching and farming, while still important, became less of a career and more of a hobby. He worked for the Federal Land Bank System (later the F.H.A.) for five years before he was elected Executive Officer/Manager of the First Security Bank in Glasgow. He remained active in the bank until his retirement.

My Grandpa Marion considered C.H. to be good friend, and they were close in age, and C.H. served as manager of the Nashua Baseball team that Grandpa played on. Grandpa always called him Charlie. Several times Grandpa needed a loan for the farm or the dairy and went to C.H. for the financial assistance. He would always say, "I guess I got to go see Charlie with my hat in my hands". C.H was involved with my first loan experience, as I had previously mentioned, and I imagine he was a part of financial assistance for many people, not only of Nashua, but of people in all areas of Valley County.

C.H. was very busy in civic and community activities as well as with professional affairs. He served as President of the Montana Bankers Association, a member of the Defense Committee for the U.S. Chamber of Commerce, director of the Federal Reserve Bank of Minneapolis, among many other professional affairs. Locally he served on the Valley County Livestock Association and was a member for the Board of Trustees of the Francis Mahon Deaconess Hospital in Glasgow for about 30 years.

C.H. married Margaret Stokes and the couple had five children, Charlyn, Patricia (who's children went to school with my own children at Nashua), Charles C. (who graduated with my wife Patty from the Glasgow High School), Kay and Margaret.

Charles C. Brocksmith, son of Charles H. and Margaret Stokes Brocksmith, lives in Nashua. He spent twenty plus years in the navy and when he retired, he moved back to Nashua, to live and work. He worked on the Brocksmith Ranch and at the Farmer's Union Co-op of Nashua. He graduated from Glasgow in 1965 and was a lifelong classmate of my wife, Patty. Charlie, (or C.C. as he is known to many) Brocksmith is very competent and knowledgeable on all electronics, especially with computers.

As mentioned above Charles C. Sargent is credited with homesteading and founding the present town of Nashua, and the roots he and his wife planted in Valley County have included children, grandchildren and great grandchildren living in and going to school in the small town he helped found at the confluence of the Porcupine Creek and Milk River. As mentioned earlier, one of the main street's in Nashua carries his family name and is familiar to all in these parts.

To the left, my great grandparents, Marion and Gertrude, and to the right, my parents, Edgar and Toni. These pictures were taken in the spring of 1945, sometime before my father went to Army training in California. It was taken east of their home place, in a field ready for spring seeding.

The hill side barn that I helped my father and grandfather build, using reclaimed railroad ties and supplies, both from Nashua and supplies that my grandparents hauled back from Ohio. It is located west of my parents house on the "home place". The chicken coop can be seen behind the tree's, just to the left of the barn. Our family has housed livestock and stored equipment in this barn for well over half a century.

This picture shows the family putting up hay, both for our own livestock, but also to be sold to help make ends meet on the farm. My Dad is on the tractor and my Grandfather is standing next to the hay trailer. I am on top of the stack of hay, with my sister's Karen and Diane to my left, along with my Beagle, fondly remembered as Buddy One.

A nice little photo of my Mom, Toni, and my youngest sister Diane. That is a mighty tall sunflower they are posing by. The screened porch in background has housed many memorable family moments.

This is my parents, Eddie and Toni, enjoying a cup of coffee on the front porch of the family farmhouse. The large white-washed timbers in the background are some of the converted bridge timbers that make up the main part of the house.

This is my grandparents, Marion and Gertrude, taken in Ohio, probably around 1937 or '38. The family had moved back to Ohio during the drought of the late 30's in Montana, and maintained a farm near Dayton, Ohio, while still having their Montana place, which was left in the hands of friends to keep up the maintenance around the place.

My dad, Edgar standing beside his pump site on the Missouri during the high water event in 2011. He was 91 years old in this picture. He was proud of this pump site and remained interested in it until the day he died.

One of my hayfields, full of small square bales (aka "idiot cubes") and a bale wagon. The equipment has changed over the years, but the tradition I learned from my Grandfather and Father remains the same. Tower Hill can be seen in the background.

CRITTERS AND SCRUB BRUSH

(flora and fauna)

"Take a quiet walk with Mother Nature. It will nurture your mind, body and soul."
-Anthony Douglas Williams

Tracks In The Snow

One of the things that I really enjoy about living on the farm near both the Milk and Missouri Rivers is that amount of wild life that traverse the land to water at the rivers. Over the years I have had the opportunity to observe much wildlife. I really enjoy going for a walk after a fresh snow! We have many animals that live here, although some of the animals will hibernate, so we do not see all the animals that live here in the winter. The winter of 2011-12 we had warmer than normal temperatures and not many snowstorms. Several days ago, we had about two inches of snow and that was about right for looking for fresh tracks.

I am a hunter and I always enjoy following deer tracks during the hunting season. To be a good hunter, it is imperative that you know as much about the species that you are hunting as is possible. Even during the rest of the year, you need to scout the areas you hunt and all around them. The best way to scout is to go out for a drive or walk after a fresh snow. It has been several days since we had about two inches of fresh snowfall, and before that, ground had been bare for about two months or so. It is always so exciting for me to see tracks in the snow, as there is a story to be told following every track you see!

I trapped for quite a few falls and into the winters for many years, but the last several years I have not trapped as much. I still do some trapping in years when we have an animal species that gets to populous for the area and I feel it needs to be thinned down some. Most animal species will come back if not over trapped. Most animal species migrate some and other species will migrate fifty or a hundred miles, especially during the mating season. Beings I have trapped and skinned a lot of animals, I have learned by experience. Reading books about animals has also been part of my learning experience. The more you are out there on the ground or walking around and looking, the more you learn!

When I see a track in the snow that I do not recognize right off, I have to follow it to try to figure out what made it, what is it doing and what is it looking for? I have followed certain tracks like elk or deer when I am hunting them to try to catch up with them for an easy shot. It sounds easy to do but you have to have the wind right and be quiet. In soft snow, it is fairly easy to be quiet but if there is a crust on the snow it is noisy and the chance of seeing your quarry is pretty tough. It also makes a difference of how fresh the sign is and how fast the animal is moving if you want to catch it. After a while on the track you can kind of get an idea if you are going to catch up to the animal. Most of the time this does not work out but following an animal tracks is about the best method if you are trying to get that particular animal. If you follow and study tracks enough, a person can tell how big and even what sex it is. A big bull or buck will have widely splayed hooves, because of their weight, and you usually can see their dewclaws on the rear of the hooves. When you are a trophy hunter and you have seen the animal and he is large, then you will make an extra effort to follow the track the best that you can. If this animal gets mixed up with a herd and is traveling together, then it can really complicate the tracking job. You can follow a herd trail pretty easy, but you have to watch out that the animal that you are after does not split off from the main herd.

Yesterday as I drove down to the Missouri River there were many tracks around as the snow was still good for tracking. The last couple of days the temperature was maybe just getting to thawing so any tracks made were really clear and distinct. In the last few years we have had some squirrels come into the Cottonwood trees and smaller brush. It took me a little while to distinguish their tracks from large weasels and small mink. Squirrel tracks are usually similar to a bounding animal like those of the weasel family, but they usually travel from tree to tree. Marten tracks that I have seen in the mountain areas travel to and then up trees, but they are larger than the squirrels that they prey on.

Some of the animal tracks that I had seen in the past here on the Missouri bottom were: whitetail deer, mule deer, raccoon, mink, weasel, skunk, mice, voles, cottontail rabbit, jack rabbit, coyote, Canada goose, red fox, ring necked pheasant, turkeys, numerous small bird species and dog!! Yes, one of my best buddies is my dog, Maxine, who I call Max. She was enjoying herself as she was running around smelling the tracks and it seems like she was having a great time! You can see why it is so exciting to live here in the rural, river bottom area in Montana. Yesterday was a beautiful winter day as the sun was shining and there was no wind. Walking around and looking at the tracks in the snow on a beautiful day was just the frosting on the cake!!

In the winter of 2003-2004 we had quite a bit of snow and it was getting pretty deep. I was checking some coyote traps on a school section west of my house. I was walking in from the road and I saw some bounding tracks that I had never seen before. They were fairly large footprints and the bounding tracks were about 5 to 6 feet apart. I could not see any sign of tail drags, so it was a bit of a mystery. If they would have had a tail mark in the snow, I would have thought it was an otter. We do not have any otters but a friend of mine who has since passed away, Merlin Ball, said he did see an otter in the Milk River. I saw an otter in Upper Cache Creek near Fort Saint John, British Columbia. I also saw one on Loon Lake during the summer at the Wesen family reunion near Bigfork, Montana. We were in a canoe on the lake when I noticed the otter come up from under the water, roll over on its back and eat a small fish. I watched it for a while and it went back down and came up with another fish.

The only animal that I thought that might make these large, bounding tracks is a wolverine! The tracks were about a hundred yards from the river and in some cottonwood trees. I followed the tracks for a while, but it was below zero and there is not a hunting season for them here in our 600 area, I decided to quit the track and walked back to the pickup. A week later, the bus driver Jim Ward who had come down to pick up my son Shawn, had told me that about a week before, he had seen a wolverine cross the road in front of his bus. He had a good look at him! What a coincidence! It is quite uncommon for wolverines to be around here. When Jim was younger, he lived and trapped near Kalispell in western Montana and he knew what they looked like. I had talked to a friend from south of Poplar and he has seen wolverines a couple of times near the badlands on his ranch near the Missouri River. The next summer my brother-in-law, Scott Forbes, said that had seen two large critters run across his field about two miles from where I had seen the tracks and he said they were not badgers, but something that was similar but bigger. When he seen a picture of a wolverine, he said it looked like the same animal. Another brother-in-law, Gary Stearns, said he seen two wolverines south of Malta, Montana after dark in the road borrow pit while he was going out on an elk hunt. We have not seen any sign of them since but they are wide rangers so who knows where they might have come from.

Back in 1964, when I was in Canada on a trip, I was hunting for moose and black bear as I had a tag for each one. Buck Musgrove and I were walking together at that time of this incident. We came upon a track of a large wolf in about three inches of snow. This was the first wolf track that I had seen, and this was the first time that I had heard them howl at night. I laid my .300 Savage down next to the track and took a picture of the large track right next to the gun. If I can locate the picture, I will try to include it in this book as it is almost blew my mind at how big of an animal it must have been! There is a really uneasy feeling when you know that there are a pack of these animals around when you are walking alone. I cannot remember if Buck and I were on foot or on horseback at the time, but I will never forget the size of those tracks. I think on that same hunting trip we seen a large elk like track that the toes curved inward to make a roundish looking track. Buck said it was probably a caribou and I have looked at caribou tracks in a magazine and they were quite similar. This sighting was in central British Columbia, north of their ranch!

I have seen black bear tracks a few times while in Canada and western Montana on past hunting trips. The fall of 1991, I drew a Shiras Moose permit in area 110, just west of Glacier National Park. Of the four subspecies of moose in North America, the Shiras is the smallest, but it is still a very large animal. It is mostly found in Montana, Idaho, Wyoming and British Columbia. As soon as I knew that I had drawn the tag for the moose, I purchased a Grizzly Bear tag from Montana Fish Wildlife and Parks. A month later I got a letter from them saying that the grizzly had just been listed on the Endangered Species Act and that I should send the grizzly tag back and they would reimburse me for it. I believe the tag was about $50.00 and it was not any good so I went ahead and sent it back for my check! Now I wish I would have saved it or just got a copy of it. We have not been able to hunt for grizzlies in Montana since that time. The day I shot my Bull Moose, I seen a grizzly track, distinctive because of the long toenails, cross the road and go up a hill. Their large tracks in the snow are just scary and amazing!

I have a picture of two black bear tracks near Lincoln, Montana, which I took while I was hunting elk from a four wheeler. Three friends were ahead of me and they crossed these tracks and did not notice them as they were on elk tracks. I had told them that I had seen the bear tracks and I had a tag. They had not noticed the tracks, the first or second time we crossed them, and I had to holler at them to come back and look at them. There were two tracks, with one being smaller, so I figured out that it was a sow and a cub. They were not legal to hunt, so we went on down the trail to look for elk, but I always appreciate getting a chance to see the tracks of animals such as this.

Unusual Animal Antics- Coyote and Antelope

Several years ago, while I was driving our contract postal mail route, I was on a straight stretch of road south of Nashua when I saw something very unusual. This occurred up above the Milk River in the hills about a mile from the river. It was springtime and there was only little snow left on the ground. I had seen movement from the left, which turned out to be two animals, one chasing the other. They were not running in a straight line, which is usually the pattern animals run in when in pursuit of another. When I first seen them, they were maybe a half a mile from me. When I got within a quarter of a mile from them, I could see an antelope and it was chasing a coyote!! I have seen coyotes chasing deer and antelope in the past when the 'Yotes were trying to get a meal! As I got closer, I could see the antelope could easily run faster than the coyote and would almost catch it. The dog was looking over his shoulder and would wait till the "prairie goat" almost caught it, and it would easily run to the side and let the faster antelope run by. Then the coyote would continue on running until the antelope caught up to it again. I stopped my car and watched this unbelievable show of nature. They did not act like they even noticed that I was there. The antelope was definitely upset with the coyote and was trying to chase it away. It was the time of the year that the doe antelopes were having their fawns and they always go off by themselves to have their young. This scenario happened at least three times before I decided to drive on. I looked back to where I had first seen the two critters but did not see a fawn. Nature has given a newborn fawn no smell so that a carnivore that is looking for a meal cannot find it easily. The antelope doe, just like a whitetail doe, will not bed by the new fawn. After they have the fawn, and it struggles to get its balance and can stand, it nurses. As soon as the fawn has suckled, its mother it will lay down to rest. Fairly soon the mother will go off a ways and have her afterbirth and watch over her fawn from a ways off. When the fawn needs nursing again she will go to it and let it suckle again.

I think what happened is that this coyote came to the smell of the mother, and she tried to chase off the coyote - which she did! I think the fawn was hidden nearby and she chased the coyote away from where it was sheltered. The antelope is the fastest animal in North America and it can maybe run 50 miles an hour! Coyotes hunt in family packs and they usually can tire out a single prey animal by taking turns running them until the prey is too tired to go on. I often wonder how that scenario turned out as there was a chance that another coyote could have been nearby, and it could have found the fawn. Like I said the newborn fawn does not have any smell and it will lie still until the coyote gets up to it and then they might get frightened and run. A newborn fawn is not very steady on its legs or fast yet!

The Rooster Pheasant and Baby Red Fox

I suppose it was maybe thirty years ago that I was driving along one of my fences and I saw some movement about a hundred yards ahead of me. I drove a little closer and I saw two reddish looking critters running in a small circle around each other. It was a full grown rooster pheasant and a very young red fox pup. I think the fox was trying to catch the rooster but the fox was smaller and slower than the pheasant. I had stopped to watch the show and I had turned the engine off, so as not to bother them. The pup would try to catch it, but the pheasant would jump up in the air and fly and land behind the fox. It really was fun to watch how this turned out. The pheasant could have easily flown off to get away, but I think it was making a game of it and it was not scared of the small fox at all. I watched this going on for a couple of minutes and the pheasant finally got tired of the game and flew on. I never get tired of watching out for these nature shows but the trouble is a person usually does not have a camera handy when they need it.

Weasels

I remember the first weasel that I had seen in the chicken house at my Dads' place. It was in the winter and I went in to gather eggs from the chicken nests. This was not a job that I particularly liked! It seemed some of the chickens did not want to give up their eggs. Their hard-worked job of laying eggs and keeping them warm, made them very protective. Sometimes they would peck your hand when you tried to get the eggs out from under them, and this was not fun on my tender hands. Looking back, it seems like very little of the time does a person actually have gloves on. A five-gallon bucket hung on a nail on the ridge pole in this old log house that we used for a chicken house. This house was dug back into the hill and it had dirt for the back wall. This is called a dugout and it might have qualified for a homestead shack or maybe something like this was used to live in while folks were building their small house to qualify for their homestead patent. After they built the house, a homesteader could use this building for their animals.

I had an egg and I reached for the bucket, but when I took the bucket down to put the egg in it, to my surprise I found a small weasel in the bucket. It was "ermine", as it was white except for the nose, eyes and tip of the tail, which were black. It was a beautiful little weasel that amazed me as it was the first one I had seen. It had gotten down in the bucket to kill and eat two mice that had gotten into the bucket and could not get out. All that was left of the mice was the intestines that the weasel did not eat. I was pretty young and I remember taking the bucket over to the house to show Mom or Dad!

Another time after I was married, I was driving down a trail to check on my irrigation water and I noticed a movement in the road that was kind of herky-jerky! As I got closer, I seen it was a larger variety weasel that had killed a cottontail rabbit and it was trying to pull it down the road. The rabbit was about three times the size of the weasel and it could not carry it, so it was jerking it to move it. I had heard that weasels or anything in the weasel family, up to the largest member of the family which is the wolverine, can kill prey several times larger than they are. They are very protective of their kill and will defend it as best as they can. This weasel finally left and ran into the weeds near the road. I stopped near the cottontail and watched. The weasel ran out and grabbed the rabbit and started to pull it and retreated again. I went on to tend to my business and when I returned later, the weasel and rabbit carcass were both gone.

Rattlesnakes

I have walked all over this river bottom all my life and I had often bragged that I had never seen a rattlesnake here. I guess that I just got used to thinking that there could not be any around. One day I was driving around checking my water when I saw a large snake on the road. I drove around the snake as I usually do not run over bull snakes. Bull snakes are very good for the environment, as they eat many pesky critter's that can tear up the fields and roads. I stopped because this snake looked different. I kept my dog in the pickup and grabbed my shovel.

I had never seen a rattlesnake on our side of the Missouri River until I found this one sunning itself on Garwood Road (when you are the only people living on a road, they name it after you). The snake was on the gravel road, and it was only 130 feet from my irrigation tubes. The tubes lie on the ditch edge, which is where I kneel on to set my water. To prime and pull a syphon tube, a person kneels on the ditch bank, submerges the syphon tube in the water, and then after sealing one end, the tube is pulled from the water in a quick, smooth motion, which causes water to flow from the ditch, through the tube and into the field. A person is very vulnerable to a snake when in a kneeling position for any length of time, especially in tall grass. When I walked up to the snake, it was trying to rattle but I could not hear it. This was a 38-inch long rattlesnake and only had one rattle. He could not make much noise but is probably the largest rattler that I have ever killed. I still wonder if there are any more of them around the farm. Since then when I walk around, I usually watch where I put my feet. I took the dead snake around to show to all my neighbors and they could hardly believe where I found it!

The fall before last, I was hunting elk during the archery season in a hunting district about forty-five miles from my house. In that secluded area, there are always those, "rattily little snakes", which is how Dave Riggin refers to them. They survive well in that rugged country out south and I have seen a lot of them out there, even in cool weather, until it finally gets to below freezing during the days. You will see them out some on real warm days near their dens, and then they den up together with other snakes for the winter. The last day of the bow season in 2011, a large bull elk had "blown out" without me getting close enough with my bow and headed over to another coulee that I had not hunted in that year yet. It was about a half of a mile away and I was creeping up to the edge of a sandstone overlook above the coulee. I saw a small rattlesnake and I approached it carefully. It got scared and slithered into a hole! I knew that this was probably a den and from past experience I knew that there were probably more snakes in the area. I walked slowly, carefully watching where I was stepping but I was also looking over the edge to try to spot elk.

Apparently, it turns out I was watching for the bull more than where I was standing. I could not see any elk, so I wanted to get a little closer to the edge of the sandstone ledge that was about fifty feet away. I looked down to step and I saw a coiled rattler that had been about a foot and a half from my boot!! It had been there the whole time that I was standing there glassing for game. The wind was blowing some and I did not even hear it rattling. This snake was only about 18 inches long. Snakes can only strike about two-third of the length of their body on level ground. If this snake would have been 30 inches or more, he would have got me! I really was not all that shook, but I did step back a step to size him up. I could not believe that I had got that close to a snake and did not know it. The wind was blowing hard and I could not hear the distinctive rattle! It was late in the afternoon of the last day of the archery season and I could not think of elk any more after that, so I stepped around the small rattler and walked the two or so miles back to my parked pickup. In the future when I am hunting out there, I will remember where that snake den is and thank the all mighty God for giving me another chance and that I did not get snake bit that day.

On an early year elk hunt out there back in the 60's with Bill Nicol, I spent a few days at his camp while hunting. We had killed a couple of rattlesnakes near his tent. Then we stumbled on to a snake den about a quarter of a mile from the tent. After having found the den and knowing there were snakes there out sunning themselves, and since we were young and dumb, we could not leave them alone. We usually played with them some as it was almost a game to us during midday when we could not find any elk. We also did not want them that close to the tent and the lookout that we climbed up to glass for the elk was near… so we killed some of them and cut off the rattles. I thought that we had killed thirteen rattlers near that camp.

After I told Bill that I had killed a large rattler about a quarter of a mile from my house, he just shook his head. We started laughing and talking about the hunt when we had killed all the snakes. Bill had remembered that it was sixteen rattlers in three days. I remember it was the last day of the hunt and we had been up on the lookout and we had not found any elk that morning. Bill decided to take his motorcycle back and start breaking camp. He had started walking back to his motorcycle and I was going to walk over and glass a little more and then started going down the trail that Bill had just walked down no more than ten minutes before. There along the trail coiled up was a large rattler, the longest that we had seen that hunting trip. Bill had just started his motorcycle when I spotted the snake and I knew he wanted to be in on the "kill". I hollered to him as hard and loud as I could and he heard me over the idling motorcycle. He stopped it and hollered back to me wondering what I wanted. When I told him that I found a large rattler, he came back up to see it. Like I said it was almost a game with us and we were almost addicted to playing with them. It was a large brown snake and was over three foot long. They are interesting and beautiful, but dangerous to be around!

Maxine Nicol told me just the other day a story about Billy when I had mentioned rattle snakes. She said Bill, Skip Ericson and some other friends had gone hunting out south, in an area where there are many rattlers. They had hunted some and when they came back home, they told Maxine that they had some snakes in a bag. Maxine was curious and she made them show her. To her surprise there were some rattle snakes in there and she made the boys take them back where they had found them. She said she does not know where they took them exactly, but it was off the farm for certain, and hopefully out south of Fort Peck.

I have seen a lot of rattlesnakes in the forty some years that I have been hunting out south in the Missouri Breaks. Most of them in the past I would kill, but with our modern bows having wheels and cables you cannot control a snake very well. I have used an arrow to try to flick them out of a hole but this is not a real safe way to mess with a large snake. My old Redwing re-curve bow was perfect for hooking a snake and pulling it out onto level ground so you can control the snake. I have a hunting buddy, Dale Borgen, that used to shoot them with an arrow with a Judo tip head on it. Judo tips have 4 wires with springs on them for practice in grassy areas as the arrows hit the grass and flip up where you can easily find them.

One year I was out hunting with Dale and he called me over to where he was standing. When I walked up to him to find out what he wanted, I noticed that he had left a small dead rattler, green in color, next to him and he wanted to see what I would do when I saw it. Like I say, I always try to watch where I put my feet and I had seen it before I walked up to him and so, much to his disappointment, I was not alarmed.

I can only carry five arrows with me on my bow quiver and I am not going to dull a sharp broad head trying to kill a rattler. I let a lot more rattle snakes live now than I used too, but that one that lives just might be the snake that will bite me or someone else in the future!

Snakes, snakes, and more snakes

I guess I have been drawn to snakes since I was young. I would catch garter snakes and blue racer snakes and play with them and keep and care for them some before I released them. I remember once when I was younger catching a blue racer and keeping in a cage. I guess I had told my parents about the snake and Mom was not real happy about me having one in a cage so close to the house. She knew it was not poisonous, but she always told me if one bit me I could get infection from a bite.

I did get bitten from a bull snake I was playing with when I was with my Grandmother Gertrude. Bull snakes can be pretty aggressive and I have found one once that was about seven feet long. No kidding!! They will coil up like a rattlesnake, wiggle their tail and hiss at you in an attempt at making you believe they are a rattler and that you will then leave them alone. The snake that bit me gave me a little more respect for them as the bite marks on my wrist were sore for a long time. I think I got Mom to help clean the wound up so it did not get infected! I guess I did learn from this mistake ... well, some!

Another time when I was young, while playing in the hills behind my parents' house, I had another snake experience. The Nicol kids were visiting us and we were playing in the hills a little ways from the house. Janice, Bill, Kathy and my sister Karen were playing hide and seek around the buildings. We did this quite often as there were numerous places to hide in the area. All I can remember is that I had only so much time to go hide and I was running on the top of the hill just behind the house. There were some cactuses and small sagebrush up there and I would jump over them trying to find a great place to make into a hiding spot. I remember that I jumped over something and a snake struck at me, although it missed. I remember looking back and I saw a brown and tan snake curled up along the side of a small sage brush. At the time I had a vivid imagination and not much knowledge of snakes in the United States. I really thought it looked like a copperhead. A little later on, I went back to really identify that snake. I could not find the snake, but it could have been a bull snake but I am still not sure. My father has seen a snake that looks similar to a bull snake, that he calls a king snake. Some king snakes are bright colored, but the prairie kingsnake mirrors the coloring of a bull or rattle snake. I know the real king snakes are not in this area of the country so it was not that. We do have a snake that looks a lot like the bull snake and it is called a gopher snake. The type of snake that struck at me has been a mystery to me since I never did find it to know for sure. This could have been the time playing in the hills when Janice fell on a cactus and needed help getting all of the spines out!

When I was in Kentucky for basic training for the National Guard, I went on a weekend pass. We were in an area where there was a small lake. We found a small snake that was about 18 inches long. This light black snake had a white mouth when it had its mouth open. I figured this snake was a cottonmouth or a water moccasin which is very poisonous. We did not want him in the area that we were picnicking so we flipped him into the water and it swam away to the other bank. I have not spent much time in the south at all, so this was the only chance for me to see a cottonmouth.

A few weeks later, I had a weekend off while I was still attending basic training at Fort Knox, Kentucky. I went to Lewisburg, Ohio to visit my Dads first cousin, Berlin "Bud" Garwood and his wife Doris on Grandpa's old farm. We also visited at the beautiful old home of Jack and his wife Jane Garwood, who live in small town near Lewisburg. Jack is Bud and Doris's oldest son. This is the northern part of the farm that my Grandparents, Marion and Gertrude, owned back in the 1930's. I really enjoyed exploring around this neat little farm. There was a ridge with the north boundary fence on it and a small creek flowing between the hill and the barn. After his dad passed away, Jack has said that selling the farm was the hardest thing he ever had to do!

While walking near the creek below the house, I noticed an old car body and I went over to look at it. As I walked up to the car, I saw a long black snake, about six feet long crawling to get under the car. I did not know if it was poisonous at the time, so I ran up close to get a better look. I found out it was called a blacksnake. It was very large and the body type was a lot like the bull snakes that we have here in Montana. I found out later that black snakes are not poisonous!

We have found a short, thick bodied snake here in Montana that is called a hognose snake. It has a thick neck, but the coloration of it is quite similar to a brown prairie rattlesnake. I have had these snakes play dead in the past when you play with it and later it will crawl off. They are fairly rare in this country and I have only seen about a dozen in the many years that I have walked around here in Valley County.

The Prairie Rattlesnakes we have here in Eastern Montana can come in many colors, but the pattern is pretty much the same. The majority of them match the color of the terrain where they are found and usually are light or dark two-toned brown with some white in the pattern. In grassy areas they can be a greenish color. One day, while walking across a thick, grassy creek bottom with Keith Meche, better known to locals as Boatride, I came across a rattle snake. Boatride was walking along side of me while going to a good glassing hill while we were out elk hunting. I was looking down, checking my steps as we were in the thick grass. Then about three feet ahead of us I spotted a large, dark brown snake moving cross ways to me, crawling through the grass. This was in yellow grass and the dark color let me see it easily. One more step and I could have stepped right in the front of him. I stopped in time, put my hand out to stop Boatride, and I told him stop. The rattlesnake was still crawling along as it had not noticed us yet. I moved my bow down toward it and it instantly coiled and started rattling. This was a large rattlesnake, being about three foot long or perhaps a little more. It was quite agitated and is very dangerous to handle snakes in thick grass if you do not have a curved snake stick. In the old days when we had re-curve bows, you could handle them as the curved ends of the bow could hook on to the snake and you could pull them out of the grass. With our compound bows with wheels on the end of the bow, you cannot get good control them. The longest Rattle snake I have seen was about forty-two inches long.

There is an area on the CMR, on the north side of Harpers Ridge that was an excellent area for elk hunting, and it is a favored place of mine to hunt. This location is where a fire burned most of this area up in the summer of 2006. That was a hot fire that was started by lightning on the south side of Harpers Ridge. Out in this area of the CMR, US Fish and Wildlife Service, does not allow vehicles off-road access, even to fight fires. The CMR fire fighters were fighting the fire with backpack sprayers in an attempt to keep the fire contained while they were waiting for air support to come in and help with the fires. As long as the wind was from the north they kind of had the fire contained along the lake, allow this was no easy task. During the night, the wind switched to coming out of the south and the fire really took off, as it was an extremely dry summer and there was plenty of dry grass. At the time of this fire, there were still a lot of live pine trees, sagebrush and junipers which was excellent elk habitat, but that fire really changed the habitat of that area.

One day when I was out hunting for elk during the archery season, I was walking on the north side of Harpers Ridge. I was creeping over a hill to look over it to the coulee below. I was looking for a place to lay my bow down and do some glassing with my binoculars. I usually look for cactus before I kneel or sit down. I put my bow down on the ground to the left side of my body and I noticed a small hole with some cobwebs in the entrance. I was only about four feet from the hole and I was keeping an eye on it while I was looking for game. I noticed something black starting to come out of the hole about a quarter of an inch. It did this several times and then would go back down. I thought it could have been a black beetle as they are quite common. I finally decided to move on and look for more game. I thought that I would hunt further on to the next hill. As I was walking down off of this hilltop, I seen a snake skin and then I saw a bull snake and another hole. Then I figured out this probably was a den area. I hunted for another hour and then I came back to this hill to have another look. I moved slowly up to the spot that I had seen the supposedly black bug. Right there about two feet from that hole was a small black rattlesnake, probably about fifteen inches long, coiled and trying to rattle. I approached the snake and he slithered over the steep edge of the hill. I decided not to go after it on this steep hillside. Sometimes I have some sense!!

This area of Harpers Ridge that burned is now almost devoid of live trees and sagebrush and it is not as good a deer and elk habitat as it was before the burn. The places where the creeping junipers were located have since become devoid of vegetation and have been replaced by Canada thistle which is a Montana noxious weed. Once Canada thistle gets started, it is incredibly hard to stop it.

I remember another incident some years ago when Bill Nicol and I had played with numerous snakes and I approached a foot-long rattlesnake when it was above me on a steep hill. The small snake was about two feet above me and I planned on pinning his head to the ground so I could then grab him behind the head like we had done to numerous snakes that hunting trip. With a few of those snakes, we would milk the venom on the ground with an arrow to just watch the venom come out. This small snake struck at me and the momentum carried it out downhill towards me and it landed right on my boot. I quickly jumped away from the snake and informed Bill what had happened. It was then I had a little more respect for rattlesnakes, especially along steep hills. There are a lot of trails in hilly country that have eroded two or more feet deep from water flowing off from rains. If a snake was waiting for game and he struck at you, he would get you at about knee level. When I am walking through these deep trail areas, I am ever alert. They say that it is the second person walking through that gets bit by a snake!!

Russian Olive Trees

The Russian olive bush is an imported plant brought into this country to help with soil erosion from wind, as well as serve as habit for small birds and animals, and is a native plant of Europe. It was commonly used for wind breaks and tree plantings in eastern Montana, as well as other areas of the country. At that time in was first introduced around here, the bush was promoted by the county extension offices as a good alternative for windbreaks in the north country because of its winter hardiness and its ability to survive and do well in a drought. Montana Fish, Wildlife and Parks planted and distributed plants because of the many species of birds and mammals that ate the seed and leaves. I feel that the mature trees that produce seed contributed greatly to the survival of many game bird and non-game bird species. In the winters of 2003-04 and 2010-2011 when we had record breaking snowfall both years. The Russian olive plantings in eastern Montana have been important in the survival of many birds and animals.

Lately, there are those that want to make Russian Olive's a Montana noxious weed, mostly because of its ability to survive and do well next to waterways. I have seen in the last years, after a season of flooding on both the Milk and the Missouri, that these trees growing along the river stopped bank erosion to a certain degree. Places on the river that did not have these trees along the river had excessive erosion from the high waters. If the Russian olive is made a noxious weed it would have to be eliminated by landowners and the agencies that have control of our public lands. It is to the betterment of wildlife that we just keep it as a species to watch. We as landowners can watch for its spread on our own property and control it if we feel it is necessary. In my opinion, this plant has too much benefit for birds, animals and erosion control to be considered a noxious weed.

Diseases That Have Effected Deer Populations
on the Milk and Missouri River Bottoms

In recent years, there have been several diseases that have had an adverse effect on the deer populations, which has really decreased the populations of deer, but also changed the patterns of migration, feeding and watering.

In the 1920's Grandpa said there were not many deer around. Then also in the early 1960's we did not have many deer here in the Missouri River bottom for a couple of years and this could have been from one of these diseases! I sure do not want to see another flooding year like this again or another winter like the 2010-11 record snow breaking of 108 inches of snow. I just hope the surviving dear have good immunities to the disease and come back to huntable numbers again.

I know we have had deaths of the deer in the past and a lot of them would go to water to drink and died near the water sources. The disease that affected animals in this way is called Blue Tongue. Blue Tongue is a disease that is viral and effects mostly sheep, goats, buffalo, deer and antelope, but does not affect cows very much. The virus is transmitted by a midge and can have quite a high mortality rate. It gets its name from the swelling of the lips and tongue of the effected animals, which get a blue or blackish appearance. This disease devastated the white tail deer population down on the river bottom but did not seem to affect the mule deer. At that time, we did not see many antelope down here, so I am not sure how it affected them, but the disease is supposed to be pretty hard on antelope.

In the last few years (2010&2011) EHD, Epizootic Hemorrhagic Disease, has hit the whitetails hard and we have lost an estimated eighty to ninety percent of them. That huge number is hard to comprehend!! It seems the Mule deer population has not been affected as much and they have begun to take over the brush area on the river bottom. In past years, only white tail roamed this river bottom, and muley's stayed to the hills, but things have certainly changed. I feel that we will have a lot more crosses between these two species in the future. This is similar to the F1 cross between two pure breeds of cattle that become better than their parent breed. I hope that the new crop of whitetails will be immune to this devastating disease! I was just sick from the death of so many deer here and all over the Milk and Missouri River valleys. This happened when both river systems were flooding and the deer were pushed in a smaller area of habitat.

In this summer of 2011, we did not have many mosquitoes, but we had a tremendous amount of Black Gnats from spring all the way through to the heavy frosts of late fall. The EHD disease is transmitted by a midge that infects a whitetail deer and several days after being infected, the animal dies. I have heard that the gnat and, maybe the midge which is similar, breeds and hatches in moving water! The animals that were affected with EHD, died out in the fields, brush and pastures. I found a young medium four-point whitetail that died only one hundred and fifty feet from my house, and I was only able to find the carcass because of the smell of it. The stink was in the area for days before I was able to find the animal. There were a lot tall weeds and grass that year so the dead animals were hard to find, but the smell of them allowed you to narrow down a location. The smell of death from the whitetails was everywhere in this whole area and was very sickening to me and others because our whitetail herd was dying off and there was nothing we could do about it! I was at a meeting when Kelvin Johnson, who is a biologist with Montana Fish Wildlife and Parks, gave a talk on Epizootic Hemorrhagic Disease. In his talk about EHD, he said that when a deer got bitten by the infected midge, the deer would die in less than a week. It is just almost unbelievable, but that it what happened to devastate the local white tail population.

Chronic Wasting Disease (CWD) has been described by wildlife professionals as possibly the largest threat to captive and to wild deer herds. The origin of CWD is unknown but first discovered in 1967 in mule deer at a research facility in Colorado. Shortly after that it was found in captive mule deer and elk in Ontario. By the 1990s it was discovered in wild white-tail deer, mule deer, elk and moose in Colorado and Wyoming. The Board of Animal Health states that this disease affects all members of the cervid family (which includes all the members of the deer family) There is no cure of for CWD, which is always fatal. The only detection right now is by checking the brain tissue from a dead animal. There is no evidence right now that humans can get the disease by eating the meat, but it is recommended that meat should be tested if the animal looks to be sickly, and it is also recommended that the meat not be consumed if it is found to be infected with CWD. It is recommended that gloves should be used to dress out the animal. Do not come in to contact with the brain or cervical fluids. As of 2017, this disease is in captive or free ranging herds in 24 states, three provinces, Norway and South Korea. The disease is slow acting, degenerative and always fatal to the infected animal. The name comes from the appearance of symptomatic animals, which get very skinny and sick-looking before they die.

As an FWP Citizen Advisory Council member for Region 6 in Montana, at one our meetings in 2016, we were warned that it was only a matter of time that CWD would come into the state as the epidemic had been reported to the south in Wyoming and Saskatchewan to the north. There were no elk or deer found to be infected at that time in the state of Montana. In the fall of 2017 there was an infected animal taken near Bridger (from tests) and two animals found infected near the Alberta Province.

At the fall 2018 CAC meeting we were notified that there were positive animals found near Bridger, several in Northern Blaine County and one positive sample from The Fort Peck Indian Reservation. It is recommended that all animal remains be put in a dumpster if under suspect. The Initial Response Area (IRA) will include a roughly 10-mile radius around where the first CWD infected deer was killed. This is an area that could have a special hunt to see how many infected animals there are in this area to measure the prevalence and spatial distribution of the disease. The heads of animals are to be taken to drop off spots during hunting season at FWP headquarters. Hunting must continue to thin out the herd so that the disease will not explode and eliminate most or all of our deer species.

Please contact FWP for more information on any of these diseases affecting wildlife in our region!

West Nile Virus (WNV)

West Nile Virus is another disease that has affected people, horses and birds in our county, state and country. It is spread by the bite from a certain strain of mosquito that is prevalent in certain regions of the country. The main spread of this disease is from the mosquito, which bites an infected bird, and then a human or another animal. Many humans who have been bitten by mosquitos have built up immunities than can protect them from WNV. Some humans have contacted this disease and have gotten very sick, weak and even has caused death in some cases. Horses are very susceptible to this disease and can die from it. I asked a birder and friend, Woody Baxter, a while back about why we do not have many magpies around like we used to. He told me the Corvid family of birds are very susceptible to this disease such as the magpie, bluejay, crow and raven, although in the last couple of years, these birds are starting to have a comeback in our area. There used to be huge numbers of magpies in this countryside, to the point that they were a problem, but now we are lucky to see more than a handful of magpies each year. It was also reported in the Charles M. Russel, (CMR) Final Environmental Impact Statement, that the Service had found that some of the Greater Sage Grouse had died with this virus in their bodies on the refuge.

Ron Stoneberg said that in the summer of 2018 the sage grouse chicks were doing fine and we had quite a bit of rain which caused some standing water which then can cause a lot of mosquitos to hatch. He later had seen hordes of mosquitos near the water and he was worried. Later he found that a lot of the chicks were gone. His wife Rose Stoneberg, who is a veterinary medical doctor, and Ron figures the sage grouse chicks got West Nile from the infected mosquitos and many died!

Dale Borgen contracted WNV from a mosquito and it weakened him for several years and maybe it still does. Some people have died from WNV and there have been many reports of this disease in Montana. Many horses have been sickened from and died from this mosquito spread disease!

There have been other diseases spread from the mosquito bite over the years, but we have learned a lot about the control of mosquitos by not having standing water around our houses. We also have some products that we can safely put in our cattle water tanks and standing water that kills the mosquito larvae!

Ticks and other Crawlies

In the spring and early summer here in Montana we have a lot of ticks that are in the grass and other vegetation. My mother would say to us kids to stay away from the sagebrush and I feel there are many ticks in this plant and other vegetation. Even walking through tall grass during tick season can leave you covered in the little critters. I also feel that ticks are in trees and they will drop on you. There several different varieties of ticks and they can spread different diseases. In this area we can get Rocky Mountain Spotted fever and there has been some reports of Lyme Disease from a certain variety of ticks.

Ron Stoneberg was bitten from a tick several years ago and almost died from a tick related disease. This affected his balance for a few years, but he has recovered well! He is retired from Montana FWP, and has a Masters Degree in wildlife conservation. He now is a Supervisor for the Valley County Conservation District, as I am. He is very active in conservation, bison and wolf issues here in eastern Montana. His daughter, Sierra Holt is an author and is very active with these same issues and also works on water right issues for farmers and ranchers!

Ticks can cause several illnesses, including Anaplasmosis, which we used to call Sleeping Sickness. This disease was more prevalent in the past. This can cause fever, severe headaches, muscle aches and nausea, vomiting and diarrhea in its early stages and in its later stages, it can cause respiratory failure, bleeding problems, organ failure and sometimes death.

We have lots of ticks in this county side and we have had problems with them on our dogs over the years. We used to try tick collars but those never seemed to work well and now we use monthly drops on our dogs in the spring and early summer, to try to keep them from being infested. Patty used to say that maybe I should wear a flea and tick collar, too!!

My Love of the Outdoors Started When I Was Young

Hunting and trapping are two of my favorite past times, and as a youth I fished quite a lot (but possibly this was an escape from helping with the farm work as a kid!) I learned Hunting from Grandpa Garwood and Dad, and it was Grandpa Garwood that taught me the basics of trapping and fishing.

The fall of 1957 was the year that I got my first hunting license and Dad, Grandpa and myself went out hunting in an area past the Pines Recreation Area. We went on a few hunting trips out in this area, on what is now called the Charles M. Russell Refuge, but at that time was known as The Fort Peck Game Range. We saw some great country and I got my first deer, a mule deer doe. I was hooked on hunting and the beauty of the Missouri breaks. We all hunted for a few years together out there. Grandpa and I always walked fairly close to each other and sometimes we would be on opposite sides of a coulee. We would work toward Dad, who was at the end of the coulee on a stand. He usually got something as we would push deer toward him.

Grandpa would use his model 99 .300 Savage or the Winchester 30-30. The Savage was the most accurate of the two guns and I liked it better. I used a .22 for a couple of years when I first got my big game hunting license, which wasn't ideal, and then Dad later got a Winchester 30-06 bolt action that he used for years, and I did too. I inherited the .300 Savage from my Grandpa Marion, which is an extremely accurate gun for a lever action. It is still my favorite gun for deer-sized game but I did take a moose in Canada in the early 1970's with it. I do not use it as much now, but only because I want to preserve it. The walnut stock has never been refinished but is still in really good shape. The workhorse gun I use most is a model 99 Savage .284 Winchester caliber. It has a clip and I reload all of my own bullets for it. It shoots flatter and hits harder and I have taken both moose and elk with it. I really like the model 99 Savage lever action rifles. I bought this rifle in 1972 at D & G Sports in Glasgow from Dale Morehouse. I had drawn a Bighorn permit west of Augusta in the Sun River Range and there were grizzlies in the area and I felt like I needed a bigger rifle. This rifle has served me well for many years and many hunts!

Grandpa taught me how to trap when I was a youngster. Grandpa was trapping with me when I caught my first skunk and a red fox on the hill above the grain bins. I caught the skunk first and then used it to lure in my first beautiful red fox. I love recreating in the outdoors and I thank Grandpa and Dad for that. Since then I have walked hundreds of miles in North America hunting, fishing and trapping, and at age 73 I still do! Even though my balance is not what it once was, I am still very fortunate that I can still walk in rough country. Walking has been good for my health and the only time I ever got over-weight was when I spent 44 days in the intensive care unit in the hospital in Glasgow and they were feeding me three milkshakes a day to help build up my skin growth from the burns that I had received from a propane fire in the fall of 1979!! I still love ice cream and milkshakes!!

I still love hunting and trapping, and the exercise I get from those favored activities!

Trapping on the River Bottom

Growing up, most of us boys that lived on the river needed a way to make extra income. We started trapping because of the excitement of it and we could make extra income to buy shells, traps and other things. I bought a years subscription to Fur, Fish and Game and my life has never been the same. I still get a subscription to it and have for about fifty years and I have most of my magazines yet. My family accuses me of being a pack-rat, but

I do not see it quite like that. I think of myself as a collector of things that may still be useful, or at least I have hope it may be useful at some time!! I have hunted, fished and trapped for most of my life. My grandfather had trapped coyotes, badgers and skunks in the old days and got me some traps and helped me get started in the "Mountain Man" lifestyle.

A neighbor that helped encourage my trapping interests was Otto Ohlson. Otto, who was a year younger than me, lived two miles to the east of my folks place on the Milk River. His parents were Sam and Gretchen Ohlson, good friends and neighbors of my parents. Otto, Buck Musgrove and I were trapping in what was probably the fall of 1963 when I was a junior at Nashua High School. We had fun competing against each other and going on each others trap line to learn from each other and we sure enjoyed the adventure of it. I remember well my first red fox caught on the hill above our house. What excitement to see the white tip of the tail of a red fox whipping back and forth as you are walking up to it.

Red fox are such a beautiful animal and none of them are quite the same color. They can be yellow, cherry red, red with gray hips, cross fox and different shades of silver. Most of them are different shades of red but if you get several you will find that some are quite similar. The last few years we have had an increase in coyotes, which have been hard on the red fox population. Also the foxes got mange really bad here several years ago. Therefore, we do not have many here now as we did in the past. We did not have any foxes here in eastern Montana until the mid-nineteen fifties when some foxes from a fox farm escaped in western North Dakota and got the population started here. They did well in this region for many years. I do not remember seeing any red fox until I was about eleven years old.

For years we did not have any coyotes here because of the use of 1080 poison to control their numbers. The 1080 controlled all the predators and predator birds, which did help increase the numbers of the sage grouse in this countryside. At that time there were thousands of sage grouse out south!! With the use of this pesticide, there was a decrease in coyote numbers, as well as fox. Since 1080 was outlawed, the coyote numbers have increased to such outlandish numbers that it is difficult to control them anymore. I shot the first coyote that I had ever seen in the fall of 1964 while I was whitetail deer hunting on the river. I shot him with my model 99-.300 savage and tore him up pretty bad. I threw him across my shoulder and headed for the house and found out he was loaded with fleas! When I realized he was infested with fleas, I dropped him like a bad habit. I came back later to retrieve him when I had something to put the carcass in that would keep the fleas off of me. My kids remember getting flea bites from my trapping habit, and at some point my wife was about to kick me out of the house!! They all would get bites, but I would not! What can I say? Oops!! I learned to put foxes and coyotes in plastic bags for a while and spray the inside of the bag with Raid, which would kill the fleas. Sometimes you learn the best lessons the hard way!!

We all had a good trapping season the year of 1964. Otto Ohlson caught three bobcats and one fox. Buck Musgrove caught four foxes and I caught two foxes, one bobcat and one ermine, or winter weasel. We all made extra money and for us redneck country kids we used that money to buy provisions for our next hunting and trapping season or for presents for Christmas. Buck and I were walking along the Milk River "beavering", when we spotted a beaver swimming along the river bank towards us. I shot it with one shot with my twenty-two and it sank immediately on the spot. We could not find it, so we went home and got a couple of fishing poles. After several casts one of us snagged something and lucked out by pulling in the medium size beaver. We had some time skinning the beaver as we had not done it before and had only seen how it was done in the Fur, Fish and Game Magazine. It was not real pretty, but we got the job done. We had some more fur to sell or keep for the wall.

One time while we were hunting down on the White place, which is south-west of my home place, and now owned by the Reimche family, we found a dead mink that some hunter had shot and left. We had never seen a mink before and it was fresh killed, so we brought it back home. Buck and I skinned and stretched it. We did not even know that there were any mink around, so it was quite exciting to discover this. Mink were worth more than anything else so we started trapping for them, but to no avail for a couple of years. Twenty years later after getting small 110 Conibear traps, I caught nine mink one trapping season. Later on, in the Montana Fish and Game survey they estimated that 100 mink had been trapped in Valley County. I realized that I had taken nine percent of the mink in Valley County. I believe the year was 1987.

The 1972 Bighorn Sheep Hunts

In the first trip on my bighorn sheep hunt, Dan Williamson went with me on a walking backpack trip into the Sun River Range west of Augusta. The weather was supposed to be pretty good for several days so we went to north of Augusta to visit his sister Linda and her husband. They lived near Choteau and told us about the best way to drive to a trailhead and walk in from there to look for some rams. This part of the mountains is pretty rough and rugged. Dad, Grandpa and I had hunted some for elk there a couple of years before, so I was a little familiar with the roads. Having been in this area before is why I put in for this area for the Bighorn sheep. Dan and I parked the pickup near an access trail that led into the Bob Marshal Wilderness Area and we walked in until the sun was starting to set and put up our tent. We had to make camp in a hurry because we were losing the light, but without access to fresh water, it was not a very good campsite. We did have time to walk around and glass for rams and did not find any. The next day we pulled camp and packed in a couple miles farther and set up camp near a small stream, which was a location that gave access to fresh water. We hiked up to a ridge where we looked over a tremendous cliff that might have been a quarter of a mile down, it was pretty much a straight drop. We saw sheep on the other side of the cliff, but they were all ewes and a few half curl rams, but nothing that I was interested in. The sheep had a mineral lick there that they were using.

We watched this area for a couple of days hoping that some mature rams would show up. This did not happen even though we were seeing plenty of young ewes. One morning we saw a few young rams move down and up this vertical cliff area that are referred to as chutes, which are hollowed out areas that the sheep used to move on the rocky surface, from below and to go up over the ridge. We were so impressed with the speed that they could go up and down this cliff area. After a couple of days watching the sheep do this, we had a decision to make. It looked like weather was moving in and we had not had any snow to deal with yet. The day before we had crossed a loose shale area to go look for some other sheep when I lost my footing on a loose rock. I had my Savage .284 slung on my back and I fell right on my rifle. I put a ding in the scope that was a deep dent. I was not hurt but my scope was! It took the brunt of my fall and was looking kind of tough. We were in sheep area and I did not want to check my rifle out to see if it was out of alignment due to the noise it would cause, though I suspected that it probably was off after that fall!!

A few years earlier on a hunt into Canada, I had found out after a day hunting by horse back and going through brush and trees all day, without a rifle scabbard on the saddle, that just from the jarring, my rifle was off about 3 inches at 100 yards. This means that at a 300 yard shot it was off 9 inches. This would have meant a missed shot or a wounded animal!! I was concerned that my fall and dented scope could cause my shot to be off too!

About the middle of the morning the next day, Dan and I broke camp and walked the 6 or 7 miles down the mountain to the pickup and drove back to Nashua.

The first hunt was early in the hunting season and I figured I would be back for another hunt. I was busy farming all fall. The last few days of the sheep season, I went back to Augusta with my father, Edgar Garwood, with only about 3 days of the Bighorn season left! These Bighorn tags are extremely hard to draw so I did not want to miss out on a chance to take one at this time. My second cousin, Bob Garwood, was working at a restaurant in Augusta at the time, so we spent the night at his place. The next morning Dad and I went back into a different part of the area that was a little ways from my first trip in. We stopped at the Augusta ranger station on the way in and talked to a warden about where a good place to find the sheep might be. This was later in the season and the "rut" was on so the rams would be with or near the ewes on this hunt.

We drove a few miles past the ranger station and we started seeing sheep. We left the pickup and walked up the mountain. Dad was getting tired, so he stayed while I walked up a ways more to be able to watch the ewes to see if a good ram would show up. I was at a pretty good glassing spot and I spent about an hour or so watching for rams with my binoculars. Then I heard a rock roll above and behind me and I looked over my shoulder and there was a pretty good ram looking right at some ewes! I did not want to move as he was watching me. I knew that this was the biggest ram that I had seen and there was only two days of the season left; the hunt would be over for the year and maybe for the rest of my life.

I knew that he was not a full curl ram, but he was only about 150 yards above me and I could pack him out fairly easy. I was in a poor position to shoot him as I was laying on my belly looking down the hill, and he was behind me and up the hillside. I had to roll over on my back in a slow and easy manner to keep from spooking him and put my rifle barrel on my toes as support. I somehow squeezed off the shot on my back and made a good one shot kill and the ram rolled down hill toward me. I was worried that he would hurt his horns as he rolled out of sight in a depression. I walked over the ridge and found him and what a beautiful sight. His horns were not damaged except for one small scrape that is noticeable only if you know where to look (as I do). I think that a bighorn ram is one of the most regal of all the big game species in North America. I am so lucky to have drawn this very illusive permit and to take a very beautiful animal species.

This shoulder mount is still the most impressive mount that I have in my den and was done by the late John Bleth, from Lewistown. Even though it is only a ¾ curl legal ram for the area, it has good bases, and I am still proud of it! I am so happy that my Dad was there on this hunt with me!

My 1991 Mountain Moose Hunt

I also got a moose tag in 1991 in the Polebridge area west of Glacier Park and north of Whitefish. I wanted a mature bull and it took three trips there in my old 1973 Dodge four-wheel drive pickup. It was 18 years old at that time and it still is driving, although I am still using it mostly to spray the fields with. With 300 gallons of water in the tank and the sprayer weight of that half ton W100 4x4 has almost 1.5 tons of weight on it and just keeps going. Patty has always said it drives like a lumber wagon, and she may be right, as it is a bit rough, but it keeps on going, Ram Tough, like the commercials say!!

The first trip out on the moose hunt was on opening day in September. Mike Buchmann and Verlin Borgen went with me. We were only out there three days and it was warm and all we managed to do was get to know the area a little. We did not see even one moose! We did hear a bear huff and run off, but we did not see it. We had black bear tags with us, too, just in case.

The second trip was out there, was on the opener of the general rifle season for elk and deer. We set up our big blue tarp tent that the north country boys had made several years earlier. They were Leroy Novak, Dale Borgen, Verlin Borgen and Mike Buchmann who all went with me along with Kendall Vaughn. It was a very memorable trip because it was severely cold, well below zero, and we set up the tent in about a foot of snow with the help of Rob Mortimer. We got up high the next morning and we seen some poles and a line of cable. It was then that we figured out that we were over the hill from The Big Mountain Ski area!! We were seeing moose tracks and Dale saw a young bull moose, but I could not find him later that day. We did see a couple of young bulls but not something that I was ready to pull the trigger on. We did not see any elk on this trip. We had previously hunted a few years before this for elk with Otto Ohlson in the White Sulphur Springs area. We had taken three elk one year there!

I managed to get a mature bull, that was 42 inches wide, on the third trip up there when Don Nybakken went with me in late November. Don had taken a spike bull moose earlier in the year in the Libby area. We picked up Gary Turner and he knew the area as he lived nearby. We talked to an elk hunter as he was glassing for game. We told him that we were looking for moose. From that spot on the road he pointed way up in a clear-cut logging area and then we could see there were four bulls, two small ones and two larger ones.

The moose were in sight of the pickup and they were getting nervous and I was afraid that they would take off, so I grabbed my rifle and headed out alone up after them. When I got up there, I found out they had moved out of site of the guys in the truck. One of the big bulls had left the other three and he was not in sight of me. I decided to try to stalk the three and get closer to them for a shot. I was not quite close enough and had to circle some to get the wind right when the other big bull blew out of a low spot and went up on a low ridge near me. I do not think the moose knew what had spooked him and I was between him and the other bulls. He stopped and looked back at about 250 yards and I held right on his ribs with my model 99 Savage 284 and squeezed one off. The bull lurched and ran into a small depression with some small brush in it. I ran up a little to get a better look, but I did not see him. I watched for a while to make sure he did not go out the other side. I then went down into the low spot and found him dead in about a foot of snow.

It was about thawing and the snow was getting sticky. I figured it would be a little while before I had help from my partners at the pickup. As it turned out, when the moose moved out of sight of the road, the guys were sitting in the truck and they did not hear the shot, so they did not know I had got a moose. I took some pictures of the bull and procrastinated some waiting for help. It took some time just getting his legs out so I could field dress him. He weighed about one thousand pounds, as he was a four and a half year old bull. By the time I got him field dressed in the wet deep snow I was almost red from the bulls' blood. When I walked up to the guys in the truck they asked "what happened to you"? I guess I looked a mess and they thought I had hurt myself. It was getting too late to get him out that day, so the next day we got two more guys and got him out in three sections with one being the head and antlers. I was carrying the head and I slipped and fell down in a small drainage with the rack kind of pinning me down in the snow for a little while. The guys laughed at the sight saying the bull had gotten payback to me by getting on top of me and pinning me in the snow!!

Hunting with Gary and Marilynn Johnson

The Johnsons are very good friends of Patty and I and have been for many years. Gary graduated from school in Glasgow and Marilynn Garsjo graduated from Nashua, a year after I did. We lived close to them for years, until they moved to Wolf Point for business, and our children were always close friends.

Patty worked with Marilynn at the Pink Poodle fixing hair when we were just married. We stood up for each other at our weddings. The Johnsons were married three months before us in 1969. We started hunting together probably in the fall of 1969 or 1970. I had given Patty a .243 Mossberg bolt action rifle for our first anniversary so she could have a rifle of her own to hunt with. She always insinuated that I bought the gun so I could use it myself! She harvested a whitetail doe and an antelope with it. Our boys Seth and Shawn both got their first deer with this rifle. I had Red Whitten from Nashua refinish the stock on the rifle and to re-bed the receiver of the rifle into the stock so it would shoot more accurate. The finish turned out to be lighter in color than the original finish and Patty never liked that lighter color, but I think it looks good. Now it is one of my favorite guns as it works well for both deer and coyotes and I do use it quite a bit! Imagine that!

One hunting season sometime in the 70's we were hunting around our place for whitetails with the Johnsons. We had not had any luck that morning hunting and the four of were hungry and decided to go to the Park Grove Bar to eat. The four of us were in Gary's old Volkswagon Bug and we just got to the top of Molly Stevens Hill where we would turn left onto Highway 117 and head toward Fort Peck. Just then, a buck crossed the road and ran down the hill at the old Stevens sheep ranch. I was sitting in the back seat with my rifle. It was deer hunting season and I usually did not go anywhere without my rifle back then. I was sitting in the back seat and I hollered at everyone to let me out so I could get a shot at it! It was not easy to get out of the back of that bug in a quick manner, let me tell you. I got a shell in the chamber just as it ran by an old combine that is just east of the turnoff on to what is now called South River Road. I missed the running buck with my first shot as it was zig-zagging through the old machinery. I got another round in the gun and the buck crossed the road near some hay bales and that second the shot it dropped dead close to the road. We all were almost in shock as it was in sight of the highway and about 200 yards from Art Neubauer's house, who I knew well as he was a neighbor of my Dad's.

We dressed it out and tagged it but we did not know what to do with it as we were really pretty close to the road to leave it while we went out to eat. In Montana, most people tie their deer on the hood or trunk but the bug did not have any room on them. Therefore, after some thought, we decided to put the deer on the roof and hold onto the legs as we did not have any rope. After we got it up there, the only way it would ride was on the stomach with the four feet hanging down over the sides so each one of us could hold onto a hoof through the windows so it would not fall off. I think the deer rack was hanging down over the windshield!! Then we went out to the Park Grove Bar to get Erma Brown to fix us a late breakfast. By the time we got to the bar there was blood running down the sides of the Volkswagon and also onto the windshield. You could not believe the looks we got as we pulled up to the bar. We did get a picture of the deer on the car for memories of this hunt!!

Another hunt we went on was out south in McCone County. The four of us had antelope permits and we went out to the Weldon Community where my Grandfather, Father and I usually went antelope hunting on Rob Schriver's place. After talking to Rob and playing some music on his old jukebox we went hunting. Rob knew that I always waited for a good buck and I very seldom took a doe. He had too many antelope around and wanted some taken out. We saw some antelope running over the hill and drove like crazy to get ahead of them. They were really spooked and we were only about a hundred yards from them. A couple of us got our guns out and Patty had a pair of binoculars with a strap around her neck and she was out in front of us hollering for us to shoot while watching them looking through the glasses. The antelope hit a fence right along the road and some stopped as they don't like to jump over the fences. They were running into each other, some falling down, some rolling over each other and they scattered in all directions. We were laughing so hard that I do not think we ever fired a shot. It was quite a show and I think none of us there will ever forget it!

We saw another herd later on so Gary and I tried to sneak up on them but the critters sensed us and started moving. The big buck did not give me a clear shot so Gary took a shot at a doe. Nothing happened so he took another shot. Then one antelope fell down, then another and then another. Gary was all excited and almost crying and he blurted out to me. "Are they ever going to stop falling down." We walked up to them and he had three antelope down with two shots and they were all lung shots with no meat wasted! Gary, Marilynn and Patty tagged them and after we gutted them out, we were heading back to Robs place. All of a sudden, here comes a lone antelope buck down the hill towards us with Rob in his pickup herding the buck right to us. This buck had his tongue hanging out and I did not want to shoot it but Rob was really trying to deliver it to me. The buck was running past me and I hit it with my second shot. Rob had a good laugh afterwards as all of us did. He said he thought that maybe he would have to shoot it for me! Rob was a very nice man and we only saw him a few more times after that as I think we quit putting in for antelope permits in McCone County.

Another hunt I remember was when the four of us were going to hunt whitetails on the White place which is just down below our house. I was driving my 73 Dodge 4x4 with the girls along in the front seat and Gary was riding in the back holding his gun. Gary started mumbling and shouting something and we could not understand what he was saying. I saw a light-colored animal run behind us in the rear view mirror and I seen that it was a large bull elk. Gary was still pointing at it and speaking jibberish. I got the shoulder strap hung up in the gun rack and could not get the gun out very smoothly. Anyway, the bull got away and we did not fire a shot!!

The Critters That Live In Our Home

I am very fortunate to live on a farm most of my life with a lot of space for pets to roam on, and it made it easy and natural to have dogs and cats for pets. I have always loved dogs and I have had many of them for pets and companions. When I lived with my parents and grandparents on their farm, we had Pumpkin, Sparky, Buddy (beagle) and Duke. It was just natural for me to have one with me while I was hunting game, irrigating, fencing or just any other work I was doing. I just love dogs and they all seem to like me. If I go to visit a friend or relative and they have a dog or dogs, they come to me with their tails wagging and greet me. I like them all and they seem to know that I like them! I am just a dog person! My kids call me "the pet whisperer"!

When Patty and I were married in 1969, we moved here to the Mattingly place that my Dad bought in 1963. I bought a Beagle pup who was called Buddy. He was the second Beagle that I had as the first one I had was killed on the county road by a vehicle. Dogs have a bad habit of chasing cars and it can be fatal for them. We lost Buddy II in the stock tank when we were gone from home on cold day in winter. Patty had friend that gave her a white miniature poodle for a wedding present that was registered and his registered name was Antwan Shawn, and we called him Tawny! We had him for many years and he was our first inside the house lap dog! He was a great companion for Patty and he traveled with us to the east coast and into Canada. He lived about 15 years and was a good friend to all.

We also had a Golden Retriever named Candy and she was given to us by John and Judy Jones. Judy was Stacy's kindergarten teacher and Stacy promised to give her dog a good home when she found out that Candy needed a new place to live. We had just lost Buddy II and Stacy must have felt like we needed a new dog. Candy lived for many years and was a great companion to the whole family. She was a trained hunting dog, very gentle and listened to commands amazingly well.

Sometime in the 1980's we were in Nashua at the annual Winterfest Festival that we always helped with and we found a small black puppy that someone apparently left for someone to take home. That someone was me, with a little manipulation from my children. We called this puppy Tyke and he would follow me everywhere in the snow while I did my cattle feeding and pumping water. He was a fluffy black dog with a patch of white on his chest. At that time, we wintered about 50 to 60 mother cows and I usually calved them out in March. Tyke did not like riding much in the pickup but would follow me up to a couple of miles while I irrigated or farmed. He was an outside dog and did not like being in the house except for some very below zero nights but he always whined and barked at the door as he wanted back outside. He would curl in the snow just like a Huskey or would go in his doghouse, which was under the front porch and was protected from the winds. He was quite a roamer and would go over to the Andersons who lived a mile away. He kept the raccoons, coyotes and foxes away from the house. He would kill racoons, skunks and one mink that wandered into the yard one spring when there was a pool of water near the house from runoff. One day when Patty and Stacy went for a mile walk, he killed two skunks that were in the borrow pits, pretty much one after the other. When he was about 15, he had started to slow down, and just before he died that summer, we think he could have been injured in a fight with another animal. I guess we will never know for sure, but he was a great dog and is still missed. We went about one year without a dog on the farm and we were getting raccoons and coyotes in the yard and I told my Stacy that I wanted a dog just like Tyke!

Stacy had gone to Billings for a visit and found a young black dog in a shelter and brought her to the farm for us. She even has a patch of white on her chest, just like Tyke did!! She was probably between 4 or 6 months old at that time. She was very well behaved and really welcome to our home. Her name is Maxine but I just call her Max! She is an inside dog at nights but when she was younger, spent a lot of the time out with the cats and cows whom she gets along with very well. She is very protective of the farmyard and she has gone with me in my pickups most of the time on the farm and to Nashua and Glasgow. She loved going with me while irrigating and she would chase gophers and gulls. She loved splashing through the cold water on hot summer days, in either the river or the irrigation ditches. When I buy a meal in town, I always share my lunch with her as she really enjoys my ole's from The Taco Shack. Sherri always says Hi to her and gives her doggie biscuit and Max looks forward to this treat! She would ride with me to Vicks to have a couple of beers in my 1991 Ford pickup. This pickup was very easy for her to get up and into the front seat when she was younger. One winter, she even would climb up in the tractor and ride with me while I cleared snow.

One day when she was less than two years old, I had left her at home when I went into Glasgow for business after having helped a neighbor with his feeding. Normally, I would take her with me to feed, but since I had to spend the whole afternoon in Glasgow, I decided to leave her home. Apparently, Max did not think this was the best plan! She must have followed me when I left home and ended up on the highway four miles from the house, near Gordon Reimche's shop on highway 117. It was cold out, it was January and that day was about -20F and someone going towards Nashua picked her up and took her to the Farmers Union gas station in Nashua. This was JR and Debbie Cusker, and they took her to the station in Nashua to see who she might belong to. Max had a collar on with a rabies tag on it, but no other form of identification. The station called the vet clinic, who tracked her down to us based on her rabies tag. I am so glad she had that tag on. The station called Patty, so we knew where she was. Stacy had realized she was missing and was out looking for her on the country roads. Patty called Stacy and Stacy brought Max home. Max has worn a name tag with her name and our number since that time. While she was at the station, Judy and Fuzz took her into the office and gave her treats and spoiled her very bad! They had no idea who Max belonged to at first but they treated her very good. Since then Max has loved going to the station and she has always been welcomed in there for a visit when I come to the station, especially from Judy. Fuzz says that she has such a soft mouth and does not bite when being given a dog treat. When I would drive up to the door at the station, she was always excited to come in for some goodies! She is such a likeable dog, and everyone knows it and pets her. She was well behaved before we adopted her from Billings and she has never tried to get on a chair or couch. She would let us know if some came to the house. She is a barker and when outside she walks around the house and farm letting the critters know to stay away!

One day when Max was young, she was with me out walking in the field south of the house. I was a couple hundred yards and I saw her running toward a coyote as it turned and ran toward the trees. I then saw a second coyote show up and the two of them ran towards her and they chased her my way. I hollered and the coyotes took off. She learned a valuable lesson about coyotes and never liked them after that experience. Max also got kicked a couple times by cows when she was young, and she learned a healthy respect of them. She is about 17 years old now and is going blind in one eye, losing her hearing and getting weaker and does not like going out of the house much! She is getting older just like the rest of us and there is not much we can do but give her lots of love and vitamins! We all love her like family!

Several years ago, when Patty was getting ready to retire from the mail route, she was thinking of getting a puppy. I though perhaps we should get some grandchildren. Patty and I do not have any grandchildren and none of our children act like they want to get married. We were visiting about things and I told her one day that we would like to have some grandchildren while we were young enough to enjoy them! Stacy told me that I should enjoy Jazz, which is her dog, and I sure do enjoy her, although she is very busy and very quick and I always have to keep an eye on what she is getting into!! A few days later Patty brought a little puppy home that Stacy had found for us!!! I guess I had my answer!!

I was hooked on this precious little puppy that is light brown and is a Shih Tzu Poodle cross. We call her a shitpoo!! The truth is, I was not crazy about the idea of Patty getting a puppy as I did not think we needed another dog at the time. But Patty won and brought her home and I was hooked from the moment I saw her. We named her Chewy which is short for Chewbacca from the Star Wars movies. She is a spoiled, loveable lap dog that our family loves. Max did not love her at first and spend a lot of time moping. It took about a month for Max to give her a chance, although Chewy loved Max from the start. We have had her about six years now and she is also a part of our family. Most nights she sleeps on our bed with Patty and I, along with our orange male cat Taz, short for Tasmanian Devil!! We love our pets!!

We have had multiple house cats over the years but we are down to just one anymore. I think at the most we have had three cats in the house at one time, although they are inside/outside cats. Two years ago my female cat Sassy died. We actually raised her on a bottle from the time she was several days old. I do not know what happened exactly, but Max found her abandoned in the farm yard and I picked her up and brought her into the house. We bottle fed her for weeks and she got so fat and sassy on the bottle, I decided to call her Sassy. She was black and white and had a mustache, which made her very unique. She was my cat from the start and she loved to curl up on my lap or on the back of my neck.

We also had two Siamese cats over the years. The first was a kitten that Patty brought home, a Siamese Persian cross she called Suky and we had her for many years. We also had a male Siamese that Stacy brought home and his name was Khan. He was beautiful colored and looked like he should be a spoiled house cat, but he loved it outside and could often be found sitting on fence posts in the corrals or hunting for mice. He loved to lay inside boxes and his personal favorite place to lay was in an 18-pack beer box, with his head poking out the open end. We could carry him around in these boxes and he would not budge!! Another cat that Stacy brought home to us was a black and grey and white tabby named C.J. who lived for almost 22 years. When we first got Max, C.J. got mad and took off for several months, but they eventually learned to be the best of buddies.

Wolf track next to my rifle, Canada, 1970's.

Myself packing into the Bob Marshall Wilderness, affectionately known as "The Bob",
in the 1970's. Rugged and beautiful countryside.

Myself, above, and my father Edgar, below, with my big horn ram.

Myself with a beautiful white tail buck, I had taken one fall. I sent this off to be mounted and unfortunately, I never got it back. At least I have the picture to remember it by.

Myself, relaxing at home. If I am still for long, I usually end up with an animal nearby. This time it was my cat Sassy, in my lap, and my dog Max, at my feet. According to my daughter, the only thing I seem to by missing in this picture is a cup of coffee in my hand.

Taking a little break from stacking hay. Chewy (the dog I never wanted but now whom I cannot imagine not having in our lives) is in front of me, while Max, my faithful companion of many years, was too busy to sit down and pose for a picture, but she is never far from my side.

SOME LOCAL CHARACTERS

(near and dear)

"Well I guess I ain't winter killed yet"!!
-Jack Nickles, Sr

"What this country needs is dirtier fingernails and cleaner minds"
-Will Rogers

A Fine Conversation with Jack Nickels, Sr.

The Nickels brothers, Jack, Lester (Swede) and Rusty, all had ranches on the Missouri River and they all irrigate out of the Missouri River. Their father was Herman Jack Nickels, who I will refer to as Herman for these stories, to help lesson confusion related to all the "Jack's" in the story. Three generations of Nickel's have shared the name Jack, leading to some confusion about just who people are talking about. Jack Senior, (who is actually Jack Herman's son), also has a son named Jack, called Jack Junior by many. Herman Jack Nickels purchased some land on the south side of the Missouri River in about 1900. At that time the ranch was in Dawson County and the county seat was in Glendive, although currently this is part of McCone County. In 1869 the old Fort Peck trading post was the county seat of Dawson County. Herman bought the original farm from Wilkins, who was a government "woodhawk". A "woodhawk" would cut and stack wood near the Missouri River to be used by the steamboats as they went up and down the river as far up as Fort Benton in central Montana. Jack thought maybe Wilkins was working for the government and maybe got the land for cutting wood for the steamboats. At one time, Fort Benton was called "The Worlds' Most Inner Port", because of the distance you could travel to get there from the sea. At one time, steamboat travel was the easiest way to get up the Missouri River to Fort Benton until the railroad was built.

Herman married Lydia Byers, whose family had a homesteaded near the Big Dry; this land is now under the Fort Peck reservoir. He also purchased land from Dykstra on the Milk River, south and east of Nashua. Herman and Lydia had three sons; Jack came along in 1920, followed by brothers Russell (Rusty) and Lester (Swede). My father was a good friend of Swede's and they were on the Valley County Conservation District Board (VCCD) together. I was on the VCCD board of supervisors with Swede for about ten years and I had a lot of respect from him. I learned a lot from him while we were on the board together and I enjoyed the few visits I had with Swede and Mildred at their farm near Wiota. Wiota is an area of river bottom north of the Missouri and east of the Milk river, which was named for the railroad siding of the same name.

Herman was killed in an irrigation accident in 1949. He was unhooking a belt from a tractor, and the tractor rolled forward and killed him. Farming is a dangerous occupation and accidents can happen quickly, even with everyday chores. At the time of the accident his son, Jack, and Bill Kirkland were in Circle at a school board meeting. Jack received word that his father was killed in an accident. He returned to the ranch and found his father still laying there by the tractor. At the time of the accident, Rusty and Swede were flying down to Pennsylvania to get an airplane they had purchased from the Etcharts. The Etchart's and Markle boys ran an aviation business together. They were informed of their dads' death when they got to Pennsylvania, after getting off the plane!

I believe Herman and his wife, Lydia, had sold some of their land near Nashua for the new High school. At that time, they still owned the land at the Nashua Airport. Herman had some land on the Milk River near Nashua which he sold and then used the proceeds to purchase more land near the confluence of the Milk and Missouri Rivers. Rusty and Swede were partners and owned some land together, mostly for summer grazing. Swede's ranch was on the north side of the Missouri, in the Wiota area east of the Milk River, and Rusty's ranch was on the south side of the Missouri river, east of Tower Hill. This was the hill that William Clark had climbed up during the Lewis and Clark Expedition. At one time, Swede's boys, Lester and Steve, ranched with Swede and Rusty. Some of the Nickel land was previously owned by Kitty Cassidy, who came from North Dakota. Rusty and Bernice's son Kenny, whose nickname was Rattlesnake, had to quit ranching for health reasons. He married and moved to North Dakota. After Rusty and his wife Bernice's (who was a Bunk) deaths, the children sold the beautiful river bottom ranch.

Herman bought a wooden ferry that they used to move cattle and machinery back and forth across the Missouri. This old ferry is aging gracefully on the southern bank of the Missouri, now in its retirement. The old wooden ferry still lies on the bank of the river and is of historical value. In the spring of 2010, I walked down to look at it; it is home to cottontail rabbits and lies very serenely, but regally, on the southern bank of the Missouri. This boat had a covered, elevated pilot cabin so the operators could look for obstructions in the river and be out of the weather. The record flows from the Spillway releases in the summer of 2011 have damaged and scattered the old ferry some, so I was happy to have the opportunity to visit the site before the high water destroyed the site. I wish I would have had a camera and taken some pictures at that time before that highwater event. It really bothers me now that I never captured the ferry in a photograph. Even though that ferry is retired, the family still operated a small metal ferry boat and used it to move cows and machinery back and forth across the Missouri river until very recently.

The Nickels pasture for their cattle is comprised of a combination of private, state, Bureau of Land Management (BLM) and Charles M. Russell National Wildlife Refuge (CMR) grasslands, located between the Missouri and Fort Peck Lake. One thing about all the Nickels boys is that regarding ranching and farming they are from the "Old School". They all raise Hereford cattle and they have the best cows and purchase the best bulls. They always got the best horned Hereford bulls that they could afford. They are one of a few cattle producers in the area that still raise Hereford cattle. At one time, they had the second largest herd of commercial Herefords in Montana.

All of the Nickels boys liked to visit with you and maybe pull your leg a little bit if they thought they could get away with it, and I loved to listen to them. Rusty passed away a several years ago and I miss visiting with him. I remember just how his voice was! I was a good listener, because they told such good stories and they knew that I loved hearing about the history of the area. I could tell them about the Musgrove family, as I keep in touch by phone with them and often went up to their ranch in British Columbia to visit. They all new Loren Musgrove as they all were good cowboys! The Nickels boys all were friends with Loren Musgrove. I have shared many enjoyable stories about visiting the Musgrove's in the "Canadian Outback".

Most of the Nickels boys were airplane pilots and used the planes to look for strays or predators that would prey on their livestock.

Jack was a good pilot and loved his flying. I visited with him in the winter of 2015 and I asked him about Rawhide Johnson and about the first thing he told me about him while grinning, is that Rawhide was a moonshiner. Well I knew that from talking to my father and Grandpa. And then I asked him about Zack Bennet, who I knew from talking to Loren Musgrove, was that Zack was also an old-time moonshiner and maybe he had spent some time elsewhere for making and selling the stuff. I do not know for sure about that and Zack may have been partnering up with someone to help moving the shine around. I later heard it may have been Zach's own parents. You see, there were a lot of pilots that flew all over the neighboring counties, who may have been making questionable deliveries! I had mentioned this to Jack when we were visiting and told him that Zack's nephew, Scott, had looked all over the coulee's in the hills looking for Zach's old still. Jack said right away, "That if I still had my plane, I'd fly over them hills and find where Zack hid that still." Jack figures that Zack hid it out in a buffalo berry patch in one of the coulees out there. Who knows where the still lies, but that information, Zack took to his grave!!!

Jack and his first wife Peggy bought a couple of sections of land to the east of Herman's land on the Missouri, which was the William Chamberlain place, where they raised three children; Holly, Jack Jr. and Sally, who all went to school at Nashua. The land to the west of his fathers' ranch was at one time owned by Wilkins the "woodhawk". Jack and Peggy built a new house there, near the river. One year when Buck Musgrove was back visiting, he and I went over to visit Jack and Peggy in their new house. It was a great visit and many a tale was told. It is too bad that I did not take notes at that time, as I was real interested in this history. I guess at that time I thought I would remember all these stories and the details involved in them. I always enjoyed visiting with Jack and Peggy. I still visit with Jack when I run into him. My Dad and Jack were classmates in Nashua through the 8th grade, when Dad's family moved back to Ohio for a couple years.

Sometime in the 1970's, Jack and Peggy Nickels ranch was recognized as "Hereford Man of The Year". Jack and Peggy were honored to be the first commercial Hereford producer to be presented the award by the Montana Hereford Association. Jack and Peggy operated an exclusively Hereford cow ranch on the Missouri River in McCone County. Jack became interested in performance testing in 1941 while attending a range tour of the Miles City Range experiment station. After serving in the Marines during WWII, he returned to the family ranch. When Herman passed away, Jack took over part of the ranch with Swede and Rusty taking over the rest. Jack and Peggy had been artificial inseminating the cows in the '60s but went back to using purebred bulls to save time. Registered bulls are used on all cows. Jack and Peggy did not like polled bulls, which are bulls that send the genetics to calves to not have any horns, as he felt the genetics with them were not as good as horned bulls. He usually traveled out of the area to get the best bulls he could afford. Jack and Peggy maintained a three hundred cow herd until the dry years of the 80's made them cut back on the numbers that they could run.

Peggy passed away after a courageous battle with cancer and I still miss her humor and stories; she was a super nice person. Jack is now married to the former Pearl Wagner. They managed their large ranch for years with one ranch hand, Victor, who has now passed away. They have Herefords, irrigated alfalfa, barley and wheat. Jack and Pearl still maintain quite a few head of cattle, but they have to buy extra hay some winters from the John Rorvik ranch.

Jack talked about Sara Apell, who lived on the south side of the Missouri River in McCone County, east of the Rawhide Johnson place. I checked with the BLM GLO records and found out that she had a homestead patent on Section 32 of Township/Range 27-42 which is just east of the Fort Peck Spillway. She was a registered nurse and an "old maid" who never married. She was a neighbor of Rawhides, but Rawhide and Sara never got along real well, and actually, from some reports they almost feuded! I do not know for sure, but some of her land may have eventually been part of Rusty's ranch and some was taken for the spillway. I know the land that Rawhide owned went to the Corps of Engineers for the Fort Peck spillway.

There is a hill nearby on BLM (Bureau of Land Management) land, which is federal public land, and it is named Dead Man Hill. This hill is a quarter of a mile east of Tower Hill. No one living that is still in the area that I have talked to seems to know why the hill is named Dead Man Hill. This is just one of those mysteries that happen when historical facts are not put on paper for the next generations to know. When my Dad and I visited with Jack once, he mentioned maybe it was from the Lewis and Clark Expedition but I do not think so. There was only one of the Lewis and Clark Expedition death, a Charles Floyd is the only man who is noted to have died on the trip and I think it was in Iowa. As to Dead Man Hill, maybe a person was buried up there but no one seems to really know? There also is a hilltop several miles to the south called Indian Hill, which is just south of Jack's turn off from the highway to go to his house. Indian Hill is about a hundred feet higher than Tower Hill and was probably named because it was used for signaling by the First People.

When Jack was younger, he trapped coyotes and bobcats to make money. He had done this for a few years while he did his chores and when going to and from school. He had some money saved up and heard that a neighbor place, that was once the John Yager homestead, was for sale. He took a day off from school and hitchhiked to Circle, the McCone County seat, to attend the auction sale. His father did not know what Jack was doing in Circle and he came home and told his dad that he had gone to Circle. His dad was kind of upset with Jack, as he had skipped school to go to Circle. Jack then told his dad that he had bought this small piece of land that bordered his fathers' ranch. This showed his father how dedicated that young Jack was to the ranch! When Jack was only a year old, his parents had secured a brand in his name, so it is no wonder he wanted his own ranch at such a young age. He was a cattleman from early on.

Jack told me that when he was trying to get his license to fly a plane, a man from the state showed up at Jacks fathers place to give him a test. Jack passed the written test but the man wanted Jack to take him for a ride in Jack's plane. Jack said that the wind was really blowing that day, maybe forty miles an hour. Jack did not want to take the plane up as it was too windy but the inspector insisted that he needed too if he wanted his license. They got up into the air but Jack did not like the windy conditions as it was too dangerous to be flying and he landed the plane soon after they had taken off. Jack told the inspector that it was just too darn windy to fly safely. The inspector was not happy with him but Jack said a couple of weeks later he got his Montana aviator license in the mail. Jacks plane was an Arotica piper Cub and he got it from Pennsylvania.

A few other stories that Jack Sr. told me, include that his father, Herman Jack Nickels donated the land north of the railroad tracks and just east of the Nashua rail crossing for an airport and he put a windsock up so the pilots could tell the wind direction. At that time Ole Brenden was keeping a milk cow in the 6-acre pasture.

It sounds like Jack Herman was quite a guy. Herman was a professional sheep shearer for many years and was quite good at it. One year after shearing many sheep, he threw the shears down and never sheared another sheep! In the early 1900's Herman rode his horse to Glendive to attend the Materson(?) murder trial, which is a fairly long trip on some rugged country on horseback, so he must have been pretty interested in that trial.

In about the winter of 2014 or 2015, I called Jack to visit and to get a little more information from him. I asked him how he was doing. He thought a little and said, "Well I guess I ain't winter killed yet"!!

I have been interviewing Jack off and on for several years or so for this book I have been writing. It has been a joy to talk to him about his ranch life. In fact, I guess I have been getting stories and information from him for quite a few years as he is such an interesting man to visit with. When I would see him at the Glasgow Stockyards auction sale, I would sit by him and visit. About a month ago, I asked him if it would be okay to put his picture on the cover of the book. He thought a little and then said it would be okay if I didn't put "WANTED" under his picture!!!!

Tales of the Musgrove's
(from both South and North of the 49th parallel)

Loren and Bernice (Leuschen) Musgrove

I will later include stories written by Buck Musgrove and Karen Musgrove Johnson about their parents, but first I have my own stories to tell about this interesting family.

The Musgrove children were near my age, and soon became good friends of my sister Karen and me, when they moved down into the Missouri River bottom full time in the late 1950's. Before this, they stayed on the river bottom during most summers irrigating and haying but we did not know each other then. Their house was just east of a school section, which the Missouri River passes through, and is south-west of my parent's house (and is due west of my current home place). We did not get to know them really well until they started school in Nashua in 1958. My sister Karen and I quickly became friends with the Musgrove's and we visited them fairly often, since they lived so close to us. We also rode the school bus together and always had a good time cutting up with the other neighbor kids. During the summer, we always got together to do something exciting for something to do. They lived about 2 miles west and 1.5 miles south from my parents home place and were good neighbors to all. The last couple of years before they moved to Canada, we were over to their place quite often.

Loren Musgrove's parents were John and Hulda (Shrowder) Musgrove. They first homesteaded about fifteen miles north of Nashua, but they also had a farm southeast of Glasgow. They eventually lost control of the homesteads or sold them, I am not sure which. This north property was part of the Vern Orth place and was at one time owned by Dale and Donna (Orth) Borgen. John and Hulda's children were Loren, Jackie, Mona and Cora. Either John or Loren Musgrove purchased the place down by the Missouri River from Earl Trotter, which is the land the Musgroves lived on up until 1964. My father, Edgar, bought the land in 1964 and I now own this property; it was after my family purchased it from the Musgrove family, when they moved to Canada.

Earl Trotter also owned more land in McCone and Valley Counties and the Missouri River split the ranch, with the other part of the ranch being out south by Fort Peck Lake and near Park Grove. Earl Trotter later sold the land in the eastern part of Valley County (the property north of the Missouri) because after Fort Peck Dam was built, there was a steady flow of water coming down river and it never had any low flows that made crossing the river easy. This constant high water made crossing the Mighty Mo much more difficult than it had been before the Dam was built.

Loren joined the Army as he wanted to be in the armed cavalry unit. Loren was always a cowboy who loved to ride and rode his horses even late into his life in the Canadian wilderness. Loren married Bernice Leuschen, who was originally from Jordan, Montana. Don Leuschen was her younger brother and he was president of Montana Power for some time. I met Don's son, David while we were both visiting the Musgroves at the Musgrove ranch in British Columbia. At that time, David had a large ranch near Yellowstone Park and ran some cows near Jordan, Montana. Bernice was raised in a log house that still stands near the Big Dry Creek. The Big Dry Creek was so named by Lewis and Clark in 1805, because the large river valley was completely dry of water. Bernice was the third child of ten. Loren was still in the service when he married Bernice. Loren ended up going to the Philippines after they were wed and their oldest child, Pat was born when he was overseas. It was a year before Loren saw his daughter, Pat, when he returned home from the war.

Loren was quite a character, especially when he was drinking. In the early days he drank mostly beer, but later on, he drank Rye. It usually was Crown Royal. When he walked into an establishment, or tavern, he would always holler "hoe hoewww!!!" and you knew the party was on. He always had some neat sayings, like "get off the table Mabel, this two bits is for a beer"!! I liked him, respected him, and he was my friend and was liked by everyone. I drank many a Schlitz or Hamm's with him in the states and Uncle Ben's beer or Labatt's Blue on their Upper Cache Creek ranch, in British Columbia. Bernice was a nice, gentle and a kind woman with a great sense of humor who always had a grin on her face.

My wife Patty met Bernice on my third trip to visit up there, in the fall of 1970. Loren and Bernice lived in log house that they had built themselves from the resources on their land and was kept up very nice. Bernice took Patty under her wing and they soon became friends. I remember one morning, after a party the night before at the ranch house in British Columbia, us guys had drank all of the beer and booze and we did not have any left for the next morning. Bernice had saved two beers for her and Patty and they drank them in front of us guys and giggled the whole time.

Patty really enjoyed staying up there, especially on our first trip, as I guess it was romantic living fifty miles from town and having no power. Everything was battery operated, even the record player, which was played for many a dance. Two years later in '72, Patty and I went up for our second visit together. We were about a half a mile away when we saw a yard light on in their yard. Patty remarked, "Oh, darn, they have power". Patty was a little disappointed, but we were happy for Bernice as she was so tickled to have electricity in the house, for a clothes washer, a refrigerator and electric lights. We were both happy for them to have these modern conveniences.

Loren and Bernice had four kids: Pat, Lee (Buck), and Karl and Karen (the twins). Bernice was a school teacher in Frazer during the years they lived in Valley County near my parents' farm, and in the previous years, when they lived out near Spring and Bobcat creeks in McCone County, east of Fort Peck Lake. She taught and home schooled the neighbor kids and her own children until they were ready for high school. Loren had a small herd of cows that he summered on the Fort Peck Indian Reservation or out there in McCone County. They put up their winter hay by stacking it in loose stacks on the farm on the Missouri. I remember well that Bernice would be gone all week while she worked as she stayed in the dorm in

Frazer and then came home on weekends. We would go over to visit the Musgroves and would not have to behave so much because she was gone teaching. She was strict but always had that smile on her face. We usually had a good time but had to behave when Loren was sleeping; we knew we did not want to wake him. We sometimes played a game called spoons and it would be real noisy at times and our laughter and the noisy spoon game would get out of hand. A holler from the back bedroom would jolt us back to soft speech and giggles and we would be quiet for a while.

Rhubarb Wine and the Wine Party

There was a patch of rhubarb that grew near the Musgrove house, and one summer Bernice started making some rhubarb wine in the shed along the side of the house. Anyway, for some time when ever there was fruit, honey or chokecherry berries available they would go in to the five-gallon crock to help make the wine. We did not show a lot of interest in the wine when Bernice was around, but we could not wait until it was ready to sample!! Later Bernice screened the wine and put it in to gallon jars to cure. We were thinking about sampling it a bit, but it was green yet and it had to cure some.

Later the Weinmeister boys, Ronnie and Donnie, decided to have a party at their place with help from the rest of us planning a wine party. Their house was about a mile from the Musgrove's. Their parents Paul and Murnie were going out for a visit and would be gone for a while. Ronnie had permission for us to come over for a visit! Therefore, Bernice said, I think, we could have one gallon of the rhubarb wine to take over to the Weinmeisters. A couple of hours later we ran out of the homemade wine and we were in a predicament.

We sure were not ready to quit partying yet, but it was raining like heck. Bernice and Loren had said only one gallon so we could not drive up to the house as we would wake them up. Buck and I decided to walk across the muddy field and go down into the root cellar quietly and get another jug. By the time we got to the root cellar our boots were so heavy we could hardly walk down the steps. We salvaged, or in all actuality, heisted, one more jug and headed across the muddy field running and giggling. Back at the Weinmeister house the party was on again. We were back to playing music on the phonograph and dancing some but mostly we were just having fun. Buck was getting pretty drunk and could not stand up anymore. All of a sudden Ronnie hollered that he could see lights coming down the road and it was his folks, coming home early. Well, another predicament!!

We were not supposed to really be drinking and Buck was drunk as a skunk!! Karl and I grabbed Buck and dragged him out and were putting him in the back of my Dad's 51 Ford pickup just as Paul and Murnie were driving up to the house. Murnie asked what was wrong with Buck and I mumbled something about he was not feeling so good. We thanked them for the party and I headed out of the yard with someone holding on to Buck so he did not fall out of the pickup as we went down the road.

We still had to get ol' Buck in to bed and I think Karl and Karen took him in as I was not in the best shape myself and I had to get my sister Karen and myself home!! It was a great party and we still talk about it when we get together. That rhubarb wine was still green but it sure was good and we had a good time with it!!!

Later, Larry Boyum said that he had gone over to the Musgroves for a visit one day sometime before the Weinmeinster party and Buck showed him the wine, when it was still fermenting and there was a dead mouse lying on top of the mash. I guess Buck grabbed it by the tail and threw it outside. I guess it is true that alcohol can kill a lot of germs!! It did not seem to hurt the taste of the wine!

It has been over fifty years since the Musgrove's left the Missouri river bottom and moved to Canada, but the rhubarb is still growing by the old water tank and there is still a patch horse radish still growing in a wheat field north of the house. These are tough plants and after spraying them every other year when we plant wheat and with letting the cows graze them every fall, they refuse to die! I still do not like the taste of horse radish but I like rhubarb wine and jelly just fine!!

The Night Hunt

Another time Buck, Karl and I decided to go rabbit hunting while Karen (my sister) and Karen (their sister) stayed back at the house to do girl things! We went down below their house in Loren's Ford pickup. I believe Buck was driving and I was riding shotgun with Dads Remington bolt action .22, but Karl thinks he was driving. Someone was driving, and it was not me!! We were in a field on the Musgrove place that was near a patch of brush under the powerline. I saw some eyes in the headlights ahead in some brush. We stopped to see if we could get a shot and could not see the eyes anymore. I had my head looking out the side window toward the front of the pickup. The rabbit took off running so Buck gunned the engine and took off after it. We had not gone even ten feet and we ran into a tree stump hidden in the snow and came to an abrupt stop. I still had my head out the window looking forward and my forehead slammed into the window guides. It got awful quiet from the Musgrove boys, but I was cussing pretty profoundly and the blood was really running down my face. Well the night's hunt was over for us!! On the way back to the house while I was holding my hankie on my eyebrow, the Musgrove boys could not keep from snickering. The next morning on the bus, with a band aid on my eyebrow, I really got a bad time from all the kids on the bus, especially from the Musgrove kids. To this day I still have two scars on my eyebrow from their Ford pickups window guide from the night hunt!!

The Bullet Hole in the Floor

On another hunt that I had with the Musgrove boys, we had gone to the river on the school section and drove around the trail along the river. We had walked around and had done some plinking. I was driving Dads' old 1951

Ford and we were going down the road heading to the hills when I heard a shot go off and dust filled the cab. Luckily the gun was pointed down and the bullet went through the floorboard. Their .22 gun was between Buck and Karl. Apparently, Karl had left a round in the chamber with the safety off. Buck, without thinking, pulled the trigger to check to see if the safety was on, and the gun went off. When the dust settled, I stopped the pickup and jumped out and looked under the truck to see if anything was hit. Luckily it had missed the transmission and went into the ground. I cannot believe how lucky we were that no one was hurt and neither was the pickup, except for the small hole that is in the floorboard. It was so small that Dad never noticed, and I surely never told him!! Maybe this could be part of the reason why I have tinitus and my ears still ring some!

The Raft Rescue on the Missouri River

It was spring and the snow was finally almost gone and us kids were itching for some activity. We had not been able to go fox or rabbit hunting for awhile because of the deep snows of the winter. Buck, Karl and I went south of the Musgrove house, along the river with our .22's looking for game. We went to the barges and looked around for cottontail rabbits that were usually there. Finding none, we headed east down the river until we came to a small island that was about 30 feet from the main shore. Out on the edge of the island on the shore side we seen a nice wooden raft with steel drums for floats. We figured that it must have floated down from Fort Peck and got stuck on the island. This was a place that all of us kids in the area swam in during the hot weather of summer. My son Seth remembers this is called a back eddy, which he always remembered because of my father's name. When the water level was high, the water flowed backwards into this channel, and when the water was low, it left a nice shallow swimming hole. The currents in the main river make it unsafe for swimming, but this area was sheltered from the current and it made it a littler warmer than the main river. Anyway, we decided to go back to the house and get a lariat rope to try to rope the raft and salvage it for the summer. We tried roping the raft, but it was a little too far to it and that plan just did not work.

It was still kind of cold outside and we knew we did not want to get into that water too bad, so Buck and I talked, well actually the truth was, we dared Karl into wading out to the raft and to tie the rope on to it. The plan was, we could tie the other end of the rope to a tree and being Karl, even though he was younger, was bigger and stronger than Buck and I, our plan was that he could just push the raft off the island, hop on the raft and float it back to the shore! It could not have been a simpler plan. Karl argued a little, but we dared him that he could not do it and he took the dare. He took off his boots and started wading out to the raft with one end of the rope.

Karl complained a little that the water was cold and wanted to come back to the shore, but we encouraged him to go on as he was halfway out to the raft. It was about two and a half feet deep but he made it to our prize. He tied the rope to the raft and we had the other end around a cottonwood tree. The only thing was, the raft was frozen down and Karl could not budge it. He just had wet socks on and getting cold feet and thought he could push more with his boots on. Buck decided to toss one of the boots across to Karl but his toss was short by about 10 feet and the boot sank and went downstream never to be found. Not by us anyway! By now, Karl was cold and did not want to walk back through the water.

After seeing what had happened to him, we sure were not about to go out and get wet, so Buck decided he would go get Loren to help and I would stay with Karl. When he got to the house after running most of the way, he had to tell Loren what a dumb thing we had done! Ronnie Weinmeister and his dad Paul and brother Donnie were there so they came along for the rescue too. When they all arrived, wow… Was I scared!! I almost think that this was my idea to rescue the raft. I told Loren that we would not do anything dumb like this again. Yea! Sure! Anyway, Loren could not talk Karl into walking back to the main shore so Loren walked over through the water to the raft following the rope, put a different rope around Karl and led him to the shore. And by led him, I mean he drug him back to shore!!! Then they took Karl back to the warmth of the house. We kind of snickered at Karl the next day on the bus, but we did not get too carried away with the jokes, as Karl was bigger than us, and it was really our fault!!

We had left the rope hooked on the raft and the tree and when we came back a week or so later the river had come up and the raft floated around and was waiting along the shore kind of like we had planned. Kinda!! We used that raft all that summer to dive off and have our noon lunches on after haying in the hot summer sun. All in all, it turned out pretty good having the raft to use, but I think Buck and I would get a deserved thumping from Karl every now and then when we reminded him about the adventure!!!

Swimming in the River

The summer of '63 was like a lot of summers in the past. A lot of the summer days were hot, getting into the 90's and a few days would get to 100 degrees. There were not that many places when we were younger to swim, but there were a few. Sometimes Mom would take us to the swimming pool at Fort Peck (which was 10 miles away), we could also swim in the Milk River by the Landis place (which had a mucky clay bottom), go to the Fort Peck dredge cuts area that is below the dam (this is the area along the Missouri river that was dredged and pumped up to form the dam), or we could go to the clear cold river that was about 45 degrees as it came from the bottom of the lake. The Missouri was the closest for us and was clean water for swimming but cold for all but us crazy kids. As mentioned above, there was the area of the back eddy that made a nice little swimming hole for us, as the currents in the main channel are not very safe. The pontoon raft was still tied to a tree and available for us to use, and boy did we use it.

The Fort Peck Dam is a "peaking" power generating facility. What that means is that it would put out more water during the day for power to the cities and therefore would raise the water level during the day. Then at night, the powerhouse would put out less water at night when the power was not needed as much. We found out that during the late afternoon when the river was up and flowing past the raft, it was too cold to really swim in. But sometimes we would but that cold water did not feel as good. We live about 8 miles below the dam, but the water does not warm up much by the time it gets here. It takes about 5 or 6 hours for the dropping river levels to get down to our swimming hole. This meant that about midnight, the river would start dropping at our pump site and also quit flowing through our swimming hole. This meant that about dark, we maybe could go swimming on really hot days. Sometimes we did but our parents liked us to be home soon after dark, as that is when some of us farmers have supper!! It was only on certain occasions that it would work out when we could swim after dark. We would need a full moon on a clear evening and only when Bernice and Loren would be gone somewhere so that us kids could dare each other into the water, you see! Our parents did not like us swimming in the Missouri after dark for safety reasons, I guess!

We later found out that about noonish our pool of water would warm up from the sun and because there was no fresh cold water flowing into the pool for the last few hours or so. This was the optimum time to swim. The trouble was, that was the year when the Musgrove boys and I were helping my Grandfather put up small square bales (some ranchers now call those small bales 'idiot cubes') and we would put in several hours haying before and after noon. We knew that we probably could not get away with the noon swimming every day, but we sure tried!! When we did try it, between eating a large meal and swimming for an hour, we were about wore out and not too good of workers in the afternoon. Bucking those bales and stacking them in our new barn at home or near the corrals where we wintered the cows was hard work every day, but a lot tougher after a swim.

This story reminds me of Adlore Bouchard, who once told his step-sons, Dave and Larry Renner about having friends over to help! He said, "One boy is worth one boy, two boys are worth one half a boy, and three boys are worth no boys at all"

Hornets and Honey Bees

The Musgroves would put up their hay in loose stacks by loading it with a buck rake on the front of their Alice Chalmers brand tractor. They would keep stacking more loose hay up on top of each load from the load before. One or two people would be on the stack with pitch forks to help form the stack to shed water. When finished the stack would have a rounded top that would shed off rain and snow, which protects the hay. This type of stack can handle a greener plant to save more leaves but is loose enough to cure without spoilage.

The Musgrove boys were always playing jokes on each other. I heard that one of them was driving the tractor and putting hay on the stack for the other and had found a hornets nest. Of course, he loaded the hornet nest along with some hay up onto the unfinished stack and then watched the other brother have to run around and jump off to get away from the wasps!! This happened a couple times, with each brother pranking the other at different times. I talked to Buck about it the other day on the phone and he remarked that the stack was pretty high and it was a long way to the ground!! There were times like that, when he could not jump off the stack and he called Karl something like, "you culprit, you"! Buck had to get on the stacker to get away from the hornets. Knowing Karl and his joking ways, he probably left Buck up in the air awhile before he let him down to the ground!

Buck always had a taste for honey and it seemed that he was always looking for a honey bee tree. If he saw where there were wild honey bees using a hollow cottonwood tree for a nest, he would keep in mind where this tree was and later in the fall when it was colder and the bees were not as active, he would come up with a plan how to extract the honey without getting stung. Or at least stung too much!

One time, twins Rick and Rob McGarvey and Larry Boyum were visiting the Musgrove family. Buck was showing them the proper way to raid a honey bee tree to get some wild honey. Buck apparently did not use enough smoke to hypnotize the bees and they swarmed after him. The twins tell the story that Buck was not running fast enough and the swarm was just about to him and they watched him try to slide or duck under and let the bee's pass over. Well…It didn't work!!! According to the story told by the McGarvey's, Buck managed to get stung several times that day. Buck always had a sweet tooth and tried to eat wild bee honey quite often! I did not really care for honey, I hated the bees and I was just smart enough not to go on one of Buck's honey hunts!!

Porcupine "meatballs"!

Buck and I were hunting together this one time and we came on to a porcupine up in a tree. Buck was telling the story about the old timers that came here would eat them when they were short of food. We were kind of hungry, so we decided to give it a try. I think that Buck shot at it a couple times and missed before he let me have a try. After I shot it and it dropped out of the tree, he got the idea to eat the hind legs as that would make the best steaks. We joked that they were "meatballs", but it was cut up more like steak. No one else was home at the Musgrove house so we started the stove and Buck started frying it up. The meat was so greasy that I decided I was not starving enough to eat, but Buck did eat some! He said it was not that bad, but I did not believe him as he kept making faces as he ate. Now that I think of it, I do not think he ate that much and said that he was full!!

Porcupines are not liked very well by us ranchers because mother cows do not like them around their calves. Calves are curious of them and will get quills in their nose and bawl. Next the cow will put her head down go after them and get stuck on the forehead. I even had a cow get a bunch of quills on her bag. She must have walked or run over the porcupine and it flipped its tail and got her in the teats. The cow would not let the calf suck and had a full bag. I had to bring her home and get her in the chute, tie her legs and pull out all the quills. Most times when I see a porcupine, I think about Buck making porcupine "meatballs"!!

Another time, I had a different cow get quills in her bag, so Seth and I brought her home. I guess I did not have her legs secured very well. I had several quills pulled out but she managed to get a hind leg free and she kicked me square in the chest!! I staggered backwards and was gasping and could not talk, and Seth thought I was going to croak!! Those darn porcupines! It is funny now, but it was not so funny at the time. That is an example of why we do not love them so much!

The Musgrove's make the move to British Columbia

In the spring of 1964, Loren and the boys took a trip up to Canada to see about buying a ranch there. They were gone a week or two and came back talking about two ranches, one on Long Pine Creek and another on Upper Cache Creek. Both places were in British Columbia, near the Alberta border, and in the beautiful Canadian Rockies. Loren and Bernice had been looking to enlarge their operation in Montana as they were not doing very well with the 154 acres that they owned in Montana and they were having trouble finding enough summer grazing. They leased 80 acres of state land that bordered their place to the west of their house, south of Nashua. It was only summer grazing for some of their cows and this is actually some land I now lease for my own cows. My father had bought the Eugene Mattingly place to the east of their home place the year before, so there was not much room for enlargement in this area, so they decided to look at property far to the north.

Bernice and Loren bought a ranch, and with the younger children Buck, Karl and Karen, all moved up to near Fort St. John in the summer of 1964. Pat, the oldest sibling was going to college at the time and stayed in Montana. She later moved up to British Columbia after she graduated with a teaching degree and had gotten married to Leroy Vossler, who was originally from the Wolf Point or the Vida area! The Musgrove family got a pretty good deal on the three quarters of a section (480 acres) of land on Upper Cache Creek and the Musgrove's made the move to Canada.

Theoretically, they had traded one quarter of land (160 acres) in Montana for three quarters of land in Canada, which was a good deal for them. My father bought their place and we started farming it and I own it now. At the time that Dad bought this place, there were irrigation ditches going to nine different fields. Dad figured he had enough irrigated land to take care of, so he used Punk Nicol's caterpillar and knocked down all the cross ditches. We cleared the trees in the south of the place and ended up with four fields in the 160 acre parcel from the original nine fields.

I was writing back and forth with the boys and I was getting quite interested in the wilderness where they had moved to. They lived south of Fort St John along the Alcan Highway (also known as the Alaskan or Alaska-Canadian) Highway, but north of the Peace River. The road from their ranch to town was about 55 miles at that time, but from Fort St John to the ranch was only about twenty-five miles away as the crow flies!! Loren, Buck and Karl took apart most of their machinery so it could be trucked up their easier. There is still some machinery in pieces on the river property that did not make it on the trucks north to British Columbia. They had several guys with trucks to help them move. One of the farmers to help truck them up was Harold Moeker, who lived about three miles from here.

About the middle of August, after most of the fall work was done Bob Strand (a friend and classmate) and I started talking about going to visit the Musgrove family. Bob was going into the Navy and I was going to MSU in Bozeman in the fall. Mail service was slow up to Canada, but I sent a letter that I was coming up for a visit. We talked to Harold Moeker and he made a map how to get to Fort St. John and to the ranch.

As it turned out, Bob and I made it up there before the letter did!! We drove right up to within one hundred yards of the house, on another trail that was just below the house, but which did not lead directly to their house. We were in an old, wore out '58 Ford car that I had bought before the trip. The engine was about shot and made some noise but we made it up there and back. They did not even know that we were coming as we had beat the letter up there! I can still remember hearing Karen hollering to everyone when she seen us walk up the hill to the house. We had missed a turn on a road near the house and had to drive across a pasture to where we could see the log house on the hillside. It had only been three months since they had left Montana and we showed up there. I did not even know we were at the right house for sure until we heard Karen hollering!!

We had stopped and had gotten one black bear tag and one moose tag at Dawson Creek, British Columbia, which was the start of the Alaskan Highway, at mile marker 1. We did get a white tail for camp meat and saw a bear but never took a shot at it. The bear was running off the road, and all I could see was the rear end as he was angling off. I was only eighteen at the time and I was not comfortable with the shot. I have since thought about it and talked to hunters who have killed black bears, they have told me that the shot probably would have killed the bear. Being that was the best chance that I ever got to get a bear, I still kick myself for not taking it!!!

While buying the license at the store, we had my Dad's pair of binoculars and a few other things stolen off the seat in the car, including Bob's camera. My grandfathers' model 99-.300 Savage was in the locked trunk and safe. Thank God for that!! That rifle is a keepsake now from my Grandfather and I would have been devastated if it would have been stolen. Bob had bought a .338 Winchester bolt action gun for the hunt in the store in Dawson Creek, which he later gave to his brother. We were quite upset about losing our binoculars but could not afford to buy another pair at this time, so we hunted the week without hunting glasses. We went to the police station and talked to the Mounties in their red uniforms, but to no avail! Bob had some traveling insurance and after we got back home Dad got another pair of binoculars and Bob got another camera. We were not able to take any pics of the trip, which was really unfortunate!!

When Bob was sighting the gun in, he took two shots and I had seen his shoulder get kicked so hard, I swear it seemed to be about a foot back each time from the recoil. He asked me if I wanted to shoot it and I said no way!! He decided that it was sighted in close enough and I do not think he fired it again on the trip. He ended up giving the gun to his brother before he went into the service. We really had a good visit and slept on the floor in our sleeping bags in the Musgrove's nice log house, a home that I would visit several times more in the future. The Musgroves later built another log house along the side of the old one. They tore the old one down later to be used the logs for other projects! I fell in love with the solitude, the wildness of the country, and the gentle people of the Peace River country.

The Trip to Upper Cache Creek in '68

I had been writing to Karl and Buck since they moved to Canada, and I was making plans for another trip to visit and it had been four years since my first trip up there. After they made the move, Karl helped his dad, Loren, on the ranch but Buck had been doing some work for a guide and outfitter. If you know Buck, he always stretched his stories a little and he kind of insinuated in his letters that he was guiding hunters, but as it turned out he probably was only a horse wrangler! I found out later, he had done that "guiding-hunting-wrangling" thing for a couple of falls while spending time with a real outfitter near Watson Lake in B.C. He worked with this guide and outfitter in prime hunting country taking care of the horses. But in the fall of '68, he was "cat skinning", which meant he was making seismograph roads with a Caterpillar tractor for an oil company. Buck was driving a Cat for an oil crew near the Half Way River, which is maybe about forty miles from the Musgrove ranch. Buck knew that I was coming as I had written to him, and after I got to the ranch, the plan was that Karl and I would go get him for the weeklong visit.

On this trip north to see them, I was driving my '66 yellow and white Ford Bronco that I had purchased a couple of years earlier. It is about a twelve-hundred mile trip from Nashua to the ranch at Fort St. John. I had left Montana on a Friday morning and drove until late that night and pulled over on a turn off somewhere for a bit of rest somewhere in Alberta. I woke up sometime after daylight and continued on until I reached the ranch in the late afternoon just before dark on the second day of the trip.

I was twenty-two then, so I bought a couple of cases of beer. When I pulled into the yard, there was a party already going on. The "Victoria fishermen" were there on a hunting trip and they had a large wall tent set up in Loren and Bernice's back yard. They were referred to as the "Victoria fishermen" because they were commercial fisherman from the coast, and they made a yearly trip up to the Musgroves for hunting trips for many years. I had drank a few of the beers I had purchased from the store on long trip out along the Peace River and then up the Upper Cache Road to the ranch. After being introduced to the fisherman from Vancouver and greeting Bernice, Loren and Karl, we then got serious about drinking and telling stories. Like I said, there was a party going on!!

All I remember is that I was tired from the trip up there and I was sitting on the kitchen counter with Loren and we were passing the vodka bottle back and forth between us. I really was not much of a hard liquor drinker as I always preferred beer. Schlitz was the preferred beer back in Montana and it was what Loren usually drank back then, as well. But I sure do not think Loren would have turned down any other beer if it was offered to him. I am a lot like him that way! If it's cold, and it's wet and it's free, and it's a beer, I am not going to turn one down!! Anyway, before long, the bottle was gone, as we passed it back and forth and I finally got tired and took a nap!! I kind of remember Loren chuckling as I was falling asleep and falling off the counter, and do not remember much more after that.

The next morning when I woke up, I know that Loren was in trouble with Bernice for getting me drunk in her kitchen and he was getting a lot of hard glares from her. I found out from one of the hunters that Loren was sticking his tongue in the bottle and was not drinking his share of the vodka so he could drink me under the table, which he did! Anyway! That is my story on the "subject" and I'm sticking with it!

After breakfast was over, Karl and I drove to the camp to get Buck. He was working down by the Halfway River and we would bring him back to the ranch for the rest of my visit. I know I did not feel very well for a while that day. We brought some beer along and on the way back the Musgrove ranch, the boys and I reminisced about the good times from the past in Montana and toasted to future visits and hunts!!!

On that same trip, the Musgroves had a dance at their place on Upper Cache Creek and invited friends over to the ranch house. I met some of their neighbors, including Bob and Inx Jackson and their daughter Linda Jackson Mroz. They had moved from Glasgow, Montana to Canada about the same time as the Musgroves, but a bit later on. Tony Trotter and his wife Claudia (Johnston), were other people from this area that moved up to British Columbia about this time. Loren and Bob and Tony had been friends when they had all lived in Montana, and all managed to move to the same area of Canada. Linda was about eight months pregnant at that time I met her. Her husband John Mroz was in the service, stationed on the island of Guam and she had come to stay with her folks and to have her baby where she could be close to family. The party and dance had gone on until almost daylight and I remember the Jacksons leaving some time during the night to go back to their home in Fort St. John.

About daylight, we were still up and got the bright idea to go out for a drive and go hunting. Buck and I got a couple of guns and went out for a drive with Dale Johnson. Dale had just married Karen Musgrove within the last year. We were in no shape to be going hunting as we had stayed up all night, but we left the beer home, I think. I guess we were not in any shape for drinking either!! We soon came on to some moose and I tried to make a shot on an average-sized bull. It seemed like a shot I could not miss on! However, I did not take into account that I had partied all night and was not seeing all that good. I think I held a little high as I thought it was farther away than it really was. When we walked to the spot that the bull had been standing, we found only long hair and no blood. I guess I had shot a little high and had clipped some hair off of the hump. Just another hunt that went awry!! This is one of a few shots that I have ever missed at big game with a rifle. With a bow and arrow, well, that it is another story!! I have missed many shots at bucks and bulls in archery season, but that has not stopped me from pursuing my favorite sport of hunting!!

My Broken Bronco after the Blown Bull Hunt

This adventure all happened the same day after the dance at Musgrove's house. Like I said before, this was the same morning that I had missed the shot at the moose. All I had to show for my efforts was some two to three inch long black hairs from the brisket or the hump, I really do not know which! We were in some poor shape from not going to sleep after a night long dance (party), and it is pretty obvious now, looking back on the situation, that we really should not have been out on a morning moose hunt.

This was the fall of 1968 and I had driven up to Fort St. John in my 1966 yellow and white Ford Bronco. It was just a basic, plain small four wheel drive vehicle that got good mileage and could climb around well in the hills. I think that I only had the Bronco for maybe a couple of years at the time of this trip. During the summer before, Buck and his mother Bernice had come to Montana to visit and my Mother took a picture of Buck and myself alongside of the Bronco in front of my folks house. It is one of my favorite pictures of the two of us.

At the time of that picture opportunity, Bernice had gone, I think, to Jordan to visit some of her relatives that still lived there. She was from Jordan and her father was a janitor at the school. They lived in the log house in the middle of Jordan near the Big Dry Creek. This log house is still there, and I think still being lived in. Jordan is about 100 miles by road from the town of Fort Peck after the lake was formed. When the Fort Peck Dam was being built, the country was going through a severe drought and the Great Depression. The Fort Peck Dam project was one of President Franklin D. Roosevelt's New Deal projects to help bring the country out of The Great Depression. There were many individuals and families that were struggling to make a living and they made their way to Fort Peck to get a job on the dam and related jobs associated with the dam project. Montana residents were supposed to be given priorities for jobs at the Fort Peck Dam. More on story this later.

The Big Dry Creek, which flows through Jordan, Montana, is the same creek that empties into the Missouri River that Lewis and Clark discovered about May 9th, 1805. They said that the flood plain of this Big Dry Creek was about a mile wide and at that time, there was not a drop of water flowing through it! This was how it got its name!! However, the surprising thing about it was that when Meriwether Lewis came down the Missouri River on his return trip in 1806, the Big Dry was flowing very high from recent rains.

After I had blown the attempt for moose meat, we continued driving on an oil company seismograph trail to look for more game. It was getting on about noon and there was not any game to see so we headed back to the ranch. It had been a wet fall and there were a lot of water holes in the trail, but the Bronco was negotiating them well as I was driving along. I do not know why I got tired of driving, maybe I needed a nap, but Buck started driving as we were hunting our way back to the house. After all, he knew the trails. We came to a low spot in the trail with water and ice on it. It would have been a long way back if we turned around to go back the way we had come so we told Buck to "give-her-heck". Well! What can I say! It sure did not work!!

These seismograph roads made by the oil companies in Canada are only wide enough for one lane of traffic, and to perhaps meet another vehicle only in a few spots. There is brush and trees everywhere along the trail, so we had to stay on the roadway and could not go around the water/ice hole. The hole was deeper than we thought and when we dropped down through the ice, we were pretty well stuck!! So much for my nap! It would have been about a three mile walk to the house across swamps and brush. In those days there was no such thing as cell phones. We had to get out the chintzy little jack that I had along and with the jack, we finally got some logs and brush under the tires for traction. After maybe an hour and with me driving, we got out and continued down the trail.

Before we got to the ranch, the rear differential was making some noise and it finally broke! It was a good thing that we had, not only some tools, but a mechanic there with us. By this, I mean Dale, not Buck! Or myself! We had enough tools to take the u-joint apart on the rear drive shaft and drove home on a better trail with the front wheel drive pulling and the rear tires freewheeling down the road. So much for the hunting for this day! We got Walt Dean to bring his truck over and we loaded the Bronco on it and took it to the nearest mechanic shop, Thompsons Repair, to get it repaired. It ended up being about a week before it could be repaired. In the meantime, all of our hunting was done by foot and closer to the house and main roads. That is just how it goes, sometimes!

On one of those days while I was waiting for the Bronco to get fixed, Karl and I went up over the hill to hunt Titas Creek. We had gone about a mile and we jumped a large moose but it was a long way off and running. I took three shots at it, or maybe I emptied my gun! Needless to say, we did not get it and we followed it over the hill to see if there was any blood but we did not find any. We hunted on foot until almost sundown and started walking back down the trail towards the house. It was almost dark and could hardly see except for the trail. We heard some thrashing in the brush next to the trail. We held both of our guns towards the noise as we did not know what it was at the time. There are black bears in the area, and a grizzly will come through a few times a year. We did not back down as we wanted to keep the muzzles of our guns pointed towards the noises. We had not heard much of any noises except the thrashing brush. Finally, out of desperation we both started hollering and the animal ran off. We walked down the dirt trail toward the house keeping a close watch behind us. It was really a welcome sight to see the lights in the ranch house. I still was wondering what it was that had tried to intercept us on the trail!

The next morning Buck and I made the trip up over the hill to go down to the spot where Karl and I had the incident with the big critter the night before. It took a while but since there was not any new snow overnight, we were still able to see the previous tracks in the snow. As we approached the place in the trail, we could see where Karl and I had danced around a little in the trail. We walked towards where we had heard the sounds the night before and found large moose tracks in snow and where he had thrashed bushes when we were near. The bull probably thought we were another bull, or maybe a cow, and was looking for a fight, or some fun!! We figured it probably was the big bull that we had seen earlier in the day before, this was probably his core area and he was protecting it from other bulls. From the tracks he was probably only fifty feet from us and we could not see him in the dark! We were pretty darn lucky that he did not come right after us!!

Bucks Homemade Beer

I think all of us redneck types that like the Barley Pop have thought about making our own beer to save money on the brew and then we can brag to our friends, or to anyone that will listen to us, about it. Making the brew is not as easy as it sounds in the instructions! To make a good homemade beer you need to be extra clean with the brewing kettle, all mixing utensils, the pot, the beer bottles and the caps. If you allow some contamination to get into anything, the batch can go bad! I am not the neatest person on the planet but Buck … well, he can make a redneck cowboy grimace at his lack of organization when watching him cooking! I cannot even imagine him making a good batch of beer. They say in the instructions that a batch of beer may not taste that great once in a while but it will not poison you! Making beer is fun but you have to do all the steps right or you can have a wreck. I think the first time we make beer, the taste of it is not the best but the alcohol content is still there and after a couple of bottles it seems to start tasting better!

I have not tasted any of Bucks brew but I have heard some stories! He told me about the first batch that they made when they went to up B.C. from the states. The reasoning was because they lived so far from the nearest liquor store that it made sense to make some beer and then they did not have to make the long drive to town as often. I know that when we were there, when we went to town to get provisions, we always stocked up with beer!

Living as far from town as they do, making your own beer really seemed like a good idea! The first batch was started but according to Buck or Karl it was a possibility that they might have bottled it a little early, maybe, before the brew had stopped working. Once you bottle it, you have to put it in a cool place that is out of the direct sunlight. Then you wait a couple of weeks or so for it to cure properly. It is just really tough to have to wait so long to taste the brew after you have worked so hard to turn spring water into something as tasty as homemade beer!! Stacy says Jesus turned water into wine and everyone got to drink it that night, but I guess we are not capable of working miracles like him! When you bottle the beer before it has stopped fermenting and maturing, the brew can build up too much pressure and there is a chance of an explosion!

Well the Musgrove boys had bottled the brew and had put it under the porch in a root cellar. This is a place underground where most pioneers had to keep vegetables from freezing in the winter. These root cellars were in the back yard or under the house. This was a perfect place for the beer to age as it was a little cooler than in the house. This was before they had electricity, so they did not have a cool fridge to cure it in. I can almost imagine how tough it would have been to wait until it cured well enough for it to be a really good beer. I think they were having a meal in the middle of the day in their dining room when they heard a loud sound from under the house. For a while they were not sure what had happened. They thought it maybe was a gunshot! They finally figured out that maybe the sound was one of their precious beers being blown all over the place!! They also had potatoes and vegetables in the area, and knew they needed to check the rest of the batch out, since they did not want glass blown all over their veggies.

They took a quick look and had seen from the mess that is indeed what happened! One or more of the beers had blown up!! What a predicament!! One of them said, I think I heard it was Loren, that maybe it had been long enough since they had bottled it, and a cool brew sounded pretty good! I guess it was Buck that volunteered to go get a bottle or two! He did not want to have a bottle blow up as he was getting it out of the cellar so he decided to go down there with a large coat spread out to protect himself from possible harm and grab a bottle with the coat and bring it out far enough to use a bottle opener to get the cap off. I guess the brew was still pretty wild and you had to put your mouth around the neck of the bottle to keep from losing any!! Well, it worked, but they had to leave the coat hanging on the cellar door to remind the person going down there to protect themselves when they got anything from the cellar until the beer was all drank up!!!

Talking to Buck last night about this story, and he told me that he remembered drinking the first two beers of this batch but he does not remember drinking a third bottle! I guess that must have been a powerful batch of beer!!

Ruttin' Music

I met Jim Arneson, who was also from Montana, at a dance in Canada at the Musgrove ranch in the fall of 1968. Jim and a friend, Walt Dean were up there from Montana to work! It was at that same party and dance at the Musgrove's house, when I had met the Jacksons, that I met Jim Arneson. I believe he was working for the Brown ranch that was about ten miles away. He and Walt Dean were from the Miles City area and were working for a neighbor of the Musgrove's. Little did I know that Jim and I would become friends as he and I would marry women who had been friends in Montana. Our wives had both had gone to school together in Glasgow.

Jim met Linda Jackson Mroz at the dance that night and Jim always said that Linda would remind him that he came to the dance that night with two blonds!! They later married and they lived on Deep Creek, south of

Fort St. John and lived in a log house that he assembled from a log kit. It was a very large and beautiful house. They later had three children together, Nathan, Jennifer and Jon Toav, and raised Linda's daughter, Pamela, from a previous marriage. At the time I met Linda Jackson Mroz, who was expecting her eldest daughter, Pamela, I had no idea how small a world we really all lived in. I later found out that my wife-to-be Patricia Wesen, was the Godmother of little baby Pam. Over the years, we visited them several times when we would go up to visit the Musgroves and they would come to Montana and see us.

Jim and Linda were very good friends to us, and when we would come to Fort St. John for a visit, we would spend some of the time visiting the Musgrove's and then some of the time staying at the Arneson's. They only lived about thirty miles from each other, so we all got together at each other's place when we were visiting in the Peace River country in British Columbia. Jim and Linda lived on Deep Creek which flows into the Peace River and the Musgrove's live on Upper Cache Creek which also flows into the Peace. The Arneson's four children were just about the same ages as our children, so the kids could entertain each other when we visited. Jim and Linda divorced later on and Linda has remarried and lives in Seattle area and Jim lived in California for several years and is now living in Miles City taking care of his mother, Betty Daniels Arneson, who wrote a book called Richland Dryland. Jim is still a friend and we visit him sometimes in Miles City. He went back to Canada for a visit in the fall of 2012, along with Patty, myself, and Dave and Sue Renner.

One of my vivid memories of Jim was one year in the seventies when we were up to see them in Canada. We stopped over at the Red Barn Saloon at Charlie Lake to have a couple of drinks. I had my first Ceasar with Jim there. He played a song on the jukebox called *Looking out My Backdoor* by Creedence Clearwater Revival. I have always liked CCR music and the lead singer John Fogerty. I think the Eagles, The Beach Boys and CCR are my favorite Golden Oldie groups! Anyway, Jim really liked this song and he said to me, "This is Ruttin' music!!" This was the first time I ever heard this particular song and I was pretty impressed with it! Whenever I hear *Looking Out My Backdoor* by Creedence Clearwater Revival, I think about Jim's remark about rutting music and chuckle!

Meeting a Good Looking Blonde

When I returned to Montana after my 1968 Canada trip, I was in Nashua on a Saturday night at the Wagon Wheel Bar. There was an older man that I knew, whose name was George Jones, at the Wheel. He was a bachelor that lived with his mother north of Nashua. He said that there was a dance going on at the old Grain Schoolhouse about twenty-five miles north of Nashua. George and I decided to get a bottle and go see what was going on up there. I was still driving my Bronco.

I had gone to this annual Grain social dance in the past and there was always good turnout there. It was not a very big wooden schoolhouse, with maybe two or three rooms and a couple outhouses out back. Most of the visiting was done outside, as there was not enough room for everyone to fit inside. There was a band playing inside and I am sure that Lee Borgen was playing guitar, singing, and probably Jack Feick was on the drums.

After drinking some of the vodka and visiting with people outside we went inside the school. I saw a good looking blonde that I did not know. She was standing by herself and I asked her to dance. We were dancing for about thirty seconds and we had not even had a chance to exchange names. George walked by and flashed what was left of the last of our booze and so I walked out the door, not wanting to miss out on what was left of the vodka. I told her I would be back and left her in the middle of the dance floor and then I went outside to have a drink. When we had finished the bottle, I ran into a friend Bill Nicol. We ended up tussling around as I always liked wrestling. After our friendly grappling was over, I was dirty and tired and I guess I kind of forgot all about the blonde in the schoolhouse.

She went back to the couple that she was with, her friend Marilynn Garsjo, with whom I later found out she worked with as a beautician, and

Marilynn's fiancée, Gary Johnson. I knew both of them, but they had not seen Patty dancing with me so there was a big mystery to who I was. I did not know her name at the time, but Patty was trying to explain to Marilyn what I looked like, but they could not figure out who I was. About two weeks later. I was at a poker game in Glasgow at Carlyle Garsjo's house. He is Marilynn's brother and she and Patty showed up to see Carlyle. When Patty came in the house and seen me in the game, she blurted out to Marilyn while pointing at me, "that's him, that's the SOB". I was pretty embarrassed as I remembered what I had done at the Grain School. The so-called mystery was over and Marilynn said "oh, I know him". I was a year older than Marilynn, and we both attended Nashua High School.

Patty and I hit it off, in spite of the awkward start, and I took her on our official first date a week later. We went out jack rabbit hunting at night in my Ford Bronco with spotlights blazing. Marilyn was along as was my best friend at the time, Dan Williamson. A perfect first date, as far as I am concerned. And Patty must not have thought it was too bad!

Patty and I were ready to settle down at the time and we got along great and we were married September 13, 1969. We have been married now for 49 years. It was some time after we met that she brought up that she had a friend in Fort St. John, British Columbia and her name was Linda, and that Linda's daughter Pam was Patty's God-daughter. I finally figured out that this Linda was the same person that I had met at Musgrove dance at the ranch and we could hardly believe the chances of that happening. This really is a small world!!

Patty's first trip to Fort St. John

In 1970, Patty and I went on a trip to see Ken and Rhonda James in Tacoma, Washington. Rhonda and Patty were classmates at Glasgow High School. We then went up to Fort Saint John via the curvy Frazer River Canyon highway at night, which was quite an experience because of a trucker who was following too close and we could not find a turn off for him to get by us for many a mile. The trucker could not pass and Patty spent some time sitting on the floor and praying. It all ended well and we made it safely.

Since Patty and I had just got married in 1969, this was her first trip to Fort St. John to meet the Musgroves. Patty was quite hesitant to go out into the boonies to see the Musgroves, whom she had never met at the time. She and Bernice ended up really getting along well so it helped make the trip up there a good experience. Patty really liked the romance of the experience of the ranch as there was no electricity there and they used kerosene lamps for light. They also used the wood stove to heat water and used batteries for everything else, including running the record player for dances. There were plenty of poplar and Douglas fir trees nearby for them to use to burn for heat. The radio station in Fort St. John would have a program on every morning to let individuals know if someone was coming to visit or anything that people in the rural areas needed to know about. It was a very good system of communication as most people in the outlying rural areas did not have phones either.

The Musgrove Kids

Pat Musgrove Vossler is the eldest of the Musgrove children. She was in college before her family moved to Canada, but after college, she ended up moving to very near where the rest of her family set down roots in the Peace River Valley. Pat is artistically talented and has done some oil paintings in the past and present. One of the things she does is making hand painted Christmas cards from patterns of cards that she found in the old barn loft here on the Missouri River. She has done a lot of oil painting in the past and still does. She also painted a large painting from a picture of her dad Loren and another man drinking beer in a bar in Montana. When you look closely at the other man, it looks just like Brownie Doke. I took a picture of it when Patty and I went up for a visit in 2007. I took the picture into the Montana Bar in Glasgow once and I showed it to the owner, Paul Monson, who has since passed away, and he said that it looked like it was from the old Buckhorn Bar in Wheeler. It is a realistic painting of those two old cowboys as they used to party it up in the Buckhorn Bar in the old days!

Buck, or Lee, as some of our classmates knew him as, because it is his real name, is the second oldest of the Musgrove kids. I have known him by Buck for so long I had almost do not remember what his real name is! Buck was an excellent pencil drawer when he was younger but he is now quite shaky from his bout with "sleeping disease" in his freshman year in Nashua. It is bothering him more as he gets older. Every letter that Buck has ever mailed to me includes almost as many sketches as words and these cartoons are worth about a thousand words each. My kids always eagerly looked forward to Buck's drawings when his letters would arrive. Buck was always a goof off and would do anything for a laugh. One day as the other kids at the bus stop were getting on the bus, Buck ran into the edge of the door. He just bounced back and we thought he was just goofing off again like he always did. Later on that same day at school day they had to take him to the hospital. This was the start of his bout with "sleeping sickness"!! He was taken to the Wolf Point hospital as it was closer to Frazer where Bernice was teaching school. He spent some time in the hospital and ended up missing the whole year of school. I think he spent a lot of time irrigating, fencing for his sheep and skipping school!!

Karl and Karen were the Musgrove's twins, the youngest of the bunch, two years younger than Buck and myself. Karen finished high school in Fort St. John with her brother Karl. Karen wanted to get married to a neighbor boy named Dale Johnson, but Dale said to her that she would have to finish school first. She graduated from high school and then married Dale. They built a beautiful log house across a creek from Dales parents house. They have three children: Leanne, Cody and Marianne. Dale worked in an oil drilling camp and Karen cooked in the camp for several years. They later took over the ranch and had about 300 head of cows with help from Cody. Sadly, both Karen and Dale have passed away, but they are certainly not forgotten. Karen was the only one of the Musgrove children that did not draw or paint and she always said that her talent was in baking and cooking, and she was known for her magnificent wedding cakes.

Artistic ability was strong in the Musgrove family, and Karl got his fair share of that talent. When Karl was in school, he would always be drawing something with pencil and paper, even when he only had a little time. He was really a good pencil artist when he was younger and would sell his drawings for a quarter or two. He took a correspondence class from Minnesota and graduated from it, which he was always very proud of. He learned how to paint with acrylic's and I have a painting of his at home with buffalo on a hillside. He prefers to paint cowboys, cows and horses.

In the summer of 2006, Karl had a severe stroke that affected the right side of his body. This left him with some blindness in the right side of his eyes and the loss of using his right hand. It is still hard for me to imagine how something like this could happen to a big strong man that could do anything he wanted with his hands and could handle most any job with ease. This was the man who was strong and talented enough to build his house from logs on his ranch with his own hands using a chain saw. He was an excellent artist with his right hand and after his stroke, he had to teach himself how to draw and paint with his left hand, which is pretty remarkable if you ask me. It has been about a dozen years since his stroke and he is painting as good or better now than he was before. His colors that he has in the paintings are unbelievable and so realistic. He loves painting horses, cowboys and wildlife. We are so proud of the advances that he has made in his artwork.

Karl married Ann Waters and she was a school teacher. Karl and Ann have two children, Ross and Heather. Ann and Ross have taken over the cow handling and farm work since Karl's stroke, so this leaves Karl with about eight hours in a day to pursue his artwork which he sells to people all over the country and United States. Karl received the Spirit of the Peace Award for his extra ordinary artwork and success as a cowboy artist! In the past he used a Dremel tool to carve figurines and horses in shed moose antlers.

He is a very talented man, and I am proud to call him my friend. Ann is an amazing woman who is helping to keep the ranch running smoothly, and they make a great team. Ann herself is a very talented photographer and I have always been impressed by her pictures.

Karl is still painting and doing pencil drawings and his wonderful work is for sale. You can contact Karl and Ann. If they don't answer leave a message and they will get back to you. 1-250-262-3278

Karl Musgrove, PO Box 106, Charlie Lake, B.C. Canada VOC1HO

Rancher and Artist

When he was first married, Karl built a log house for he and Ann to live in and that home was only about three hundred yards from Loren's house. Karl was a big strong man who could do anything with a chainsaw, with a rope or a paintbrush. A few years later, they moved their house over to their own ranch, which was about two miles away. Their home is decorated by Ann's photographic pictures and Karl's artwork. He has pencil drawings, acrylic paintings, horn engravings, bison skull paintings and much more. When we were up there in 1993, I asked Karl why he was not doing more artwork and he told me he just did not have time! He was keeping so busy at making a living and building up the ranch for them and their kids, that he had little time to pursue his art.

Karl was always a hard worker and very driven to get things done. Loren had shown Karl and Buck how to braid rawhide for horse tack when they were young, a skill which they both still do. Loren was all cowboy and made his own tack from rawhide or horse hair. Stacy still has a hackamore that Loren braided for her many years ago. Karl had built his first saddle by age twenty.

As I mentioned earlier, he was always artistically talented and for much of his life he always painted with his right hand even though he was normally a lefty. Then in the summer of 2006, he had a severe stroke and laid out in the yard for some time until he was found. It was a devastating stroke that affected his right side of the body. He was in the hospital and treatment for many months. He has made great strides to make a comeback, but the stroke paralyzed the right arm that he painted with and he also cannot see from the right side of his eyes. He had to retire from ranching and he has learned how to draw and paint with his left hand. It has been great therapy to do his artwork and he is almost as good as he once was or maybe even better! He works on more than one painting at a time, and gets maybe two done a month or more. He has time to paint more now than he had done for a long time and he is getting better. He paints from memory and his memory of colors is amazing. When he looks at snow, he does not see just white but the shades of whites, which is pretty darn impressive if you ask me.

Bucks Redneck Flagpole Fence

Buck had some sheep here in Montana and while he was recuperating from his bout of what we call his "sleeping sickness", he spent a lot more time fencing for them sheep. He fixed a fence around the Crow place and the school section so he could run his sheep all fall and winter. He used diamond willow trees for posts, which were quite common on the river bottom. The fence was made from old used barbed wire that had been rolled up from old fences around the place and diamond willow posts. Some of this fence is still there but not nearly as high as it was when he constructed it. Buck had some crazy ideas about fencing, but some of them worked pretty well. Such as leaving the post stick up about three feet higher than it needed to be. His idea was if the posts rotted off, he could dig the post back into the ground and rehook the wires to the posts higher and it would save having to kill or cut another bush to fix the fence! In Canada he also would dig the post hole, put the post in and then he did not fill in the dirt around the post. You see it is a lot of work to tamp dirt in around the post to make it a little more solid. His redneck reasoning for that is the posts under the ground could dry out after a rain and the water would go into the soil under the post and it would not rot off. I have seen some of these posts he put in the ground in the early sixties's and some are still standing after fifty years. These posts stuck so far out of the ground they looked like flagpoles. I asked his dad Loren about the flagpole posts that were sticking up in their fence and finally he blurted out to me coming home late one night, "Buck!"

Bird and Bull hunting in B.C. with Buck

On one of our trips up to the Peace River country, in 1972 I think, Buck, Patty and I were hunting for camp meat. We were above the log house that rests above Upper Cache Creek, and we had walked from the house up into the trees to go for a little hunt. We were mostly thinking to get a moose or deer. We were walking down a trail and all of a sudden, a blue grouse or maybe a "Fool's hen", flew up into a tree. I think they are the same but I do not know for sure? Buck told me to hand him the .22 caliber single shot and he shot the bird. Well, now what to do as we were kind of "big game hunting" and the shot probably scared off any thing within hearing distance. Buck had a clean, kind of light-colored shirt on and he took it off to dress the bird out, as he did not want to get it dirty or Bernice would give him "the look". It was fairly warm out and sunny, maybe forty degrees, and if you know Buck like I do, he cannot take the heat as it bothers him and right away his shirt has to come off, although this time he took the shirt off in hopes of keeping it clean! He finished dressing out the grouse and wiped off his hands on some dry grass nearby, put his clean shirt back on and we continued down the trail in our quest for "the one"!

As we continued on the trail, danged if we did not run into another dumb grouse that sat there in a low tree and looked down at us. Buck said if we had to fry up one, we might as well take another one home. Well, another bird down on the ground and the shirt came off again! Again, he had to wipe his hands off on some dry grass to clean up. He put the shirt back on again and I thought that we are finally going to get some hunting done, maybe, hopefully!! We got into some thick spruce timber and it got quite dark in that heavy cover, hoping there was a good chance of a bull or buck to be laying in there, out of the sun and heat. Would you believe it, but another spruce hen was chirping at us. I sure did not want to hand him the gun and I almost scared off the bird. I actually think I tried pretty hard, but that dumb bird stayed right there. I guess it made Buck almost mad too, and so, guess what, after a shot or two we had another bird down!

In the spruce thickets, the sun does not get in very well and there is very little grass growing. Off came the shirt and he laid it down behind him; I guess it was his job to clean the bird because he had shot it. Well this bird was a little messier than the first two, but he got the job done. He was looking around for something to wipe his hands off on, and I was giving him some encouragement to "hurry it up". There was not any grass to use for a towel and he did not know what to use, so he cussed and grabbed his shirt and wiped it vigorously with his hands. I could not help but laugh at him, as he had tried so hard all morning to keep his white shirt clean and now he dirtied it up just for a laugh. That is Buck, and that is why I like to hang out with him as he is always fun to be with! Patty still laughs and shakes her head about the incident after more than forty years.

Buck and the attempted butchering of a cow with a .22 rifle

I was not around when this incident happened but I feel it is worth sharing. This story was seen and told by his brother Karl, and I felt it was worthy of a repeat. I might mention that this story has changed a bit on each retelling, so hard to know the truth from the fiction. Anyway, it was time to kill a fat cow for some burger and steaks. They usually took the old 30-30 lever action Winchester to kill a cow to butcher. Buck decided to use the .22 rifle because he heard some people have used one to kill a cow. Karl kind of complained to Buck about using the small rifle, but beings they only had a few shells left in the 30-30 box and being Buck was the eldest and

Loren was not around at the time to decide for them, they would give it a try. Maybe it might work?

Well the cow was not behaving real well and she was moving around the pen while Buck was walking around stalking her. There are times that some people will put a little bit of hay or grain down on the ground to get the animal to stop for a clean shot in this process. But not Buck!! You got to remember that Karl is telling this story and he is encouraging Buck by telling him to hurry up, and I got an idea that the hollering was making the old cow a little nervous!

Well Buck finally got steady enough to try to get a shot between the eyes to hit the brain for a clean kill. Well… apparently, he missed the proper spot for a good hit and he jacked another shell into the chamber, leaned against a post to steady the rifle and he lined up the sights. I guess he tried to squeeze off the shot but missed the spot again and maybe he hit the horn!! Well with all the encouragement from Karl and the cow racing around the corral it was starting to get a little intense! One thing with this .22 rifle is it holds 12 shells, so Buck was not too concerned yet. Well after the third miss, the cow was starting to get a little wild and running around in circles and bouncing off the corral panels!

Karl was starting to get a little worried that the fence would not hold so he headed to the house to get the bigger gun. As Karl got close to the house, he looked back to see the fray and Buck was running around chasing the cow and getting pretty excited. He could see Buck running after the cow and shooting from the hip whenever he got close to the wild-eyed critter. Karl could hear bullets zinging around and he went into the house for his own security. After he got the bigger gun, he looked out the door to see that apparently Buck had not gotten the job done but that the rifle was not empty yet. Again, I would like to remind everyone that this was Karl's version of the story and he might have juiced up the details more than a little bit!!

Karl thought that maybe he would have to saddle a horse if the cow got out and he would need to chase it down to finish the job. I do not know if

Buck maybe ran out of shells in the .22 or not, but he had stopped shooting. Like I said before, as this story has changed some in the last few years! Karl hollered at Buck to get out of the way! Buck finally heard the shout and allowed Karl to finish off the cow with the 30-30. The story is that they did not dare tell the folks about this, so they just skinned out the cow and hung her to cool. Apparently, later on when they were eating the beef steaks the family would find small .22 bullets in the meat!!! I think this was the last time that Karl allowed Buck to try to kill a beef with a .22 rifle.

This story was told to me by Karl quite a few years ago and I will let you decide how truthful it is!!!!!!

The Day of the Wild Horse Ride

In 1986, Patty and myself, along with Stacy, Seth and Shawn went up to Fort St. John for a visit with the Musgroves and Arnesons. The Arnesons had company coming in a few days so we went to visit Jim and Linda first. We called the Musgroves and told them that we had just gotten to the Arneson's so Buck and Vonnie, Karl and Ann and Loren came over and we had quite a party. We were playing, singing and telling stories. We stayed at the Arneson,s for a couple of days, then we were planning to stay with the Musgroves for a couple days before we had to leave for home in three days.

On the last morning that we were at the Arneson,s, I went out to help Jim try to get a moose for winter meat. We went out and Jim went through some brush and I circled around to see if anything came out. I heard a shot and then a little later I heard another. I then walked in and found that Jim had shot a young spike bull and a cow moose. Apparently, Jim had shot the cow first and she ran off. He saw the bull walking with his head down and thought it was the wounded cow and shot him. When I walked to where I had heard him shoot, he had two moose down. I went and got Patty and Linda for pictures and then we had to go to Musgroves. I hated to leave Jim with the moose to dress out, but he understood and said he could call his brother-in-law Chet Jackson to help him. The weather was cool so the meat would not spoil. The good news was that they had plenty of meat for the winter.

When we got to the Musgrove Ranch, the kids had seen the horses in the corral and wanted to go for a ride. Buck was all for it and Loren said okay. We saddled three horses Drifter, Guy and Rigo. Patty would ride Rigo, the horse I like to ride when I am up there. Rigo was Buck's wife Vonnie's horse. Seth was on Guy and Stacy was on Drifter. Shawn wanted to ride too, but Loren said no, which turned out to be a good thing. We did put him in front of Seth for a picture. We took a few pictures and then they went for a ride down to Upper Cache Creek, which is about a quarter of a mile away.

Buck, Loren and I opened a beer and watched them ride off. Then, all of a sudden, the horses were trotting and then the race was on. We watched as they galloped down to the fence near the creek. Buck was not sure if the gate was open but the horses apparently knew that it was. Patty did not know, so she was trying to catch Stacy and Seth, but she ended in front because Rigo liked to race and there was no stopping him. We could see them ride through the gate but when they got close to the creek they all circled and stopped. We could see one rider had come off a horse.

Buck and I jumped on the quad (four-wheeler) and headed down to see how everyone was. When we got down there everyone was standing around and laughing, as everyone was okay. Stacy had slid off the back of her horse when he reared up in the air trying to keep from running into one of the other horses. I know Seth rode his all the way and I think Patty did too. We stood around and laughed and visited for a while. Buck, Patty and Stacy rode back, but Seth and I went for a ride on the quad. When we got back to the house, Loren decided for us that was enough of a horse ride for one day. Loren and Shawn had gone into the house and I think Loren was very happy to see that no one got hurt. The kids, Patty, I and Buck still talk about the wild ride but it was very exciting and we have a lot of pictures before the ride for memories.

Traveling with the Boyum Kid

Larry Boyum and I had gone to school together in Nashua, but I had not seen Larry since he had gone into the Navy. It had to have been about 1970 when I saw Larry again, at least five years since I had seen him last. One night while sleeping (I remember vividly that I had National Guard training the next morning at 8:00 am), about three in the morning, I heard some noises out in front of the trailer house. I looked out the window and seen a car outside and the driver was revving up the pipes pretty loudly. I turned on the lights and opened the door and Larry shut off the car and came inside. He had just driven up from California to visit his folks, who lived about four miles from my place. It was not daylight yet and he did not want to wake up his folks, so he came to my place to see if I would wake up. It worked!! All that engine revving is better than any alarm clock!! We had a couple of beers and Patty did come out of the bedroom for a bit to meet LB. She pretty much said "Hi" and then went back to bed. Anyway, this was the first time I had seen LB in several years, and the first time Patty had ever met him. It was a heck of a way to wake up!

On a side note, both LB and Gary Meyer have very nice heads of hair and they keep it greased up and combed back in the 50's look. I think between the two of them they have kept butch wax and brill cream in business all these years!!

In 1993, Larry Boyum and I went up to visit the Musgroves. I had been up there more times that I can count, but this was Larry's first trip up to visit. Karl was just building a barn with help from his neighbor and best friend, Lynn Bovee, when Larry and I drove up into the yard. We had two cases of Schlitz beer in the front seat between us so it would not freeze. This beer was mostly for Loren, as he drank a lot of that brand in the states, but we all helped Loren drink this beer!! It was a great visit and Larry remarked of how quiet it was up there, and we all really slept well, either from the quiet or the beer, or maybe a bit of both!

On the trip up there, I took a nap and when I woke up, we were on the interstate heading straight for the Calgary Space Needle, which I guess is really called The Calgary Tower. I said "oh-oh" to Larry, and I told him we were on the wrong interstate! We went quite a bit further until we came to the first place to turn around. It was about 2:00 in the morning and the only place open in a dark street was a small store. Larry just reminded me that only one person in the store spoke English! He told us how to get back on the interstate and continue on toward on Edmonton on Wild Horse Road. I think we were in a bad part of Calgary and I am so glad we made it out of there unscathed!

The Stool Chair Wrestling Incident with Buck

The year was 1993 and LB (aka Larry Boyum) and I went up for a visit to see the Musgrove family. Several months earlier, I had hurt my knee wrestling with a friend of mine, Larry Lloyd (as I have never really grown up) and I had to wear a brace for a while as I had stretched the ACL in my left knee. It had healed up nicely and I did not need the brace anymore, or so I thought! Loren Musgrove had gone to bed and the three of us youngsters, LB, Buck and myself, were in the kitchen drinking and telling stories.

Well Buck and I were pushing each other around kind of friendly like. All of a sudden, my knee went out and I fell to the floor in pain. Buck set his chair on me and sat down on it so I could not get up. I guess Larry and Buck both about died laughing at me still moaning while Buck was sitting in his chair over me while he was drinking a beer. He finally let me up and I had to limp around after that kind of gingerly-like. Buck really got me good that time!!! A couple of months later, Buck sent Larry and I a letter and he had doodled on the letter like he usually did showing him straddling a chair and me under it, and in color. Larry and I laugh whenever we bring up the incident.

Hopefully you have enjoyed my stories of the Musgrove family. Trust me when I say there are plenty more stories than these that could be told. Both Buck and Karen have contributed some memories to add to my reminiscing and those will be included later in this book.

George and Maxine (Turner) Nicol

George Raymond Nicol, or Punk, as I have known him for 60 years or so, has also gone by "Nick" from the days when he worked at AVCO after the Glasgow Air Force Base closed in the 1960's. Punk and Maxine were always very close friends of my parents (Edgar and Toni Garwood). My Dad and Punk farmed close to each other and helped each other out when each other needed it. The Nicol's had five children: Janice married to Dennis Shanks and they have two girls, Janelle and Jamie. Bill and Kareen Nicol had two children, Shane and Shelley. Kathy who was married to Bob Steele and they have two children, Joy and Scott. Twins Connie (Steve) and Bonnie were born later and Maxine called them "A Godsend"!

Maxine was from the Jordan area and her father homesteaded there but because of the depression and the dry times, the Turner family went to the Fort Peck Dam to find work. They built a small house in Wheeler and found jobs with the Fort Peck Dam Project. Maxine and my mother were the best of friends until my mothers' death in 2006.

Maxine's brother Kenneth Turner started working in Fort Peck when he was 15 and a couple of years later he was a foreman on a project. He later was a contractor who worked on the building of the second powerhouse. He was a building contractor for many years in the Nashua area. He was a very kind and good person and he passed away after celebrating his 90th birthday. His wife Marjorie continued to live in their home in Nashua for several years after Kenny died, before moving to Nemont Manor in Glasgow. There is a write up about Ken on the wall of the Fort Peck Interpretive Center, which hosted a 75th celebration of the Fort Peck Project in June, 2012.

Punks' father, George Raymond Nicol Sr., homesteaded south of the Missouri River near Bear Creek but with the flooding out of the lands around Fort Peck by the dam project, they were moved to resettlement land on the south side of the Milk River near Nashua. He farmed land that was his and rented or leased other land to make a living off of the land. He also was a great welder for AVCO, which operated at the old Glasgow Air Force Base and he could weld anything. His son Bill is also a great welder and did welding for the Valley County Roads Department Maintenance shop before his retirement. Punk used to talk about how he loved living in the rugged hills of the south country until the family was relocated into the Milk River Valley.

This is a story that Grandpa Marion (and later Punk) told me. Punk was at my grandparents farm and he was working on an implement after a breakdown in Grandpa's yard with Grandpa helping him. Apparently, he had a breakdown at his land up on the hill and it was closer to grandpas than to go to his house to repair it. They had worked on it for a while and Punk saw someone walking down the hill to the house and he looked up and said, "Look! Here comes Eddie". That was my dad walking down the hill to the house after he was released from the Army in the fall of 1945 after medical complications of unknown problems (the military was unable to diagnose him, but it made him very ill and landed him in a military hospital for a long time) before being discharged. Grandpa Marion always called Punk, "Raymond" which I think was his middle name, but I do not know any other people who called him that. Grandpa Marion was also about the only person who called my mother Theona, which was her given name, instead of Toni, which she mostly went by.

Punk was always telling stories about different things (rather far-fetched but very entertaining) but he was so good at it that they were believable. One of the stories he told to me (when I was younger) and I am sure to many others was about snow snakes. We were over visiting the Nicol's one day in winter and he told me that he had seen a snake the other day. It being winter, I scoffed at him and told him there were not any snakes around during winter. He persisted and said that he had seen a snake cross the road when he was coming home from Nashua. In the end, I almost believed him and I think he let it go. On the way home with my folks the wind was blowing snow across the road and dad says son, "there's Punks snow snakes"!!! I always think of them as Punk's Snow Snakes!

I was hunting with him and Dad during antelope season and we had a few tags. I think that I got a medium sized buck and I was going to go get the pickup. This was back in the late 1960's and at that time we could drive into BLM lands for game retrieval if you needed to. We decided we could just carry it back and I carried it a ways on my shoulders but eventually had to give up. Punk told me to get it up on his shoulders and we started to walk to the truck while I carried the guns, knowing that we could go get the truck if we needed to. He stopped one time to sit on a rock and rest but did not take the antelope buck off his shoulders. It was probably a half a mile to the truck and he carried it all the way. He told me how much he loved this rugged country that at that time was called The Fort Peck Game Range, as he had to up and leave this country when he was a young boy. He told me that his father had to sell the ranch with the coming of Fort Peck Dam. We were maybe 10 miles from where their ranch house used be, which is now located under Fort Peck Lake!

Here is a story that was told to me by Maxine that Punk had told her about when he was younger. When he was a boy, he had been out riding his horse on a ridge trail and he found small golden chain. He had shown it to his father and his father asked him to show him just where he found it. Punk and his father went to the spot and they dug around some and they found the watch that had been attached to the small chain and lost years before. Apparently, this watch had been lost by his grandfather while riding horse back on this trail many years before. What luck!

Punk and Maxine's farm was near the Milk River and prone to flooding. They had had flood damage in the past and Punk and my Dad decided that maybe the best thing to do was build a dirt dike around Punk's home and buildings. With a small dirt mover that my Dad used to level some of his own land, Dad moved dirt and built a raised dike around the property. Dad remembered that when it was close to completion, the river had started to flood, and that he had to drive through flooded water to complete working on the dike. I am not sure what year that was (middle sixties, I think), but that dike is still in place and still protecting those buildings from the flood waters of the Milk River. In exchange for the dirt work that my Dad did for the Nicol's, Punk let my Dad borrow his Caterpillar to clear trees from property that Dad had recently purchased from the Musgroves.

Punk was always an early riser and I know he would be up a three or four in the morning. When he was working as a welder at the old base, he would have to get up early to get all of his farm work done. I always admired him holding down a full-time job and being a full-time farmer because I know how much time he put into his work.

He and my Dad went elk hunting a couple of times and one time in particular, a hunt that Dad always talked about, was when they went to Lincoln, as I have a few times. I think that Punk fixed his grain truck up with a tarp across the grain bed with some supports to give them head room, which is what they planned to camp in on their hunting trip. There was a wood stove in there to keep warm with. I do not think they got an elk that trip but they saw some crossing the road as they were going in to where they were going to camp. I know that they had a good time just like I do every time I am in elk camp. Can you imagine taking a grain truck into the mountains to hunt?

Punk and Maxine lived on their farm south of Nashua for many years, probably into the early 2010's. Punk's hearing was pretty bad and it got harder to visit with him in his later years, but I am very thankful for all the stories and conversation I had with a man I very much respected. He was also a great musician and used to play the guitar really well, although in later years he did not play anymore. He was always a reader and I have some of his old books, and he also read the Great Falls Tribune daily for many years. He was a good friend to my father, just as Maxine was a good friend to my mother, and they even stood as witnesses as my parents wedding and I think my parents stood as witnesses for Punk and Maxine. For several years, my parents and the Nicol's spent some winter months in Arizona and they always spent time with each other down there. They loved to go to the "Montana Picnic" down there because it was a great way to see people and friends from home. The farmhouse and buildings have since been sold, but there was a great red barn on that place that is still impressive to see. Punk had lived at the retirement home in Glasgow for several years before he passed away and Maxine is now living in Glasgow at Prairie Ridge Village and still enjoys good health.

Punk was a great friend and neighbor to both my Dad and Grandpa over the years, and he was a man I really admired. My Mom and Maxine were great friends until my mother passed away. I am still friends with their children, especially Bill and Janice.

Homer and Marilyn Peters

Homer was the neighbor who lived just east of my parents' farmstead. His farm was right at the confluence of the Milk River and the Missouri River. Many years ago, the confluence of the Milk River was about a mile east of where it is now. According to Jack Nickels, it was about 1915 when the Milk River flooded and went over the river bank and formed the new channel where it is today. Back in 1805 when Lewis and Clark came up the Missouri River, I really do not know where the confluence would have been. At one time, either the Missouri River or the Milk River, or perhaps both, flowed closer to the hills than they do today.

Homer was the son of Abe and Maud Peters. She was a second cousin or aunt of my grandmother Gertrude, I think, so that made us relatives of some sort. Old Abe Peters was rumored to have gotten in trouble with the law in Kentucky and left in the middle of the night! I had heard he was on the lamb for a while in Texas before settling in eastern Montana and changing his name from Peterson to Peters. Abe was known to be very ornery and had a mean streak, or so I have been told. Homer inherited the land from him, and maybe a little bit of ornery, too.

Homer was kind of crippled and had a bad limp; he had suffered from polio, I think, as a child. He was about five years older than my Dad and five years younger than Rufus Anderson. Their places were all close to each of the others and they worked together some and were pretty good friends. Homer was a distant relation to my Dad and Ken Bales. Ken Bales had a striking resemblance to Homer and even more so now that he is older. I have not seen Ken for a few years, but he should be in his late nineties by now. Dad and I spoke to him a couple of winters before Dad passed away, it was after Christmas and at that time, Ken was still getting around pretty well. He lives near Ferndale, Montana, which is near Big Fork. Ken's family once had a place at second point, but they left this countryside after the lake flooded them out.

Homer and his wife, Marilyn Bell, whom he met and married later in his life, sold their place on the confluence around twenty years ago and moved to Arizona for retirement. Homer passed away several years ago and his widow Marilyn, has since passed away too. My sister Diane and her husband Scott live in Apache Junction during the winter, near where the Peter's moved to. Diane helped take care of both Homer and Marilyn in their retirement years. Diane and Marilyn were very good friends and Diane had helped care for Homer and Marilyn in a retirement community, at first when they went down for the winter season and later when they lived in Arizona full time.

Homer's land bordered my own to the east for a quarter of a mile of fence line between us. On both sides of this fence is pretty heavy brush with numerous cottonwood trees that are over a hundred years old. There are also water willows, red osier dogwood, diamond willow and eastern ash trees in this area that is perfect habitat for the whitetail deer. Homer and I liked to hunt whitetails so we kind of competed with each other to see who could get the biggest buck each year. At that time, a Montana resident could get an A and B tag, with these two tags a resident could take two bucks in a hunting season. I believe that you could only take one muley buck and one whitetail buck, but a hunter could legally take two whitetail bucks in the hunting season many years ago!! I liked this old system as a hunter could kill a small buck first, and then hunt the rest of the season for a really big one! Now a days, a B tag is only for does, and an A tag is for bucks.

In those days there were a lot of deer around and not as many hunters as we have now. Homer loved venison but did not like to kill does, so he did what most of us hunters did at that time period, we would take a small buck for excellent eating and then look the rest of the season for a wall hanger. Which never happened!! He was an excellent cook as he was single for most of his life. We would help each other out if the other needed help tracking or pulling the deer out. Homer had a small hoist on his pickup to help in his later years on the farm. He built this hoist himself, as he was an excellent welder, to lift the deer up into his pickup and take back to his heated shop for processing.

Homer was an excellent shot with a rifle. He practiced a lot and shot almost every day. He reloaded all of his shells for his guns and was very precise with his reloading, as accuracy was very important to him. He taught me to reload my own shells and I now reload all of my own shells. I still have some 300 Savage bullets that I bought from Gary Lloyd. I did not have any loading die for my 300 Savage so I bought these several boxes of shells and I do not shoot this gun much anymore as it is a classic gun that I had gotten from my grandfather. Homer had one special small room in his house that was just for reloading and he kept it very organized. I spent several days over several years with Homer reloading with him to learn proper and safe reloading. I have enough powder, bullets and caps to reload for my guns for the future because we do not know what will happen in the future with gun control laws. Homer was always sending off one of his guns to have worked on to make it hotter, therefore faster, and more accurate. He had an old 30-40 Krag high wall rifle that he liked and he had a different barrel put in it and retooled it to handle .25 caliber bullets. This rifle turned out to be a flat shooting and hot gun that he was proud of. There were times that I would hear him practicing down in the brush next to my place where there were some old buildings from his older brother Riley's homestead property.

I would walk up to his pickup because he always shot out of the window from his Chevy. I then would ask what he was shooting at. He then would tell me he was trying to drive nails! His objective was to shoot a nail further into the wood of the old building. Later on, I noticed on this old metal sided shed that he did drive some nails in, but he also missed some shots, too.

Homer shot enough, and was so accurate, that it was a little unnerving at times. One thing was when he was around, he controlled the driving access to the Mouth and would not let people drive down our pump road. He always said this pump trail was not to be used for access to the Mouth of the Milk River!! Many local's may tell you that one time or another Homer would shoot over their heads, and they would probably be right. He was a good shot, so they could be assured he was just warning them away. He also was rumored to control a section line road north of his house in this way.

He owned one of the best places to fish in the area and a lot of people fished there, including him. He owned the property just north of the mouth of the Milk River and the Missouri River. This was generally pretty good fishing most of the time, and still is pretty good. We generally caught sauger, channel cats and drum there then and they are all native fish species. We caught a lot of shiners and some carp, but neither was a very good eating fish. I caught my first walleye there in the early 1970's and I did not know what it was for sure. I had it weighed and it was 9 pounds and 10 ounces. Jim Liebelt, who worked for Montana Fish and Game fisheries, checked it out and thought it was a walleye but it did not have the real distinct white marking on the lower dorsal fin. At that time the Montana State record was 12 pounds and 2 ounces for a walleye and it had been taken at Nelson Reservoir.

Later on, there was a new species for the records called a saugeye which is a cross between a sauger and a walleye. I think that fish could have been one. At that time, I do not think there was a saugeye listing in the Montana records. Homer did not want anyone to know that a fish that big was caught at the point, so in the press, I said I caught it at the cable car crossing about a mile up the Missouri near where the School Trust

Fishing site is. I fished this point at the confluence quite a bit with both of my grandfathers, when I was younger. Later on I fished there by myself; I would ride my bike there from my Dad's place, which is about 1.5 miles away. At times the fishing was so good that I would fill up two stringers on the handle bars for the trip home. My kids grew up fishing some at this site, as well.

There were a lot of different people that Homer would let them fish there, but not all the time, as Homer was real moody about this and he did not always give permission. There were some people that he would not let go down there fishing so he got kind of a bad reputation from some people. This was always a hassle for him to stop his farming to talk to a stranger about fishing at the mouth of the Milk River. Homer always left his house locked when he was not in the house as too many people would stop in to ask to go fishing and he did not trust a lot of people. There were a lot of guys around from the Glasgow Air Base and the work being done on the second Fort Peck Powerhouse that were unfamiliar to him and he did not have a very trusting nature.

Homer had a lot of pain in his hip and he drank a lot of blackberry brandy to kill the pain, so it depended on how much he drank to know what kind of mood he was in. My Dad was a good friend of his and said the best way to get along with Homer is, and I quote, "let him think that he got the best of every deal with you". There are times I sure wish that he was still here as a neighbor. He was a pretty good neighbor and those of us that lived near him knew what to expect from him and he usually treated a neighbor fairly!

Orville and Phyllis Landis

There were many neighbors near my parents farm, and one of those neighbors in the late 1950's were Orville and Phyllis Landis until they sold the farm and moved to South Dakota, which was I believe in the summer of 1962. They had 6 children: Shari, Mary Ann, Julie, James, Thomas and

Margaret. My parents Edgar and Theona "Toni" Garwood were very good friends with Orville and Phyllis. Therefore, we spent a lot of time visiting at each others farms. My sister Karen and I were about the same ages of MaryAnn, Jim and Julie. Jim was about three years younger than me, but he was big for his age and I was small for my age, so we got along well and we were best of friends until they moved away in 1962.

The Wiota railroad bridge crossed the Milk River at the Landis place. This was the bridge that was built and used to move equipment, lumber, building materials and even rocks for the face of the dam from the Snake Butte quarry, and most everything else that was needed at the Fort Peck Dam construction site and later for the power house projects. The bridge abutment still remains at the site down below the high crest of the river!

In January of 1934 The Corps of Engineers needed a railroad from the Great Northern Railroad to bring in most of what the Corps of Engineers needed at the Fort Peck Dam Site. They decided on a route from Wiota, which is east of Nashua, to bring supplies from the Great Northern Railroad. The right of way was 100 feet wide, crossed the Milk River and went up the Missouri River bottom on the north side of the Missouri River, which split my grandfathers' farm, as I have previously mentioned. The bridge and tracks were one of the first things that the Corps started to work on as there was not a good highway to the dam site. This railroad was finished probably in less than a year.

I have a picture of the Wiota bridge with the tractor on it was probably taken in the summer of 1952. You can see that the water was up very high and I myself cannot remember the water being normally closer than twenty feet from touching the steel girders on the bridge. Julie Landis Johnson gave me the picture and it is probably from her parents. She remembers the river flooding one year and they had to stay in an old school bus out near the hills. They had an old school bus that they had converted for some living quarters in times of need, and as their family grew. She could not remember what year it was, she was really young, but she could remember the flood. I know that there was a major flood on the Milk River in 1952 and I remember seeing the flood when I was a youngster going to Nashua, as we had to cross the old Milk River Bridge just south of Nashua.

I remember when we would go over to visit the Landis family, the Milk River Railroad Bridge was a real draw for me. It was probably only about a half of a mile from their house and we could ride our bikes on a trail to it that went along the river. The bridge had two steel housing abutments and the major part of the river flow went between them. We would walk over on the ties that hold the steel rails in position on the bridge. It was real exciting for us as kids, since across the river and bridge was the Fort Peck Indian Reservation. We would go over there from time to time and fantasize and play cowboys and Indians. I remember going onto the bridge when we could hear the train coming from a long ways off. At times, we would crawl down one of the steel housings to get down to the gravel at the bottom of the bridge abutment and wait for the train to come overhead on the rails. This was pretty exciting for us and we did it more than once. One time, when the train was only about a quarter mile away, we were walking out and crawling down to the hidey hole under the tracks on the bridge when the train was coming. As we waited at the bottom, the train stopped. We had been spotted by the engineer when we were climbing down to our hiding spot. One of the train crewmen came over and hollered to us to come out and not to come back or he would tell our parents. For some reason, later on our folks found out about the incident and we had to stay away from the bridge for a while!

We went back later one spring and we were fishing off the top off the bridge. I caught something and it was too big to pull up, so I had to let off-line trying to keep it snug while I walked around the end and down to the river. I pulled in about a three pound fish (well, maybe it was two pounds) and it was not a catfish like we usually catch in the Milk River. Jim and I did not know what it was. I got it on the bank to grab a hold of it and it wrapped around my arm. To us young boys it almost looked like an eel that we had seen pictures of that come from the ocean. We found out it was a burbot, otherwise known as a ling, and they are very good eating. They are a native fish to the Milk and Missouri Rivers, as well as are channel catfish, sauger, paddlefish and sturgeon.

Julie, Jim, Karen and I were close in ages and spent a lot of time biking or riding their two horses Dixie and Olly Con. We inherited the horses from them when they left as we had just got the Mattingly place, which is now my home place, so we had pasture for them. Julie came back with a girlfriend from Minnesota about twenty years ago with their horses to ride around the old farm. Her dad Orville brought his motor home to stay down by their old house and showed them how to fish for catfish. Julie had dreamed of fishing for channel cats for years since they moved and she caught one on that trip. I remember talking to Orville in his motorhome as he was telling about Julie coming up from the river with the fish still hanging from the fishing pole. He said she was grinning, and so proud of herself. They were camped in the yard of their old house, which is about a hundred yards from the river. The old two-story house that they had lived in for years is still standing. It was built on a concrete foundation by Orville and is standing up well to the test of time.

Phyllis was a full-time mother and also was a volunteer 4-H leader who I respected very much. I think it was the Lucky Clover club here in Valley County that she was a part of. It was a good youth organization that enabled us to be a part of a great organization and be able to go to a lot of activities around the county. Most of the neighbor kids belonged so we could go to activities together and to meet other great kids from all over the county. The Valley County fair was the most important event of the year and we had a lot of fun the few days we were there. Phyllis was such a great person and leader we were so blessed. After she moved out of the area our 4-H club was not quite the same without her leadership. I was heart-broken, when we found out a few years later after they had moved away, that she had died of a heart attack and I was so saddened for the family for their loss!!

One day, when they were still on the farm, Orville had come over to our farm in his old Chevy grain truck. It was in the evening and it was after he had gotten off work from doing concrete work at the old air force base north of Glasgow. This place is now a town called St. Marie. He needed some seed wheat to plant in his own wheat fields. I always liked Orville; he was our school bus driver and was a nice man. They got the wheat loaded on the truck and they were doing some other things and I was following them around. Mom was always baking cinnamon rolls or pie so I think we went into the house for a while to get a bite to eat. When we came out the sun was already down and it was almost dark. He had a couple of things to do to his truck and before we knew it, it was dark. He got into the truck and found out that the lights did not work. He walked around the truck looking for the problem and still he had no lights. I think there was a little bit of a moon out, so it was not completely dark. It was about four or five miles to his place around the bend to his farm on the county road, to the place we still call the Landis place. He started to get in and go and I asked him how he was going to see the road. He told me something then that I will never forget about Orville. He said, "I'll be fine unless I meet some fool on the road with no lights on!!" Ha! Then he went on home.

Orville worked with concrete for a contractor at the Glasgow Air Force Base north of Glasgow. He also farmed. He was a good neighbor and was a good friend of my fathers. He also drove a school bus for us kids going to the Nashua School. He was a hard worker all his life. In 1962 he had a chance to sell the farm and take over a liquor store in South Dakota after his mother passed away, so they moved from Montana.

Back in the days when I was going to school, there were families living every half mile or mile around was is now known as South River Road and we had a bus full of kids when we got to Nashua. Right now, we do not have any children of school age so a bus is not needed on South River Road. On the far end of the road, which is known as North River Road, there are two children at "Rorville" that are in school. "Rorville" is the nickname of the area where John and Donna Rorvik, Wesley and Teresa

Rorvik, and Jeffrey and Kayla Rorvik have their houses. It is Jeffrey and Kayla's boys, Reese and Carson, who are in school. The bus does not come onto the gravel road any more so the bus stop is a couple of miles away from their place, along the highway!

About a year after the Landis family moved away, my folks took us on a trip back to Ohio. We stopped at Flandreau, South Dakota to see the Landis family. Jim and I were walking around town and he said we could try to get served a beer at a local bar! The drinking age in South Dakota was 18 at the time. We got served and drank a couple of tap beers. This was my 'first time', being served in a bar, that is!!!

Rufus and Martha (Weinmeister) Anderson

The Andersons were and still are close neighbors of my parents and only live about 3/8 of a mile away to the Southwest. From my house now where I live now on the Mattingly place, their farm house is about a mile north. They had three children, Larry, Rita and David. I remember when my sister Karen and I would walk over to the Andersons to visit we would have to walk along or on the rails of the Corps of Engineers railroad track. At this time, it wasn't being used much so we could walk on it safely and it was quiet here so you could hear it coming a long ways away. It was a slow-moving train and it did not come by every day. There was a vehicle crossing over the railroad tracks about 400 yards away from the house that we would walk over in wet weather or snow conditions. Under this wooden crossing there were blue racer snakes that lived there. They were a nonpoisonous fast moving small bluish green snake that you would have to run to keep up with them. We would see these snakes under this crossing quite often.

Rufus was the youngest of the Anderson children, his parents being Martin and Molly Anderson. The other Anderson brothers that I knew were Tom and Simon and I just barely remember Amos. Amos was a bachelor like Larry and Lavore, and he lived and farmed here in the Milk and Missouri river bottom. Simon lived north of Nashua and he married Irene Keil. They had two children, Myrna Anderson Lauckner and Lavore Anderson. Lavore has a few cows and he still lives on Simon's farm northeast of Nashua. Myrna married neighbor Bill Lauckner and they have two children, Will and Gwen. Tom and Doris lived on a farm 2 miles east of my parents' farm. They had two children, Leila who was my age and a classmate and Tom who was the same age as Karen and they were classmates of ours. We were good friends of them as they lived close to us and we rode the bus together to Nashua. Leila lives near Billings now and Tommy passed away from heart trouble many years ago. Leila and I have always been good friends. Rufus lost his father, Martin, when he was struck and killed by a hit and run driver near Park Grove during The Fort Peck Dam days.

Martha, Rufus's wife was a Weinmeister, the daughter of David and Mary, who lived and farmed in the Nashua area, and she had three brothers that also farmed on this river bottom land.

I always liked to shoot my .22 rifle and one day I rode my bike down to the river to our pump site. Tom was there and he was shooting down into the water next to the intakes. I was curious what he was shooting at. I didn't have my gun along as I didn't have a scabbard on it to carry it safely with me. Tom was trying to scare the carp away that were always sucking the gunk from the water surface. His method seemed like he was trying to herd the carp; after the carp would swim away he would shoot in front of it and make it change directions. In the past I would shoot carp, but since they weren't any good to eat, I would leave them in the water for other fish to eat. The trouble is that when they were dead, they would be sucked up to the screen on the pump intakes and someone would have to get them out with a pitchfork as they would restrict the flow of water. I was warned by Dad and Rufus not to shoot anymore carp by the pump! Tom let me shoot the semi auto .22 to scare the carp back and forth and it was great fun. I never did buy a semi automatic rifle as I thought that they were too dangerous as after a shot another round would go into the chamber and would be ready to fire again. Then you would have to put the safety on, but there was always a round in the chamber. I don't trust the safety on most rifles and I would rather have an empty shot shell in the chamber. If I have a live round in the chamber, I leave the action open so it can't fire. It was fun shooting a semi automatic though!

Rufus and my Dad were good friends and next door neighbors and they owned a irrigation right-of-way together; they had purchased this land from Homer Peters to have access to the Missouri so they could irrigate their own land. We farm side by side with them and our properties are inter-twined and we own machinery together as well as sharing a pump site on the river. I don't know how much schooling Rufus had on metallurgy but he could build just about anything with steel. He was an excellent welder and he also had a forge so he could repair any broken equipment. He built a lot of his machinery and when he was finished you would have thought it was designed by an engineer. Along with my father, Edgar, they designed and built a concrete platform for two irrigation intake pumps on the river. Within a few years the high spring water runoff had eroded the pump site enough they had to move the pumps back about 10 feet. This second time they purchased some metal from the old Wiota railroad bridge that was taken down in the early 1960's. This metal was driven down into the river sand until it hit a solid surface, just like the engineers did under Fort Peck Dam. The next piece of metal would inter lock with the last and slide down to make a solid wall at the water level to stop the erosion of the river bank under the pumps into the river. This has lasted for over 50 years without major sloughing of the riverbank at the pump site. It withstood the 65,000 cubic feet per second flooding event from the Fort Peck spillway which is almost directly across the river from the pump site. This 2011 flood event lasted from June until September with very little damage to the protected pump site. The native trees and the Russian olives that are on the river bank stopped a lot of erosion on the river banks. Where there wasn't any protection on the banks from brush and trees, there was a lot of major erosion along the Missouri River. Therefore, Rufus and Dads' efforts and engineering on the pump site is very correct and will be stable for years to come.

Rufus worked for a while at the Fort Peck project on the Administration Building which is still used by the Corps of Engineers up on the hill looking down on the river and power houses. He worked with Harold Moeker who was a neighbor about three miles north of Dads' farm. Rufus learned a lot about working with steel and concrete while working on this construction.

My dad bought a 3 yard, pull type scraper to level his land and build ditches to distribute the water to the other parts of his property. This piece of machinery or a can, as my dad calls the scraper, worked so well that Rufus used the dimensions from it and built one just like it from scratch. Rufus used this one for many years on his property to level land and make ditches. These scrapers are still on the farms and are still in use, both being pulled by an IH tractor. Rufus built so many pieces of machinery that they are too numerous to mention. He built a small Steam engine that operated but I don't think that he put it to work. He liked to do many things, so he spent a lot of time in his heated shop. He had a stone cutter and he collected agates and cut them. He was always tinkering or repairing machinery when he wasn't farming. When he was a young man, he had a motorcycle that he used. During winter snow conditions he built and put a ski on the front of it. I talked to his son Dave and it was an Indian motorcycle. I really liked Rufus, even though he usually had a cigar in his mouth and a bottle of whiskey behind the seat. Just about every evening he would drive around his property to see what needed to be done on the farm the next day. Dave still drives around, checking out the countryside and he is alike Rufus in many ways.

My children remember Martha and Rufus fondly. They would often ride their bikes through the Anderson's yard on the way over to visit my parents. Stacy is a bit of a rock hound, like me, and she would take rocks she had found to Rufus, and he would cut and polish them and give them back. Martha was a sweet lady and she always had a smile on her face. There were often treats and always smiles and friendly waves for my kids when they went through the yard. Larry and Dave both farmed with Rufus and eventually took over the place. Larry still lives on the home place, Dave and his wife live just north of there, and raised their three children very close to my own. Rita lives in Glasgow and worked as a county dispatcher for years.

The Weinmeister Family

There were three Weimeister brother's who had farmland on this river bottom, Victor, Paul and Harvey, and a sister, Martha, and I knew them all. Their parents were David and Mary, who had immigrated from Russia to California in 1910.This family was of German heritage but lived and farmed in Russia. After a few years, they started farming in Kansas. Times were lean and consisted of much hard work, but they persevered and had nine children. In the 40's, they moved to Montana to be near David's brother Jacob, who had also immigrated and ended up farming south of Nashua. David and Mary farmed southwest of Nashua until David retired in the late 50's.

Victor and Amarylis (Moeker) Weinmeister's farm was located about one and a half miles east of the Edgar Garwood farm. Vic had bought the Tom and Doris Anderson place in the 1950's. This farm had irrigated land next to The Milk River where they grew alfalfa for their cows. On the dryland up on the bench, they raised wheat and barley. They were always good neighbors to everyone in the area. All of their children were tall and very good athletes in school and college. Their daughters Cynthia and Marylou would babysit our children at times when we had Jaycee meetings and conventions when our parents couldn't. Duane. Randy and Gene helped with their cows and the farm. They were all good kids and never were in any trouble! Amarylis had bought a farm east of her parents, Harold and Celia Moeker, farm near Nashua when she was about 18 years old. This farm had mostly grazing land for their Santa Gertrudis cross cows that they had purchased from the King Ranch, that was in Texas. Their farm later was sold to Merlin and Shirley Ball. Vic and Amarylis Weinmeister left a tall blue Harvestore silo on the river bottom which is a local landmark on the Milk River bottom and can be seen for miles.

Paul and Murnie (White) Weinmeister farmed west of my Dads farm, and this place was owned back in the 1930's by Ted Steagal and John E. Paul. Therefore, this crooked hill north of School Section Road was always called Johnny Paul Hill. This is the same John E. Paul that bought Marion Garwoods (my Grandfather) dairy about 1936. Paul and Murnie had three boys: Gerry, Ronnie and Donnie. Paul farmed and lived on the Crow/Pattison place until 1968. This was an irrigated farm that had an irrigation ditch easement that went through the Lee Merrick/Terry Pointer property to get irrigation water from the Missouri River, property that I now own. Paul was good friends with the Loren Musgrove family, and I knew the boys well and we were on the same South Nashua bus together. Gerry and Don both worked many years for grain elevators. Ron farmed the Steagell property and was a good friend of mine and he helped me out more than a few times. Paul worked for a contractor at the former Glasgow Air Force Base after the base was closed down. There were several companies that operated at the bases location after it closed, but I am not sure which one Paul worked for. Paul and Murnie bought a house in Nashua and lived there until they passed away. Ronnie lived in the house several years and sold it to Mike and Shandy (Cook) Stingley.

Harvey Weinmeister was a bachelor and he bought his farm from Armund Ceruleus, who then used the money to buy The Park Grove Bar, which is a long time local favorite establishment. This farmstead went west almost to the Pickthorn Dredge Cut. There is an old Fort Peck barge there and us Garwood, Musgrove and Weinmeister kids would drive there to play on the barge and swim in the warmer water of the Dredge Cut back in the early 1960's. It was a good fishing spot and was usually nice and out of the wind there. This property was bought by Rufus and Martha Anderson. They had the land next to the Missouri River leveled and he put up a metal building Quonset that I helped put together. It was used for storage and is near some pretty neat river frontage property!

Frank and Lucy Bales

I owe a lot to the Bales family, Frank, Lucy and their children, that my family is even living here in eastern Montana. They homesteaded this countryside during some tough times in eastern Montana and were much of the reason my family has roots in Valley County. I personally never met Frank and Lucy but I have visited with their son Ken Bales several times. Frank and Lucy homesteaded land along the Missouri River, south of Fort Peck, on second point in the early nineteen hundreds. The Bales farmed, ranched and ran a bed and breakfast, which they called a roadhouse. I believe it was near the road that was serviced by one of the ferries that provided a means to transport people and goods to the south side of the Missouri River and back

My Dad, Edgar, said that Frank Bales had built up the large log house with an axe, and he worked for so long on the logs that he could hardly open his hands!

The reason I feel like I owe thanks to the Bales family is because, you see, my Grandpa and Grandma Marion and Gertrude Garwood on their honeymoon in the fall of 1920, came out to visit the Bales. Lucy was Grandma's aunt. My grandparents had worked their way west from Ohio working on a wheat threshing crew to this area. If they would not have come to visit here, they would not have homesteaded and my family would not have had any roots here in Valley County.

I visited with Ken Bales, son of Frank and Lucy, a few years ago. At the time he was 92 years old and he could remember names and stories very well, especially of the pre-Fort Peck Dam days. The building of Fort Peck Dam brought a lot of people here to work for "fifty cents an hour" during the recession but also caused a lot of families to lose their homesteads and farms to the waters of Fort Peck Reservoir. Frank and Lucy Bales were among these people who lost their land. I know that these people had some hard feelings toward the dam project for taking their properties at the time, when they had worked so hard to establish their farms and ranches. They were paid money for their properties, but I am not sure if they were compensated enough. I kind of doubt it was fair compensation. Certainly, they were told to take the money that was offered, and if they did not, when the dam was finished, then they would be flooded out and left with nothing. It was too bad that these people who lived upriver of Fort Peck Dam had to sacrifice their hard work to the future generations whom have benefitted from the dam. Not only to we need to thank the people that worked so hard to construct the Fort Peck Dam, spillway and power houses, but we need to be thankful and appreciate the many hard working people and families that lost everything they had worked years for making a home and a living on prime river bottom land which is now under the waters of Fort Peck Reservoir. People such as Ken and Lucy Bales!

I do not know how much money that was paid an acre to these hard-working people, but it probably was not near enough. I know that my Grandpa and Grandma were paid $10 an acre for five acres, which was for a 100ft wide right-of-way, from the Bureau of Reclamation, for the building of the railroad spur line from Wiota to Fort Peck. The railroad split their farm in half during a time when they were running a twelve to fifteen cow dairy herd. There were two crossings with two gates on the fence that needed to be opened and closed each time they moved the milk cows home to be milked, which needed to be done twice a day. It certainly created extra work for my grandparents.

The Bureau of Reclamation man that made the deal with my grand-parents told them that they would get the land back when the railroad was no longer needed by The Fort Peck Project. The only thing was that statement about them getting the land back was not in the written document that took the land for the railroad, and that caused considerable problems for the land owners years later. After the rails and good ties were taken off the line in about 1963, this property was determined to be given to any agency that wanted it. My father, Edgar Garwood, Homer Peters, Rufus Anderson, Victor Weinmeister and others fought hard to get the property back for the landowners. The trouble is they had to pay $80 an acre to get it back. I remember Grandpa saying he sure was happy to get the land back, but he wished the Corps would have taken the dirt and gravel for the raised grade back to the hills where they had gotten it! The railroad grade is still noticeable in several areas along the river bottom!

After Frank and Lucy had to leave their homestead along the Missouri and the life that they had worked so hard to build, they packed up their children and what belongings they could, and moved back to Indiana, which is where Frank's family came from. There are many stories like this from the construction of the Fort Peck Dam. Many people came here for a job (some eventually stayed and some moved on), but many others left this countryside, never to return.

Zack Bennett

I met Zack for the first time when I went out south with the Musgroves to visit to Zack and Cecil (Lingle) Bennett. Let me just say that Cecil was a wonderful woman to put up with Zack's shenanigans. Cecil Lingle Bennet was the aunt of a very good family friend, Donna Rees Rorvik. It seems like everyone is related to someone in this countryside. It was at the Bennet place that the Musgrove's lived and leased for several years, until the Musgrove kids needed to go to high school and moved to the north side of the Missouri. This is when I started seeing the kids on the school bus and got to know them.

The next time I remember seeing Zack was when I was having a "cold one" at the Park Grove Bar when I was old enough and Ol' Zack had been there for a while. At that time Zack and Cecil were living in their house in Park Grove and he could walk over to the watering hole. Harold Brown owned the bar at that time and was cleaning and cooking in the kitchen. Harold would come out front once in a while to check on things. There was just Zack and I in the bar at that time. We were visiting in between the naps that Zack was having. It seemed it happened quite often that his head would rest on the bar to take a nap. He drank Crème de Mint, you know that "green medicine", and would take a little drink once in a while. I noticed that Zack was sleeping and Harold went back to the kitchen and right away Zack's head popped up. He reached over the bar, grabbed the bottle of green syrup, poured him a little shot, took a drink and pretended to nap again. He did this at least one more time that night and I could not hardly believe it! I chuckled at his guts and ingenuity! About twenty years later, after Zack was gone and Harold had long sold the bar, I brought that night up and told Harold of Zack's doings. Harold chuckled and replied "Aw, he was my best customer and I figured maybe he was doing it a little, and he was a friend of mine." Let's just say, that Harold was not surprised. Harold was a bit of a character himself. Zack Bennett and Brownie Doke were about the only two that drank the "green medicine", that I knew, anyway.

Brownie Doke and Wib Dolson

Brownie Doke and Loren Musgrove were old friends, so when Loren would come down from Canada to visit, I would get a chance to visit with Brownie. I remember one day when Patty and I were shopping in Glasgow at Beede's Men's Wear, when three old "loud" cowboys staggered down the sidewalk from the Montana Bar, headed toward the Oasis to visit with Frosty. I had heard that Loren was in the country but had not seen him yet. It turned out that the cowboys were Loren, Brownie Doke and Wib Dolson. I had to go over and greet Loren and he introduced them to me. I shook their hands and that was the first time that I had met Brownie and Wib, although I had seen them around before. Patty and I followed along to the Oasis and had a couple beers with them and listened to their stories. I sure wished I would have had a tape recorder during that session. When Loren would come down to visit, he would always spend a couple days staying with Brownie, and I would visit with them and have a beer and spend hours listening to the great stories they would tell.

After us running into Loren, Brownie and Wib, Loren ended up coming to our house for a few days, like he usually did and would continue to do for quite a few years. In earlier years during the winter, Bernice and

Loren would come and stay with us. After she passed away, Loren would come down to visit on his own, bringing an assortment of family and friends along for the trip. One year he brought his granddaughter Leanne along as a driver from Fort St. John and he called her his "Chofeeere"!! The Musgrove's have been good friends continuously since the 50's. I remember when the Musgrove's were about to move to Canada, my sister Karen and I went over to visit them. Jack and Peggy Nickels were there visiting at the same time and we all had a good time reminiscing. This was in the spring of 1964 and it probably was the first time that I really got to hear Jack's and Peggy's stories!!!

Larry and Judy (Rorvik) Boyum

Larry was a year younger than me and so was a year behind me at school in Nashua. I have forgot many of the stories that happened when I was with him but the stories that I hear about him from others are especially interesting, mostly from events that happened in the South Country when he was younger, which is where Larry grew up. Larry married Judy Rorvik and for years they owned Vick's Bar in Nashua (the Rorvik family has become great family friends over the years). Judy also was also raised out in the country south of the spillway. This area is in McCone County, which is south of Valley County and is south of the Missouri River and east of Fort Peck Lake, is sagebrush steppe, brushed coulees, rugged badlands, sandstone ridged, mostly grazing country and inhabited by more than a few interesting cowboys and characters.

This is a story told to me by Larry Boyum. One time, Kris Sorensen had bought a Chevrolet Corvair car and one day Kris and Loren Musgrove had taken it into town. Loren was driving for some reason and they stopped in front of Vick's Bar in downtown Nashua. They had been in the bar too long and were about to leave and go home later that night. It was cold and someone started the car to warm up and they left it run for a while. A little while later they came out to go home. These Corvair cars had a shape that the front of the car was similar to the back end, especially in the dark! Loren had been driving and was expected to drive home. He opened the door and turned the lights on. Someone on the sidewalk said, "you can't drive this home as your head lights don't work". Loren got out and walked to the back of the car and said "they do too" as they are on. That is when it was more than apparent that he was in no shape to drive home!!

This story was told by Buck Musgrove or maybe Larry to me, so you can decide yourself on its reliability. Larry and Buck were working for Tony Trotter doing some haying, down on the Missouri River near Park Grove. They both got up in the morning and went down to the river to wash up for breakfast. Buck was kneeling down along the water and using his hands to flick water in his face like most of us do. Larry gave him a little nudge and Buck lost his balance and fell in the water. This water coming from the power houses, comes off the bottom of Fort Peck Lake, and it is cold, maybe about 45 to 50 degrees. Buck crawled out of the water and came running after Larry mumbling something like, "if I ever catch you. I'm going to kill ya". Larry was keeping just ahead of Buck as they made little loops around the alfalfa hayfield. Buck did not give up easily as he was really mad! They both got winded and Buck finally gave up the chase. All I know is that neither one of them was "for Shit!" the rest of the day stacking hay and Larry kept an eye on Buck the rest of the day worried about retaliation! Maybe he still should!!

This story happened out south of the spillway at Zack and Cecil Bennet's place, when the Musgroves were living out there. Larry and his brother Terry were over visiting Buck and Karl, and for fun, they were pulling the little red wagon up the hill a little ways and then one or two would get in and get an exciting ride to the bottom toward the dry creek near the house. Buck said it was Larry's turn to get to ride in the wagon down the hill, right by the house. Bernice was starting to wash clothes and she had a fire under a tub of water that she was starting to heat. Things had been going pretty well for all, until the boys gave Larry a push down the hill towards the house. Larry did not want to hit the house, so he steered away and ran right into the wash tub of water, knocking it over and spilling the water and in the process put out the fire. Bernice was almost beside herself and was "big time mad" according to Buck and Karen. After she found that Larry was okay, she started hollering at the boys. With the kids all snickering and grinning to themselves, she really was unhappy with them. They all had to help clean up the mess and carry up more water from the long-handled pump at the well, which was near the bottom of the creek.

Judy Rorvik Boyum is married to Larry and is a daughter of daughter of Carl and Peggy (Burman) Rorvik, who lived out south in McCone County near Shade Creek. Her siblings are John, Jim, Jean, Jerry, Jesse and Janet (and a sister named Jenny who is deceased). Larry and Judy have three children who are God-children to Patty and myself. They are Naomi, Kathy and Raymond. Larry and I have been friends since we were in grade school and I met Judy when she started school in Nashua. After they were married, they lived down the road from us about a mile away. We have a lot of memories from living so close to each other. It was great for our kid's to be so close to each other then, and the kids have always been close friends. Stacy, Naomi, Kathy and Janice Rorvik are the best of friends and they have had a lot of good times together.

More than once when Patty and I would be going home we would find Larry sleeping in his pickup on the gravel road and taking a nap. We would wake him up to see if he was alright and then he would go to his house. One night, Patty decided to drive him home while I followed in our car. That spring, there was a water hole just before you drove up to his house and the pickup quit in the water hole. Patty and Larry both had to wade out of the water. The next morning Larry figured out that the one gas tank had ran out of gas and then after switching tanks it started and he got out of the water hole.

Larry and Judy lived in Nashua for years and we are all still great friends, but for a while, they also lived between Nashua and Fort Peck near Larry's mother's place. Larry and Judy bought the Vick's Bar on the main street of Nashua many years ago. They needed some help bartending and my wife Patty started bartending for them. She is still working there and has gone through working for three owners of the bar. Someone remarked that she just goes with the bar!! She enjoys the people that she has met there and patrons come back to the bar to visit her! When friends and relatives come here for a visit, Vick's Bar is the place to socialize!

In January of 1993, Larry and I drove his Chevy pickup up to visit the Musgrove clan. All of the Musgroves live near the Fort Saint John and Charlie Lake, British Columbia, Canada area. Larry had known the Musgrove family before I did but he had never been up to Canada to visit them before, so we headed out on a two-week trip in the middle of winter. At that time, Bernice, had been gone for some time and Larry wanted to go visit them while Loren was still alive. I am not sure but I think John Rorvik fed my cows as Patty was driving the mail route. My Dad might have helped some. When we got up there to the Musgrove ranch there was about two-foot of snow on the ground. It was such a great visit as we stayed at Loren's log house and we visited and partied with Buck and Karl every day and we had a great time.

I remember that Karl was a pretty good skater and the community club had a hockey rink where they would play hockey. One day when they were practicing and I got talked into being the goalie for Karl's team and Buck was the goalie for the opposing team. I had a great time, but I did not put skates on as I probably would have spent most of my time on my back! I remember that I did not wear a mask as I could not see through it. I am lucky that I still have my front teeth!! I had some padding on for protection and a glove, and I did catch one or two pucks with it. I am glad that Karl was on my team as he would have been tough on me if he would have been on the opposing team. It was a great time for us, Larry and Loren sat in the pickup watching and drinking barley pop!

It is so quiet up there that we usually slept so well but being around the Musgroves we usually had our share of beer to drink, so that helped us sleep well at nights. We also got to see Linda Jackson Arneson, and two of her children, Jennifer and John Toav, on that visit. We had a few beers at the Fort Bar together, that I had gone to many years ago with them. It almost seems that the beers were about five bucks a piece at that time, so we did not stay too long in the bar. Yeah, you can you believe that, or not! It was a great trip up there to see good friends and I am always excited to get up there again.

Mick Trotter was a friend of George Boyum, who was Larry's father. Mick was married and had two children. He was later divorced and no one seems to know where they went. Sonny Bergan married Marie Trotter and had a cabin in western Montana next to his brother Terry, who was a 1964 classmate of myself. Clint Trotter, the eldest son, who now lives in Deer Lodge showed up at the 2006 Nashua High School reunion. He pulled up out behind the school with a cooler of beer! Buck told me he was a Trotter, so we went over and had a brew with him and we visited some. When we were talking, I said that I owned the Musgrove place on the Missouri. He said that he had helped his dad, Earl, clear some brush and trees of the property, which Earl owned before Loren Musgrove bought it. I told him that I had helped my dad, Edgar, clear almost the whole place and that there were not many trees left there anymore. He could not hardly believe that most of the cottonwoods were gone and there were only about three big fields now! Earline Trotter was a classmate of Terry Boyum, and she now farms west of Jordan and is married to Rick Lawrence. Jo Trotter and Blake Luse are married, and they live in Great Falls. They come back to school reunions in Glasgow and Nashua. Earl and Marie Rose Trotter lived in Park Grove and Nashua for a while.

As youths, Larry Boyum and Buck Musgrove were working for Tony Trotter haying near Park Grove. They went to Wolf Point for the Wild Horse Stampede. After the rodeo the boys were waiting in the pickup behind a bar when Tony came out staggering and threw the keys to Larry and said "you drive, boy!" It was dark and Tony was sleeping in the back of the pickup and a cow was out in the road near the Wiota hill. Larry hit the brakes to keep from hitting the cow and they heard a thump in the back of the pickup. They found that Tony was not moving so they stopped into Larry's folks place, which was nearby, across Highway 2 from the now Jim Gartside place! They told Larry's mother Gerry about Tony, thinking he might be dead as he was not moving! She looked at him and seen that he was alive and deduced that he was just passed out! Larry drove back to Tony's house near Park Grove and told his wife Claudia about him being in the back of the pickup. She cussed Tony out, brought out a blanket and told them to cover him up. The next morning, he was fine and ready to go back to haying!!!

The last story brings to mind another story worth sharing, a story about when Larry and Judy (Rorvik) Boyum had gone to Miles City for a basketball tournament. Their son Ray was playing basketball on the Nashua team. They were staying in a large motel. Larry had had quite a bit to drink and they had gone to bed. In the middle of the night Larry had gotten up to go into the bathroom. In the dark he opened a door thinking he was going into the bathroom. In his stupor he had opened and closed the door going out into the hall by the lobby. The room door was locked and he was in his shorts. It almost seemed like I heard that he forgot what room he was in and he surely did not have a key on him. He kept calling for Judy to open the door and let him back in. Finally, Judy woke up and let him back in the room before he woke up everyone in the area. The first time I heard Judy tell the story I almost died laughing and I still do when I think of Larry in his shorts knocking on doors, hollering and trying to wake Judy up. And all the while, he still had to go to the bathroom!

John and Donna (Rees) Rorvik

John and Donna are very good friends of Patty and I. They are neighbors living about four miles away from our farmhouse. He is known as Uncle John to many of us as he will help anyone out if they need help even though he is busy at the time! Patty and I have travelled a lot with them to destinations, just to get away! It is always fun to 'get away' with them even though we have things to do on the farm. On the farm and ranch there is always something that you can do.

We were involved in the Jaycees and Jayceens together in the 1970's in Nashua. John was the Nashua Jaycee Charter President and I was the secretary. John has been on several boards including the local Farmers Union board in Nashua for several years. He is very knowledgeable in the business of the Farmers Union Cooperative.

Uncle John has helped me out many times and I needed help while I had calving problems back in the 70's. I had a cow that was trying to have a calf that was breeched in the cow, and I needed to get her to a vet. It was very cold out and I couldn't get the cow into the rack in the back of my pickup. He came up with the idea to get a lariat rope on the cow, string the other end through the rack and attach it to his pickup. With a short section of plywood, we were able to slide the cow up into the pickup, and I was able to take the cow into the vet. I can't remember if we were able to save the calf or not, but I was able to save the cow and I wouldn't have been able to do that without his help.

John is one of my very best friends that I have known since high school. Donna and Patty are very good friends and the four of us bowled as a mixed league team together for several years. They only live about four miles away, just across a couple of hills from us on the Milk River and we are on the Missouri, but we farm and ranch next to each other and are great neighbors. John and Donna Rees Rorvik grew up in the South country on the East side of the highway near Hungry Creek. They both have a rural contract Post Office route just like my wife Patty did, so we have a lot in common.

John and I were both officers when we started the Nashua Jaycee chapter in about 1972 and kept it together for about 10 years even with the few people we had in our small community. The Nashua Jaycees did a lot of community work and it was great for individual development. We started the chapter with the help of Gary Meyer who is married to Bonnie, Donn's' sister. The Meyer's lived in Scobey at that time and now live nearby in Fort

Peck. Gary is a great guy that is always ready to help and usually has a joke or story to tell. I think he could have been a great stand-up comedian. He is a good lead singer and sings in a band along with Larry Boyum. We play cards together and are all friends. We are so fortunate to live close to each other and we are all pretty healthy, even though we are getting older!!

Almost everyone that knows John, calls him "Uncle John" because he is so helpful to other people even though he has a lot to do with his own farm and ranch. John and Donna's have two sons, Wesley and Jeffrey, who work on the ranch while working full time jobs. John and Donna's daughter Janice is a school teacher here locally and has a daughter Tia with Tim Dees. Wesley is married to Theresa who is a nutritionist at the hospitals in Glasgow, Poplar and Wolf Point. She is turning in to be a great farm and ranch woman and isn't scared to operate any farm equipment. Jeffry is married to Kayla Skolrud Rorvik, also a great help with the farm work, and they are raising two great kids, Reese and Carson.

John and the boys use four wheelers and motorcycles for their horses and still trail their cows between pastures as they have a lot of cows and that saves a lot of fuel for the trucking. They have a large pasture up north on the Fort Peck Indian Reservation and they have leased land next to me that they hay and graze later on in the fall. John still has some land out south in McCone County that they hay in the wet years but always use it for grazing normally with their yearling heifer calves.

John parents were Karl and Peggy (Berman) Rorvik and they started ranching in McCone County after they were married. Karl and Peggy both were in the Armed Service when WWII was going on. They met while they were in the service. Peggy was from Wibaux, Montana and Karl was from near Brockway, Montana. They took over a piece of land that Karl's sister had promised him if he came back from the war safe. They had eight children, John, Jim, Jerry, Judy, Jean, Jennie, Jesse and Janet. Karl Rorvik's father was Elias and he ranched near Brockton, but he lost his land during WWII. Donna's parents were Harold and Margaret (Lingle) Rees, and their ranch was out south in McCone County. The Rorvik, Rees, and Boyum's all grew up very near each other in that rugged south country.

John, Donna, Patty and I have been going somewhere most falls to relax after the harvest is done. We have a lot of stories to tell about our gambling escapades. One year we went to Deadwood, South Dakota. Patty and Donna were playing the machines upstairs in an old building. John and I had gotten in a blackjack game in the basement of a building. I had way too much beer to drink to be playing but I was lucky, and the dealer was being good to me. I was winning pretty good with the help of this real patient dealer. Any way they decided to close the game for the night as John and I were winning most hands. We had to take our chips upstairs to cash them in. I had taken a little spill going up the steps and dropped a lot of my chips, which John helped pick up. When we got up to the cashier office, I had given them all my chips, I thought. I had made some money and they paid me. I found some more chips in a couple of other of my pockets, so they had to give me more money. John and I still laugh about that as I was pretty well wasted at the time.

I was talking to John a while back while he was recuperating from knee surgery. I told him about his story in this book, and I said that we had never done anything really, crazy together. He reminded me of the boat ride after one of my brandings. At that in the seventies I had about fifty or sixty head of mother cows. At my brandings we always had plenty of beer on hand and even though we didn't use horses to rope with, the brandings could get pretty western! I didn't have a calf table at that time, so we had to wrestle every calf to brand and vaccinate them. I always calved in February and March so by the middle of April I could start seeding wheat and I didn't have to worry about much about the cows while I was farming. My calves would be big by the time we got them branded, and we had to work hard to get the job done. That year we got the branding done early in the afternoon and we were looking for something to do.

After we had gotten the calves mothered up, Dave Anderson mentioned that we could go fishing in his dads' (Rufus) small aluminum boat. John always liked fishing and probably had never fished much from a boat before. It was only about a mile to where Dave had his boat in the Missouri River at our irrigation pump site. There were four of us heading the half of a mile to the mouth of the Milk River where the best fishing was. I remember we were out of beer, but Jeff Wagner, a good friend of Dave's, had a fifth of Canadian Mist and we had some poles and bait, so we motored the boat out in the river. I can't remember if we got any fish or not but there was a little leak in the back of the boat and we would have to bail water some to keep our feet dry. About sundown we headed back to shore into a little head wind. We were kind of drunk and overloaded in the small boat and probably only had a couple of life jackets along. We were a couple of feet from shore and John leaped out of the boat to the safety of dry land! He exclaimed something like he thought were going to get drownded!!! It was then we found out that he couldn't swim! The Missouri River is very cold and unforgiving, and John remembers the incident very well to this day! On the way back to shore everyone but Dave had gotten wet from the mist from the bow of the boat. Dave was in the back and hadn't gotten as wet, so we had to throw some water on him accidently, as we were bailing the boat out. Back at the house I went out to check on the cows and calves. I went back into the house and to my dismay found Dave in my robe. Patty was drying his overalls as they were wet!! Ha!

Speaking of boating on the Missouri, anther time about thirty years later John, Patty and I headed out down the Missouri in my old boat to go see Jack Nickels who has a house on the river, and liquor was involved. We got about a mile from Jacks place and we took a wrong way around an island and I grounded the boat on a gravel bar. Patty, who had shorts on, had to get out and push us off to open water. It was getting late and we got back to the dock about dark! I guess maybe we learn eventually from these sometimes, fun adventure filled circumstances, as we haven't been boating on the Missouri much since!

Allyn and Dorothy (Evenson) Skyberg

Allyn and Dorothy Skyberg first lived on the Skyberg ranch south of the Missouri River for a couple of years after they were married. The ranch needed a good source of irrigated hay so they bought a farm on the Milk River in 1958, and so they moved to Valley County. They had three children, Debra, Jeff and Audrey. They lived about four miles from my parents' farm. Debbie Skyberg and my youngest sister Diane were classmates in school, so our families spent time together, allowing the children to swim in the Milk River, Missouri River or the Fort Peck Dredge cuts. Allyn, whose nickname is Buster, had irrigated alfalfa that raised for use on the ranch or sold to other cattlemen. He started to work at the Montana Dakota Utilities (MDU) compressor station near Fort Peck alongside his farming. He later became the manager of the compressor station and they sold the farm and moved into the house on the station site. All of the Skyberg children graduated from Nashua High School.

A story that Dorothy tells is that my mother, Toni Garwood, did not like onions in her cooking and so she did not put any in her potato salad. The Skyberg's were over at my folks place having supper and young Jeff made a remark about how "flat" tasting the potato salad was to his mom. Dorothy said she was so glad that Jeff had made the remark when Toni was in another room so she did not hear it. Dorothy said that she would have been so embarrassed if my mom would have heard. Mom definitely did not like onions or very spicy herbs in her cooking. I guess I was the same way when Patty and I got married. Patty said I did not want onions in my food, but I do now!

After Buster retired from MDU, they moved "out south" to the ranch where they built a very nice house. Dorothy has written a very nice story about Melvin and Thora Skyberg, who had pioneered and homesteaded on the prairies in the badlands, and has agreed to share this story with us. Her sister Karen Bender also has a story included, which is about the Evenson family, and those will be shared later in the book.

Jack Nickels and my father, Edgar Garwood, taken at a Nashua All School Reunion. They were classmates for many years and were both around 90 years old in this picture, which was taken in Fort Peck at Kiwanis Park.

Myself and Buck Musgrove posing with my 1966 Ford Bronco. This was taken in front of my parents' farmhouse when Buck and Bernice made it back to Montana for a visit.

Patty and myself, taken on our first trip to Canada after we were married. This was taken out in front of Loren and Bernice's homeplace in the Canadian Rockies, beautiful countryside.

This picture was taken in front of the Musgrove place in British Columbia, from left to right, myself, Karl, Buck, Loren and Bernice. The photo was taken by Patty.

Picture of me and the Musgrove boys, Buck and I in the back and Karl in the front. We made him sit down so he didn't tower over us.

Karl posing with some of his artwork and sketches. He is very talented.

The day of the "wild horse race". From left to right, Stacy on Drifter, Buck, Shawn riding in front of Seth on Guy, and Patty on Rigo.

Loren Musgrove, relaxed and having a brew. There was no other person in this world quite like Loren Musgrove. I greatly admired him and was proud to call him my friend.

This was the bridge that crossed the Milk River on the railroad spur line that ran from Wiota to the Fort Peck Dam Site. It was right by the Landis place and we played on it a time or two, even though we were not supposed to. One of the bridge footings is still in place on the river.

This picture was taken when the Musgrove clan came down for a Nashua All School Reunion. From left to right, Buck, Karl, Karen and Ann, Karl's lovely wife.

A FEW WORDS FROM MY FRIENDS

(shared stories)

contributed by

Karen Musgrove Johnson

Dorothy Evenson Skyberg

Karen Evenson Bender

And

Lee "Buck" Musgrove

"There is no greater agony than bearing an untold story inside you"

-Maya Angelou

A Few Memories of My Family

by Karen Musgrove Johnson

Loren Oral Musgrove was born November 26, 1911 at Glasgow. He passed away December 2, 1998 at Fort St. John, British Columbia, Canada. He married Ann Bernice Leuschen on November 20, YEAR in Needles, California. Mom was born December 26, 1919 at Jordan, Montana and passed away December 20, 1984 in Upper Cache Creek.

Dad grew up north of Nashua, with two older sisters, Mona, Cora and a younger brother Jackie, who passed away at a young age, from a ruptured appendix. Dad broke horses for Abe Friesen until he entered the army in March of 1942. He served in the 112th Cavalry for 21 months, mainly in the South Pacific. His daughter Patricia Ann (March 23, 1944) was almost a year old before he saw her. On his return his family lived with John and Huldah Musgrove on the home place north of Nashua. Bernice taught school at the Big Four School starting in December of 1940 until May of 1946. She stayed at Cherney's before marrying dad.

It was then that the family moved to the home place below the Fort Peck Dam, where the ranching and farming was started. Lee Allen (Buck) was born November 2, 1946. Karl John and Karen Jean followed on May 25th, 1948. We spent most summers there, but wintered at the Zack Bennett's place on Fort Peck Lake, to feed cows. Mom taught at Frazer school for three years and then two years at home with correspondence courses.

Some of my memories of the old place were: the white morning glory flowers, which I used to decorate my mud pies, which gave me a good base for my future as a camp cook and wedding cake decorator, playing in the irrigation ditches on hot summer days, as kids I stayed close to the house while the three "OLDER" kids rode horses and did ranch things. After we turned 40 years of age Karl said that I could be the older twin!

Our home always drew friends. Many hours Lee Merrick would come and play rummy with me. But some visitors would not like it when dad brought in the hind leg of a horse to slice off for steaks for supper. We also went visiting on Sundays. The Kirklunds, Mr. and Mrs. Pointer, Mr. and Mrs. John French, Palmer Strand, Kris Sorensen, Gus Anderson, Mr. and Mrs. Earl Trotter, Mr. and Mrs. George Boyum, Mr. and Mrs. Glenn Daley, just to name a few.

Then in the fall of 1958 we stayed on the home place year round and started going to Nashua School. Meeting new lifelong friends like the Garwoods and Wienmasters. Mrs. Snyder became a big influence on me as

I worked in the lunchroom for two years; she made the best turkey dressing and gravy, potato soup with bologna sandwiches and of course her chili burgers. When I asked for her recipes in my Christmas letter she said she never used a recipe.

In the spring of 1964, Dad ventured north to the Peace River area looking for a ranch, as we were getting short of grazing to summer the cows on. He found his ideal land in the Upper Cache Creek area. There was the log home he and mom had dreamed of, lots of grass, far from town, no power, and lots of water (if you packed it in). So, in July we moved from the "Big Sky Country" Montana to British Columbia and the "Wide Sky Country", just fifty miles from another of the biggest earth filled dams in the world.

Life on the Skyberg Homestead

By Dorothy Evenson Skyberg, wife of Allyn Skyberg

Before I get into the story, "Life on The Homestead", it would be helpful to have some kind of an understanding of just what was involved in becoming a homesteader.

It was on May 20, 1862, that the Free Homestead Act was passed and signed by President Abraham Lincoln. The law took effect on January 1, 1863.

Under this law any man or woman who was a citizen (or was in the act of becoming a citizen) twenty-one years old, or the head of a family, could have 160 acres of undeveloped land by living on it five years and paying eighteen dollars in fees. They were also required to build a house, make improvements, such as fences, and farm the land before they could own it outright and receive their patent. Alternatively, the homesteader could purchase the land for $1.25 per acre after having filed and lived on the land for six months.

As with any law, there are wrinkles that have to be ironed out. The original law had such a wrinkle. The authors simply stated that the homesteader was required to build a 12X14 house, making no indication of feet or inches. Well, you can easily guess what happened. Speculators took great advantage of that error quickly taking up large areas of the best land.

Another way to get around the housing requirement, though obviously not used quite as often, found family members filing on adjacent sections, building one house, and putting it on the section line between them. Brothers found this a handy way of accomplishing the housing requirement.

It was soon found that the land in the west was no comparison to that in the eastern or mid-section of the country. It was simply impossible for the homesteader to make a living on so little land so the law changed and homesteaders were allowed to file on 320 acres.

How does one make the decision to move from the known to the totally unknown? How do you make the decision to leave family and friends behind, perhaps to never see them again? After all, you are planning to move many hundreds of miles away all in the hope of a better life, on the promise of free land.

What does that land hold for you? Will it be a land of rich soil and plenteous rainfall? Such were the hopes of Melvin Charles Skyberg as he stepped from the train in Wolf Point, Montana on that day in 1917.

To properly tell the story of his homesteading experience I must go back a bit. Melvin, the son of a Lutheran pastor, married Thora Wangsness on March 9, 1916 at the rural Rock Prairie Lutheran Church near Elbow Lake, Minnesota.

Melvin had a small farm where they lived for about two years before it was lost to foreclosure. In his case that is, no doubt, what prompted the move to Montana. By this time their first son, Kristian Syvert had been born, April 6, 1917.

Later that year, 1917, Melvin came searching for a new life in "Montana, The Land of Opportunity". I wonder if he might have read the book, "Montana 1917" in which the above proclamation is given. I quote from the foreword of the book: *"Issued by the authority of the State of*

Montana, "Montana-1917" seeks to give home seekers, investors, young people who are looking for a new field, those who are seeking a place where they can start life anew, reliable and accurate information of the opportunities which are offered them in the Treasure State. " The book goes on to give glowing reports of all the rich grain fields, cattle, swine, mining, fruit growing, gas and oil. The book proclaimed that scenically, *Montana may be called the Switzerland of America.* I don't believe they were writing of the badlands of eastern Montana.

What a disappointment it must have been, upon arrival, to find that all the best land, along the Missouri and Milk Rivers, was taken. It isn't known how he got from Wolf Point to Glasgow but after hearing reports of land still available in Dawson County, Melvin walked out to the area about 25 miles south of present-day Fort Peck where he staked his claim on 320 acres which was filed at the land office in Glasgow. In 1919 this area became part of the newly formed McCone County.

What could his feelings have been as he surveyed the area of buttes, gullies, sagebrush, and rattlesnakes? This had to have been a shock after coming from the fertile, black soil of Minnesota. If he couldn't make a living on that farm, what in the world could he do here?

He returned to Minnesota for the winter. In the spring the family arrived in Montana, by train. Debbie recalled hearing that they had brought their household furnishings and small farm equipment with them on the train. Upon arriving in Wolf Point they had to make arrangements for a team and wagon. I have a postcard Melvin had written to Thora's father on which he wrote; "Frazer, Montana, Thursday. We got here alright this morning, had to stay overnight at Minot and Wolf Point. We will cross the river tonight. Address, Bonin, Montana." The postmark on the card is Frazer, April 4, 1918. And so began the life of these homesteaders, Melvin 26 years of age and Thora 22 years. As we look back to all that they would have to face, they were so very young.

On January 2, 1917, the so-called 640-acre homestead law became effective. Under the provisions of this law, settlers were allowed to file upon as much as 640 acres of land, provided the land was designated as being of more value for stock-raising and grazing, than farming purposes. So, Melvin filed for as additional 320 acres. He received the patent for the first filing dated, June 26, 1924. The second claim was filed with the land office in Great Falls. The patent for that land is dated, March 12, 1928. Both patents are signed by President, Calvin Coolidge. A patent is a 'Deed of Title' from the Federal Government giving the holder the right to do as he wishes with the land – sell it if he wishes.

The land is his! Now, what to do with it. Those first years were hard. There was a house to build and land to break, seed and harvest. Ready cash was a thing few homesteaders had. The homestead laws had recently been greatly liberalized. Before, the settler had to live on and cultivate his land continuously for a period of five years. Under a recent act of congress this period had been reduced to three years, and the homesteader was allowed to be absent from the land for not over five months of any year. Melvin and Thora took advantage of this change. They moved to Eureka, in western Montana, in the fall of 1919 where Melvin found a job at a saw mill, grading lumber.

It was while they were in Eureka that their second son, Melvin Thomas, was born on November 23, 1919. They returned to the homestead in the spring and never left it again.

I have often wondered what Thora thought of her new home; a one-room tarpaper shack. She grew up in a two-story home, complete with a summer kitchen. No one ever thought to ask just what they may have brought with them to furnish the homestead. There are so many questions we would like answers to now, but when one is living the day to day life those things do not seem important.

The family increased to six as Margaret Lois was born July 5, 1922 and Allyn Walter born on December 14, 1924.

When one thinks back to what those days were like it is rather daunting. The ranch was a very long way from anywhere. And roads. There were no roads – only established trails to be traveled with team or horseback. Should there be an illness or accident, there were no quick trips to a doctor or emergency room. They simply made-do the best way they could. The women were usually tended in childbirth, by a neighbor lady who acted as her midwife; this was the case for Thora.

It is my personal feeling that life on those homesteads was especially hard on the wife. She spent many long lonely days with just her family and the endless hours of work to keep her company. If she didn't put in a large enough garden, tend it well enough, and preserve enough, they could be very hungry before there would be fresh produce again. Of course, the weather had a lot to do with her success. Would there be enough rain? Would everything be hailed out? Would the grasshoppers eat the tender plants into the ground? All these disasters hit the homesteaders at one time or another. Much responsibility fell directly on the shoulders of the women.

Thora had to can much of their meat as well. The fat was saved and rendered and made into lye laundry soap. Allyn recalls that during those times when the lye soap ran out she used purchased P & G laundry soap.

In her "spare" time she sewed clothing, mended, and darned. This kind of work was usually saved to do in the evening in the dim light of a kerosene or Aladdin lamp. Homesteaders were true recyclers. Thora turned the skirts of her worn dresses into dresses or shirts for Margaret and the boys. Legs of the worn-out overalls were made into little boy's pants or into durable rugs.

If there was to be bread on the table Thora baked it, as well as the cookies, cakes and pies and she did them all marvelously, all without the aid of modern day conveniences we take for granted. Most of her recipes were in her head and few exact measurements were used. She saved and churned cream to make all the butter needed for the table, cooking and baking. She picked wild plums, buffalo berries and chokecherries to make jams, jellies and syrup. A bachelor neighbor, Charles Nelson, would always let her know when the cherries were ripe down on Spring Creek and he would go along to help with the picking so, of course, she would make him a few jars of syrup and jelly. He also enjoyed her home-canned tomatoes.

Doing the laundry was an all-day job. The water had to be carried in, a bucket full at a time from the spring, heated on the stove and poured into tubs. Then it was to scrub all the clothing on a washboard. (A product called Mrs. Stewart's Bluing was used in the rinse water to help keep the white clothes beautifully white.) This was a back breaking job and so very hard on the hands. Just imagine what it was like to wash sheets and blankets by hand and to wring them out. I remember Thora once telling of how sore and cracked her hands would get from all that homemade lye soap and the scrubbing action, plus wringing out all those heavy work pants.

Of course, washing the clothes was just the first step. Then came the drying of them; usually they were hung on lines out of doors, until it became so cold that they froze instead of drying. When that time of year came, lines were strung up indoors, which was not always easy in that small homestead shack.

After the washing and drying came the inevitable ironing. Thora set up her ironing board next to the cook stove where the sad irons would be heated. That might not be an unwelcome place to be in the winter months, but in the heat of summer it was miserable. It was necessary to have, at least, two of the heavy cast-iron irons so one could be heating as the other was in use. Thora's irons were the kind that allowed a wooden handle to be attached or removed. The advantage of the removable handle was that the wooden part did not get hot while the base was being heated. It was most important to be able to judge just how hot the iron was lest she have the misfortune of scorching something. Shirts and dresses worn "for good" were starched. The starch burned quickly and it also had a tendency to want to stick to the iron. A piece of course, rough fabric was usually kept nearby.

The iron was run over this to help remove any starch that may have stuck to it. It also helped to judge the heat of the iron.

The wash water was never wasted. Its next use was to scrub the floor, the front steps, and the outhouse. Oh, those necessities of the prairie! (And the Badlands!) Depending upon the season they tended to be either too hot or too cold; and they usually did not smell the best either. Even as smelly and fly-infested as they often were in the warmer months, the winter months were the worst. Because of the fly problem, they were usually placed a good distance from the house. Now one had to "bundle up" and make a dash out through the wind and snow only to face that very cold bench to sit on. That also brings up the topic of bathroom tissue – there was none. The Montgomery Ward and Sears catalogs were about the best there was available.

I don't know what year it was, but the spring near the shack dried up and, as was often the case in those days of one-room shacks, the house was moved further north. Where the shack stood originally is only a few yards southeast from where our house stands today.

In choosing their land the homesteader had to make sure there was water available. They were dependant upon the spring-fed creeks for their sheep and cattle. In those early days there were many more springs than there are now. Most have dried up causing the ranchers of today to have to drill wells and sometimes to pipe the water great distances.

Besides farming, and all that entailed, as if that wasn't enough, Melvin also had other things to do such as bringing in a supply of coal to heat the poorly insulated shack during the winter months. Coal was blasted out and hauled from mines found in the local hillsides. Allyn remembers using a team and wagon to haul coal. Over the years they hauled from several different mines. The closest one was ten miles away, south of the homestead, through some very rugged country. Using a team and wagon, many trips had to be made to be sure there would be enough coal for all winter and at least well into the spring when one could get to the mine again.

Remember, those stoves had to be fueled even on the hottest days of summer for baking, cooking meals and to do all the canning! Wood was usually the fuel of choice during the summer months. The usual wood was dead, badland cedar gathered from the surrounding buttes – another long arduous job!

At some point during the winter the Skybergs went to Charles Nelson's dam where they cut their supply of ice to be used for refrigeration. Melvin dug a cave into a hill and built a low roof over it. This was covered with dirt. The blocks of ice were stacked in this and sawdust was packed between each block. What a treat it was when some of the ice was crushed, in a gunny sack, and used to make ice cream.

Farm equipment on that early-day homestead was sparse. The earliest implement Melvin used for breaking sod was a horse-drawn walking plow. That had to have been a long and exhausting process both for the horses and for Melvin. It is doubtful that the soil gave in easily to being torn apart for the first time.

The binder was used to cut the grain and tie it into bundles. Next the bundles were "shocked". Shocking was a method of standing each bundle on its cut end, in groups of seven or eight bundles each. At least, that is the number Melvin preferred to use. When the stationary threshing machine was brought to the ranch, the bundles were loaded on hay racks and hauled to the machine. This machine was often called a 'separator' as that is technically what it did. It separated the grain from the straw. Melvin threshed wheat and a few oats.

Allyn recalls his Dad saying that the best crop he ever had was in 1927. They made two trips a week for a month to haul it to the elevators. To make the trip to either Frazer or Oswego would take two days going in. There were ferries at both towns so it would depend upon river conditions as to which place they went. There were three elevators in Frazer and two in Oswego. On the trip into town they quite often stopped for the night at

Leo McNabb's place. Coming home was a one-day trip, with the horses trotting right along.

When the last trip was made that year Melvin bought a new Chevrolet 4-door car and a wagon load of groceries. As Allyn recalled, the price of the car was a bit over $800.00. The groceries would have consisted of sugar, flour, coffee and any other items they couldn't provide for themselves – enough to last until there was grain to sell again next year. There were, quite possibly, also crates of dried peaches and apples as those were available the year around and were certainly a welcome addition to the daily fare.

Kris had gone to town with his Dad on that trip. He gave an account of the car and how it got to the ranch. The car was purchased from Lein Motor Sales, in Frazer.

When the supplies had been purchased and loaded, Melvin took the team and wagon to the river and put them on the ferry, leaving Kris to take it on home. Melvin had never driven a vehicle before so he returned to the dealership as Martin Lein had agreed to give him driving lessons.

Because of the late start from town, Kris had to camp out for the night. He recalled leading the horses for water and staking them out to graze; then spending the night alone with only the horses for company. The next day he and his Dad arrived back at the ranch at nearly the same time. He was so very proud of having been given the responsibility of driving that team, and wagon load of supplies, all by himself, at only ten and a half years of age.

In about 1929, 200 head of sheep became the livestock on the ranch. Over the next years the sheep built up to a flock of about 1200. Of course, there were a few milk cows, four work horses and a few chickens. Up until the coming of the sheep the only income was derived from grain.

Shearing was a back-breaking job, mostly done by a crew made up of area ranchers working to supplement their meager incomes. Kristian and Melvin Jr., when they were old enough, did the shearing for a couple of years. The bags were large and, when fully and properly packed and sewn shut, they weighed about 300 pounds. The team to haul that load was made up of three horses abreast. A bag of oats was also included to feed the horses on the trip to town. The wool was hauled to Circle, a distance of about 45 miles which meant it was a three-day trip – two over and one back. On the way to town their usual stopping place was at the Spillum ranch. *(In here I intend to tell more about trailing sheep to Circle to sell)*

There were a few years when prairie dogs moved in. They eventually took over an area of the ranch about eighty acres in size. Although many of them were shot it was impossible to control them. Then badgers found the town and cleared out the entire thing in one year. The next year Allyn planted that field to corn. However, it was a poor crop. No ears ever formed. Although it was a scant crop it did make good fodder for winter feed.

In those early homesteading days Melvin also tried to find blue-joint hay to cut for winter feed. A good rain would run off those slick, steep buttes and the grass at the bottom made good hay; it just meant moving around from place to place to find it.

Thinking of those slick, steep buttes brings to mind the type of soil covering much of the area – gumbo. Just what is gumbo? Well, it certainly is not the soup or stew made with okra. Gumbo is a clay soil that, when wet, becomes both slick and sticky. That doesn't seem possible but if you have ever encountered it you will immediately understand. It can be so slick you can hardly stand up on it and at the same time it will cling to your feet till you can no longer pick them up. Then just try to scrape it off. It is nearly impossible! It will build up in the wheel wells of vehicles till the wheels can no longer turn. Dealing with wet gumbo is an experience one does not soon forget and the Skybergs had their share of incidents to recall. It is great that the lapse of time can make such misfortunes funny in the telling. It certainly wasn't funny when it happened!

With all the heavy, exhausting work there had to be times for relaxation and recouping of ones strength and determination to continue on. The school houses in each area became the community centers. The main entertainment was the many dances held in these schools. It seems that almost every neighborhood had someone who could play a violin, an accordion or maybe a mouth organ. Those events were always well attended, with a lunch served to round out the evening, and of course, the ladies provided the best they could afford. When the children grew tired they were put down to sleep, on coats or blankets, along the walls and the dancing and socializing continued.

Those occasions were especially important to the women. This was likely one of the few times for them to socialize. The men, though it was in the line of work, had more opportunities as they hauled grain or wool to town and stayed overnight with families along the way. They also shared work with neighbors and would, in that way also, hear what was happening in the communities beyond their usual neighborhood.

The schools provided their share of socializing also as the parents were invited to the Christmas programs and "last-day-of-school" picnics, among other things.

A point of interest concerning those schools of the early 1900s was that each family was required to furnish a share of the coal needed for heat and they took turns supplying the drinking water.

The Skyberg children attended several schools in those early days. When Kristian and Melvin were old enough they started school in the South Rock Creek School. This school was south of the ranch and they stayed with the Hoskin family during the term. From the fall of 1924 through the spring of 1928 they attended the North Rock Creek School. In the fall of 1928, Thora and the children lived in a small house near Patton Hill, so the children could attend Illmont School. This was the year Margaret started school. They were there only the one year. After that they attended the North Rock Creek School again. That is where Allyn went for his first five years of schooling; then two years in Frazer, followed by four years in Nashua and then back to Frazer. Frazer is where Allyn would have graduated but with both Kristian and Melvin gone from home, during WWII, he was needed at home. Although he had planned to finish school by correspondence, that became impossible.

Thora and the children set up housekeeping in both Nashua and Frazer during the years of schooling in those towns.

It was in November of 1928, while Thora and the children were at Patton Hill, that the Skyberg family lost their home to fire. Melvin, and a man by the name of Vincent Strecker, who had stopped for the night, were asleep when the fire started. Melvin was severely burned about the face, neck, arms, hands and feet. He lost part of his right ear due to the burns he received that night. Many times, as he answered some inquisitive questions asked about his strange ear, he told the story and remarked on how fortunate they were to have gotten out at all.

The battery for that new car had been brought in that evening to run the radio, so it was lost in the fire. Vincent rode his horse to Charles Nelson's place and carried a battery back so the car could be used. Allyn doesn't remember where the two men went from there. However, they surely must have gone to one of the neighbors for Melvin's burns to be treated. With the house gone, Melvin moved into the root cellar.

Sometime after the fire the family moved into a stone house which was on the homestead of Harold Crosby. Melvin purchased the land for taxes, paying a total of $848.71 for 321 acres, on June 29, 1929. The house was located where the present ranch house now stands. It wasn't until 1941 that work began on a new home. The stone house was torn down and the stones used for the foundation of the new dwelling, which was built mostly of railroad ties. Most of the flooring, studding, and Celotex came from a McCone City school. Dalton Brown and Melvin bought the school and shared the material. It was several years before the house was finished but it must have seemed like a mansion after the previous houses they had lived in, especially as it eventually had electricity and running water put in also.

I have a secretary-treasurer's notebook for "The Farmers Educational and Co-operative Union of America". Melvin was the last secretary before the group disbanded in 1936. The minutes are for 1932 – 1936. In 1932 there were 42 members with addresses at Frazer and Bonin.

In December of 1932 they were greatly concerned over the 'Holiday Movement'. This was a movement to withhold farm products from the market, in essence creating a farmer's strike. They used such slogans as "Stay at Home-Buy Nothing-Sell Nothing" and "Lets call a Farmer's Holiday, a Holiday let's hold. We'll eat our wheat and ham and eggs, and let them eat their gold." This movement had mostly gone by the wayside by 1934. There was no indication that the farmers and ranchers of McCone County ever participated.

In the minutes dated March 3, 1934 note is made of the election of officers. I quote, "This election was carried on giving the delinquent members the same privilege to vote and hold office as the dues paying members on account of hard times". Those years of the depression were most certainly hard times for everyone.

Later in 1934 they were searching for information on where they could buy winter feed for their livestock. They were also contacting the Grazing Board, in Jordan, about getting dams built.

I feel that, possibly even more important than anything they ever accomplished as an organization, it was an organized time for the homesteaders to simply get together. It was a time to discuss problems and to support each other.

The great thing about this group is that the wives were also members. This was not a men-only organization. This gave the women an outing and a voice in what went on. Almost every meeting ended with a dance and supper. The disbursements for one meeting noted: coffee and milk, $.60; Stationary, $.30; Music (Hoskin, Tew and Lucky) $3.85. The income to pay the musicians appears to have been a .25 ticket for the dance. Even that must have been hard to come by during those dark days.

We have the Avon lady who comes to the door selling her wares. Well, the homesteaders looked for the Raleigh man. He came by horse and wagon about twice a year. The one who made the rounds in the area of the Skyberg ranch had built a box-like house on his wagon. This allowed him not only a place for his wares but also a place to sleep and protection from the weather. Thora bought her seasonings and spices from him. These fellows had a knack for timing their appearances about meal time. One could wonder whether they hid out just over the hill until the appropriate time!

When Melvin and Thora arrived at their homestead they got their mail at Bonin. It was approximately an eight mile round trip, on horseback, to fetch it. The Bonin post office opened the same year Melvin came to Dawson County to file for his homestead, 1917. It closed in 1933. Depending upon the season of the year, the mail either crossed the river from Frazer by row boat or on the ice. The rowboat came into use for those who had vehicles; otherwise they simply rode their horse across. Some of those early-day mail carriers were Bill Kirkland Sr., Oscar Gribble, Louis Loges, Fay Davis, George DeLeary, King Walton, John Walton, and Zacharie Bennet. John Rorvik is the current mail carrier.

The early route was from Frazer, across the river, down Spring Creek, across Sand Arroyo, to the Maurice Tew place (where the post office was after the one at Bonin burned) to Ed Nelson's, on to Dave Brown's and back to the river and to Frazer. This was a route encompassing approximately 50 miles. When John Walton rode the route in winter he fashioned a toboggan on a pair of skis to haul packages, and larger quantities of mail and supplies.

The mailman carried more than the mail in those days. He often delivered medicine and groceries and at times, a passenger. The homesteaders could order almost anything they could possibly need from the catalogs, so he might be faced with hauling a large crate of dried fruit, which was not only awkward but also heavy. I once heard of one thing that none of the mailmen wanted to deliver. Baby chicks! They were not only fragile but very smelly!

The following incident happened many years after the actual home-steading days but it is an example of the way things were and the things those early-day mailmen encountered.

If it had not been for lemons left in the mailbox, Charles Nelson would not have been found as soon as he was after his accident. He had asked Zack Bennet to bring him out some lemons, which he did. When Zack came two days later and found them still in the mailbox he knew something wasn't right. The neighbors were notified and a search was begun. Charles was found the following morning, by Lyle Nelson, when he flew the area. Charles never totally recovered from that accident with his horse.

Thinking of Zack Bennet, there is a story told on him we have all enjoyed over the years. It seems he was invited to have dinner with the Skybergs. Zack was a man of short stature so when he wanted a second helping he simply stood up and reached, sometimes clear across the table. Once, when this happened, he apparently notices some looks and snickers around the table. His response was, "It's alright, just as long as you keep one foot of the floor".

I noted previously that sheep came to the Skyberg ranch in 1929. During lambing season Melvin Sr. was usually the one to stay with the ewes, using the sheep wagon for his home. About every ten days, or so, the new lambs would be docked and castrated. During that time, someone would take the remainder of the band out for grazing. At night they would be corralled.

Allyn recalls an experience he would just as soon forget. The previous day the threshing of the grain had finally finished. That evening, after supper, he had shoveled off the load of grain from the truck. He got to bed late and extremely tired. The next morning found him out herding those sheep. It was usual for the sheep to graze most of the forenoon and then to bed down around noon. Allyn took that opportunity to get some rest. In his words he said, "I was sleeping on my belly with my chin resting on my hands. When I woke up there was that rattler, looking me right in the eye. I guess I moved faster than he did."

One can never quite get used to those creatures. You never know where they will be; perhaps under a tomato plant, or in the strawberry bed, in the hay, or sunning themselves on your doorstep. They are a part of life in the badlands. None of the family was ever bitten by one; however, the dog and occasionally livestock were not so fortunate. It is very painful as several neighbors learned firstxhand. Dalton Brown was bit while picking tomatoes and Donnie Ferguson was bitten when he slid off a straw stack onto one. It is not a good experience.

As I think back on the homesteading years and what it has meant to, not only to our country at large, but to generations of families who came looking for a better life; I can't help but think of what brought them. It was the advertising of all the free land. This advertising that was, more often than not, greatly glorified and often just plain false. One promotion I read stated that the settlers were drawn to Montana by, "The liberal provisions of the homestead law, under which the government seeks to give its citizens an opportunity to make it productive". Merely the time and labor-how simple it sounds. Little did the homesteaders know just what this 'free land' would cost to them.

When one reflects on what went into surviving on their 'free land' it was really quite costly. For most, there was first the emotional price of leaving family and friends behind. Then there was the price of building a dwelling and putting up fences; purchasing a team of horses, a wagon, and the equipment necessary for breaking the soil; buying the seed for planting, harvesting and hauling the grain to market over many miles of rough trails. There were the day to day things like food for the table and the clothes on their back. They would have to with the lack of medical help. They soon learned that they were on their own to deal with all things, even death. Where did they bury a loved one when they were so far from anywhere? Some were able to send the body back to their original homes but many were buried on the homesteads and left there when the family moved on. In some cases if the death occurred in the winter months. The body was kept until spring and then taken to Frazer, Circle or Wolf Point for burial.

As I think on the homesteading years and what it has meant to, not only our country at large but to generations of families who came looking for a better way of life; I can't help but think of what brought them. It was the advertising of all that free land. Advertising, that was more often than not, greatly glorified and often just plain false. One promotion I read stated that the settlers were drawn to Montana by, "The liberal provisions of the homestead law, under which the government seeks to give to its citizens an opportunity to secure a home at the expenditure of merely the time and labor necessary to make it productive". Merely the time and labor-how simple it all sounds. Little did the homesteaders know just how much this 'free land' would cost them.!

Though there were many who lost their homesteads due to loss of funds, drought, or stamina there were many who simply gave up! They had come having no idea what homesteading would demand of then financially, physically or emotionally; and it demanded a lot. It is amazing that there were so many who survived the homesteading experience. Melvin and Thora Skyberg were two of those who survived. Thanks Be To God!

Memories of My Parents, Orval and Fay Evenson

By Karen Evenson Bender

Dad and Mom were married in Beach North Dakota on June 28th, 1936. It was shortly after they arrived home from a honeymoon to the Yellowstone Park that Dad got his card to work on the Fort Peck Dam. On July 18th he started working for the spillway builders, making 50 cents an hour. His first shift started at three o'clock in the morning. His favorite shift was from afternoon till midnight because that was the coolest part of the day. He said that when it was real hot all you could smell was tar.

When he first started working, they had the biggest share of the cut out of the spillway done and they had quite a lot of the floor laid. He said that when they laid the cement, they laid the forms in checkerboard design. After that set up, they came back and laid the spaces in between. His first job was working at the bottom end of the spillway floor. They were blasting and moving dirt in preparation for laying the last of the floor. Later he went on to do other jobs. If things got slow they would be lent to another foreman. Dad said that one foreman wore suntan shirts and trousers, white buckskin gloves, a helmet like hat and wore both Rouge and lipstick!

When my folks first moved to Park Grove they lived with mother's sister and her husband (Ruby and Paul Barringer) for a few days until they found a small homemade trailer house in Midway. They paid $60 dollars for it. It was 8x12 foot on the outside. On July 29th, they found a guy to move it to Park Grove. Mother said he worked really hard for the $4 he charged them. Dad worked until the end of November when he was laid off. In December, he hooked the trailer behind their 1929 Plymouth car and they went to Beach, North Dakota for the winter. While there, Dad and mothers brother Ray worked on W.P.A., which was a national work relief program initiated by during President Roosevelt's administration.

Mother spent most of her time with her mother, Lavina, who was sick. She would go back and forth to their trailer to keep the fire going. Her brother had the screen door covered with building paper and one time when she opened the door the wind caught it and yanked her off the porch. She didn't feel good the rest of the day and the next night my oldest sister Dorothy was born. She arrived three weeks early.

Shortly after Dorothy was born they returned to Park Grove and Dad went back to work on the dam. One day when they came home from Glasgow, they found a sheriff sign on their door. It said they had not paid their rent all winter. Off they went with their receipts to show the sheriff. They showed him that they had paid their rent till they had gone to Beach, and again since they had been back. Mother said that he sure was mad. The sheriff had told him that the woman they had paid the rent to, had given him a long list of names of people that she said had not paid their rent all winter. They were the seventh ones to bring in their receipts. She said that taught them a good lesson to always save your receipts.

Later they bought another trailer for $9 and joined to the first one. The next spring they were notified that the west end of Park Grove, where they lived, was going to be dredged out and they would have to move. They found a nice two room house in New Deal which they bought for $20. They moved the first trailer house to New Deal and joined it to the house. The government gave them $9 for the other trailer house.

My oldest brother, Orwin was born in this house September 21, 1938. The next day the dam slid, and eight men lost their lives, with six still buried somewhere in the dam. Dad had been working from midnight till eight a.m. When he came home that morning, he was all excited and told mother that they were keeping too much water in the core pool. He went to bed and at 1:15 p.m. the slide happened. Mother was lying in bed facing the door, which was open, when a man came yelling. "The dam's going out, the dam's going out". She said he still had his tools in his hands, and had run all the way from the dam to New Deal. A man and a woman that she did not know came and parked a wooden camp trailer outside their door. They told mother that they had heard that there was a woman in that house who had just had a baby and they were going to be there for them in case the dam went out and they had to get to higher ground. They had a farm north of Nashua and a home about a block from the folks. They were the Bill Broast family, later dad and mother went to visit them at their farm.

When I asked dad about the slide, this is what he had to say, "I was working on the graveyard shift and I was working right in the place where it went out. At that time we had a pump boat that was broke down. We had two pump boats in the core pool right in the middle of the dam. That's where the water drains when they are bringing in the dirt. It drains down into the core pool in the middle and then it is pumped out. One of those pump boats broke down and the big shots were keeping everybody up there, afraid the water was going over when they were dredging, instead of shutting down a couple of the dredges for a while, or at least one. When I was there, there were seven crews there with shovels, laying up an edge. It was building up just like an eggshell. You could expect it to go out. Then they even got a dozer up there to help, because the men couldn't pile dirt fast enough. The water should have been pumped out. It was no accident that it went out. It was just foolishness on the part of those big shots. They wanted to do everything to fast. It was just the Lord that took care of us, I could have gone. We all could have been drowned!"

When I asked him if they called everyone back to help, he said. "Yes, we went back and it was to get down there and dig around in the mud and poke around. There were a lot of deep holes in the place where the water left. We were out there poking around and hanging pumps. It stunk to high heaven. You were expecting to find men, you know, in that cut. Well, that one general foreman, Red something, I've forgotten what his name was, anyway he used to drive a red Dodge pickup, he was there and he went out and he drowned. They sent boats out to hunt for some of those men that drowned. Some got buried right over the edge, and some got carried out further".

On the night of June 24th, 1939, Orval Evenson fell from a traveling gantry on a trestle and broke his leg. My sister Dorothy found the following records:

According to "SAFETY MEMORANDUM NO. 33" published July 6, 1939

On June 24, 1939, Orval Evenson, laborer, sustained a simple fracture to his leg, when he fell from a traveling gantry on a trestle, landing approximately 15 feet below among some quarry stone.

CAUSE; defective agencies
SUPERVISION; H. H. Harries, Assoc. Superintendent, Walter Roark, General Foreman, Frank Annalora, Foreman

When I asked Dad about his accident, where he fell from high in the sky and broke his leg. He said, "I was on the Missouri cross over. That was where they could raise the pipes high up in the air because they had to go under them with those big cranes. They would have to lay the doggone crane down and back through underneath it. We were laying these, it was after the slide, and we were raising these pipes with flanges on them. It was around midnight in the dark and in the rain. I was working on this and I had lifted up several pipes and set them across and I got this one just about up, so had the other guy, and all of a sudden mine sheared a key. I was standing up lifting, straddling a pipe on the track, and lifted right up underneath there. That wheel that I turned weighed more than I did. I was standing on an angle iron frame turning it. All of a sudden that wheel sheered and that shaft spun right in the wheel and all of a sudden, I went backward and down". At this time Dad was working just west of where the dam went out.

Dad went on to say, "When I got hurt, they promised me a job. Three of them came around my bed in the morning, saying that they would see that I got back to working, even if they had to hide me out some of the time. They would see that I had a job all winter. I went through that hardship of trying to work, and during the hot weather with the cast that went from the heal of my foot up to my crotch. It was bad enough wearing that doggone cast let alone traveling to and from work besides staying down there. I don't know how I managed to do it."

I remember mother saying that there was always constant nose from the dredges. She said that one fall when the leaves fell off of the trees, they found they had neighbors living in the trees right behind them. They had no idea when they had moved in.

In March of 1940 Dad and Mother traded their Plymouth Coup for a 1933 Chevrolet Coach, they got $67 trade in on their Plymouth and paid $189 difference. On March 22, 1940 the man that owned New Deal, Charlie Whisennand, asked Dad to farm his land. They rented the land on shares. They moved into a house across from where Ivan and Helen Miller lived.

Dad talked about how difficult it was to make the move up there. It was a Sunday when they started moving and they went as far as the Galpin Church, and when they made the corner they got stuck. He said they went up on the bank and got some long grass to pack in the tracks so they could get out. The next load they went around by Park Grove and I asked Dad if he went by the Ivan Miller place. "Yah, C. M. Peterson lived up there then. We went up with one load, unloaded it, and went for a second load. I got just pretty near to breaking over the top of the hill and the motor quit. It wasn't getting near enough gas enough. So, shoot, I had to walk over to C.M.'s and get some wire and patch the up that fuel pump cause it had slack in there. By the time we got up there it was starting to get dark and here I had two sows that were going to have pigs in a little bit. All I had was just a roof piled with straw for shade, is about all it was. But, anyway I found some gates, and some lumber, and tacked it all together. I started carrying old rotten hay and piling it around there so I would have shelter for the pigs. During the night it snowed and I was going out there to check on those pigs. The next morning it just shows the top of the tire on the back of the truck. It snowed that much! I had seventeen pigs during the night. I sure hit it right and all by the time it got daylight. I left them out there, it was't very cold. It was all the fresh snow come and covered up all the straw and stuff, so it made it nice in there. The worst place was where I went in and out with the kind of a door I made and working with a lantern light. I rigged up a post and hung a lantern; shut the door and put a prop on it. Then by the afternoon I stepped in that deep snow and the water would go over my four-buckles, it was melting that fast."

Dad said that first year they had a hard time putting in the crop, it stayed wet for so long but they ended up with a beautiful crop. The truck was he was using had a flatbed on it, so he had to build side boards so he could bring in the wheat. He said, "I brought the truck over toward the house after I painted the side boards. I put them on and got them all ready for harvest. I threw the grain scoops in and got ready to go. The air got funny and it was just sultry and hot. Then all of a sudden we thought it was going to rain.

We was worried that about it was going to lodge the grain, cause it would rain so hard, instead of that it come hail. We had vines growing along the south side of the house, on wire, and they went up and curled around the chimney. When the hailstorm was over you couldn't see a sign of the vines any place. It was all beat up; and I had six inches of hail in the truck. That was the first time I even thought about going and looking in it. That was the first year. It wasn't much of a beginning and here we had nice crop and the hail took the whole smear."

On February 2, 1942 I was born in the New Deal home. All of us were born at home except for Dorothy who was born in a maternity home. My sister Janice was born July 7, 1944, in this same home. When she was 9 months old my folks bought the Biddle farm from Albert Lizicar for $1200. When they were cleaning it to get ready to move in, our new neighbor Art Blue, who lived just across the road, came over and told us that President Roosevelt had died.

My younger brother Kenneth was born in this home on April 20, 1946 and the next spring on March 31, 1947, our youngest sister Eileen was born there also. Mother said it was fun having two babies 11 months apart. She always wanted twins and this was as close as she got.

The fall of 1946 Dad started driving the school bus for the Newton School District. The first bus was a panel, with two long bench seats that Dad built in, going the length of the bus. Later they bought a 30 passenger, yellow school bus. He drove the bus for 18 years. He quit when the youngest member of the family, Eileen graduated from Glasgow High School. Because we were a family of eight and didn't fit in a car, the buses were our everyday ride. We went everywhere in them!

1948 was a year of big change. Us older ones remember it quite vividly, as that was the year the farm was hooked up to electricity. Dad ordered a how to book on electricity from the Sears and Roebuck catalog. He studied that until he was sure he knew how to hook the house, barn and shop to the electricity.

When I asked my older brother, Orwin, what he remembered about it, he said, "Dad studied that book until he could sit down and figure out how much wire he needed to right down to the foot. He and mother ordered everything for our house, for Art Blue, Art and Margaret Boyum and the John Yager family. He would sit down with each of them and they would figure out what lights they wanted for each room, how many outlets they wanted and it was all ordered from the catalog.

When we got down to Yagers, Bud was helping. Dad had brought two long bits. Bud was down stairs drilling and he was supposed to drill thru the ceiling with the large drill and then take the small drill thru the floor above so they would know where to take up the floor board. Well, instead he drilled all the way thru with the large bit. When this happened he went up into where they stored the sugar. The sugar started pouring down the large hole into the living room!

My brother Ken remembers Dad later hooking Kennon Stapp's place up to electricity. The Stapp's place was east of Yagers. My brother said they cut down a tall straight tree to use for an electrical pole for his place.

Orwin remembered another time when a guy (from the electric company) got electrocuted over at Art Blues, which was across the road from us. Dad said, "Go over and tell those guys that there's some juice running around that pole". He had gotten shocked earlier, well the only way you could get shocked on the ground was because it was so cotton picking dry, there was no moisture and there was something goofy going on up there, otherwise it would have shorted out and popped a fuse and they would have known the pole hadn't grounded. Anyway, I went over, there were two of them in this pretty new truck. I said, "Daddy said to look out when you go up there because there is juice running around that pole. He got shocked on that wire". The guy said, okay, "I'll bring you down a bucket full of juice". He goes up that sucker and he just got up there and grabbed something and all of a sudden there is this terrible gut quivering noise come out of him. The other guy run up the pole (without climbers) and he got about half way up when the other guy falls backward right on the fence. The other guy pulled him over on the ground and set him against the tire. The guy was talking but his words were real shaky. The other guy called an ambulance and said it was on the way. This guy lived for several months but he was all burnt up inside. He just got worse and worse and finally died. You don't ever forget a thing like that when you are a little kid!

March of 1951 was another time that sticks in my mind. It was Friday, and I was in the fourth grade. A blizzard came up in the afternoon but I do not think any of us realized how bad it was until Walter Newton walked through the door looking like a snowman. He had ice and snow hanging off his face and clothes. He had hooked up their pickup behind the tractor, and pulled it with Francis steering it all the way to the school. They had high boards on the pickup with tarps over the top. They put us all in the back and went back the same way that they had come. They scattered us between Schroeders, their place, and Grandma Newtons. Our teacher, Mrs. Sheffer, had written a note on the blackboard in case anyone comes looking for us. She also left the lights on in hopes anyone might get lost or stuck would see the lights and find their way to shelter. A group of men did find their way to the school and stayed overnight. They were Sheriff Richter, Highway Patrolman Hugh Borton of Glasgow, Pete Lehman of Malta and Border Patrolman Neil Bowen. They were in radio contact with Glasgow and got the message out on the radio station so word went out and at least some of the parents heard where we were and that we were okay. We had no telephones back then.

In the meantime Dad was out with the bus trying to get to the school. He could not see through the windshield so he had to stick his head out the window and try to see that way. It was impossible to for him to keep on going so he finally had to turn around and almost did not make it back home. It was a good thing Art Boyum had walked up to our farm to find out where his daughter was. He was there to help mother get Dad into the house. They opened up the oven door on the old wood and coal stove and sat him there to warm him up. He was probably suffering from hyperthermia and was having trouble breathing. It was Sunday afternoon before he was able to come pick us up.

There was another time when Dad looked at the thermometer in the West window and found it had broken at 53 below zero. Dad said, "If it's colder than that then it's too darn cold to run the bus". But he went out anyway with a blow torch and got the bus running anyway. To this day I cannot understand why he did that, unless he thought the thermometer had broken and it was not until we got to the corner towards Whisennands that the bus was getting real sluggish and then when we turned into Fullertons driveway it stopped altogether. God was watching out for us that day. It was 61 below and we were so thank full when Mr. Fullerton told us kids to go to the house and get warm. He and dad spent quite a while getting the bus running again and we were finally able to make it back home.

Dad's Story

by Lee "Buck" Musgrove

Dad used to tell me these stories and more. And like a story can be better or worse with the translation or telling. When I started writing stuff down it was this last year that dad was alive. Dad had stopped drinking for health reasons. So of course his stories weren't as colorful as when he was on the bottle. Also he was trying to tell the truth which in itself wrecks a good story! So if you will bear with me, here it goes. You will get this story as Dad told it to me.

Dad went to school at Big Four which was a one room school house north of Nashua, Montana. Dad said he had the longest ride to school of all the kids that went there. It was on his dads' second homestead. I'm not sure if the school was on grandpas' land or maybe that's where dad rode from, as they moved the school a mile.

The Big Four School was started by John Musgrove, the Shuckeys, the Dearstead's and Haydon. All Dad knew about Haydon was that he was from Kentucky and didn't stay long in Montana. I'll be bouncing around writing stories about different people and happenings quite a lot so just keep your shirt on and bear with me!!

Uncle Ade came from Illinois and he homesteaded in North Dakota. Grandpaw worked on the railroad and helped Uncle Ade for 2 or 3 years. Grandpaw shoveled snow for the railroad and said the snow would drift over the top of the boxcars and the tracks had to be kept clean so the train could run.

Dads' sisters, had two pigs in North Dakota that they fed them through a trapdoor under the house till they were ready to butcher, and table scraps and whatever they would eat. Uncle Ade was forty miles from town at his place in North Dakota. He had six or seven oxen and one that was gentle enough that Grandpaw Johns' mother could plow the garden with. He used the oxen mostly for plowing. I guess it was a pretty long trip to town with them. If it was cold weather they traveled pretty good but if it was hot weather they had to stop and rest. Later on Uncle Ade got horses and they weren't as strong but they were faster. That's probably where the term "bull low" came from when discussing gears in tractors or pickups! Uncle Ade later moved to Montana where he farmed and ranched near Roundup, Montana.

The name of the coulee that Dad lived in was Dead Lamb Coulee. This was because of a lot of lambs had died there. When Dad was a young man he stayed one year with Uncle Ade. He also threshed up there for two or three years. When Dad was staying there his uncle went someplace, maybe back east. Ade Shrowder had a good dog, but when Ade left the dog took off too. Ade was gone for a month or so and the dog showed up about the same time! I believe the dogs' name was Teddy. Dad used to tell that Teddy had a certain bowl that he ate out of. Ade also had a cat but of course the dog and cat didn't get along. The dog and cat both ate out of the same bowl. Uncle Ade would make them take turns just with voice commands.

Dad worked for John Etchart for two or three years. John had 13 bands of sheep with 4000 to the bunch. There were two or three campsites, one tent and one sheep wagon.

Old Ed Roberts: Ed was a neighbor down on the Missouri and he was a fiddle player. Old Ed would get drunk for about two or three months and had a bad temper. Ed would come over and play rummie cards with Karen. He built a three or four cow barn and he beat his cows to teach them not to leave droppings on the floor. There was always lots of parties at Ed's place. He was a dirty person and his hands were usually shitty from milking cows. One time when he played the song pop goes the weasel he would stick his finger in his mouth and make it go pop at the right time in the song. He would play round and round the mulberry bush the monkey chased the weasel. "Pop goes the weasel". Then he would put his finger in his mouth and make the pop sound. By the end of the night his finger was white as snow! Another time he wanted the rear end checked for oil on his old Model T. It was pretty cold so Alford Barent took the plug out and stuck his finger in the hole to check it. Well his finger got stuck and he was getting pretty cold before they got his finger out!

Dad told me this story and also said that he told it at Bovee's and Edna said she didn't believe it. I guess she leads a more of a sheltered life in Canada. It was reported that Mack Hunter had killed Bill Kirklunds' Dad. This was when Bill Kirklund had sheep and a few cows. Loren used to ride by after the shooting took place, Mack had a place by the Galpin Church.

Zack Bennit: Zacks dad was kind of shiftless and he started making moonshine whiskey, and when they came to this county he would sell it! Dad told me that his mother would sit on the bottle on the stool to protect it. Zacks grandpaw was a doctor in Saint Lewis, Missouri. The reason they came here was they were in a place that was packed and his mother poked a lady to move her with a hat pin and it got infected. This was at the world fair and they figured the woman might die from blood poisoning so the Bennits came west!

Tom Pointer was at Sixth Point when they built the dam and he moved to the place that they are now.

Dad and another kid were riding yearling colts in the corral after dark, I think they had a lantern hanging on a post. The colts didn't have anything on them. Dad got a wood sliver in his arm about a foot long from one of the corral boards. The doc said it would fester out. It finally did but it took about a half a year. Doc Curoy was most famous for castor oil, it was the cure for all!

Dad's Mom and Dad, who originally came from Indiana, raised lots of musk melons on the reservation. They had a good well. They watered just before dark so the cold water wouldn't shock the plants so bad. Johnny French was a neighbor of John Musgrove. John's first place was 8 or 9 miles northeast of his present place. The Federal loan bank finally got the best of Johnny and he lost that place. But after that his luck changed and he improved on his second homestead. Johnny was younger than grandpaw John. Herkits were one of the few homesteaders to keep their original homestead. Johnny French and Myrtle had the three oldest kids in North Dakota: Faye, Albert and Buella. Albert was wild and harum scarum! Dad got the old Model T from Johnny French after it run over Buella F. They didn't want it around after that and it was 1 or 2 years old. Buella married Ted Alley.

Dad was in the Army when the accident happened; Dan French got out before dad. Thinking about the old car Dad had crossed bear creek, he took the fan belt off and made it to the middle and then the motor stopped. Dad had to walk to Zacks place. It was the same year that Castella had those "mex" steers and Johnny McDonald rode for them and a lot of the steers died in a May 24th storm. This Castella guy was mixed up with Lawyers during the bootlegger days and helped put Rawhide Johnson in jail.

Grandpa John Musgrove got wood from Rawhide Johnson. He got planks and 2x4s as he had a sawmill. Sid Vollin lived on the Castella place and dad knew him all his life. Sid was up north for a while and then moved south of the river. Sid had about 50 cows, 10 saddle horses and 20 mares. Rambling Sam had a homestead where Park Grove is now.

The way I hear it is Sid and some men had been gambling or not but Sid had been tormenting this kid. They were at Rambling Sams and the kid had a 22 gun. Sid had been down to the barn and he told the kid to put the gun down and started for him with the pitch fork. The kid shot Sid 13 times. He left after the shooting and went down around Sidney. Sid met and married Gertrude White and he met her in the hospital when he was recuperating. Gertrude was a nurse.

Joe Butch cut wood for the sternwheelers. He was related to Walter Clark. They were crossing the river with some whiskey when the Indians shot two of Joes partners. They burnt the fort on the Missouri down. It was where Trotters lived. It was built up where the bar is now.

Ross (Karl and Ann Musgroves son), was up visiting and we got to talking about Ed Roberts and Dad said that old Ed was a good cook. He was a dirty but a top notched cook. He was quite the boozer and he would get on a drunk and stay that way for 2 or 3 months. Towards the end he got religion and didn't drink for a couple of months getting ready for the hereafter.

Bud Nicol was quite a boxer and father of Dick and Pete. They all liked to scrap some and Jim Arnison hung the name nick on to Dick.

Dads folks came from back east Indiana and Illinois. Her Dad was kind of cranky and he was out at Grandpa Johns gardening with a hoe. Dads mom had a small pet bird that was real gentle and the old guy had a hole in the top of his straw hat. That little bird would land on the hat and try to peck the white hairs on the old guys head. That made the old guy mad and he kept trying to bat the bird out of the sky with his hoe!

One time we were gathering cows at Zacks. Dad, Cris, Tony and me. It was late fall and getting a little chilly. Zack shows up in his big truck and he's purty drunk. He gets out with a half full bottle of whiskey. He offers a drink to all of us guys. Old Cris grabs the bottle and throws it in the brush.

Zack never stopped smiling and grabs another bottle from his truck. Cris tried to grab that one too but Zack jumps at Cris and got him by both hands around his neck choking Cris and rode him to the ground. They finally stopped, and we went out riding looking for cows!!

Zack had a mail route that started in Frazer and in the winter he crossed the Missouri. It took care of the people in the badlands and they got their mail 2 or 3 times a week. Zack only weighed 100 pounds but he could be pretty tough.

Dalton Browns father once said that he would rather see a herd of rattlesnakes come over the hill instead of seeing Zack come riding on a horse!

Plus a little more from Buck...

Zack (Bennet) had a mail route that started in Frazer and crossed the ice on the Missouri. It took care of the people in the bad lands and they got the mail once or twice a week.

He liked cats and one time he rode thirty miles in the winter to get catnip for it when his old cat got sick.

He was good hearted as hell but he could be purty tough and mean, like when his old white and black team. They were inclined to be balky so he would tie them down on the ground and rub tobacco in their eyes, which is darn painful. Just ask my brother Karl. One time when he was fixin his hair in front of the meare, before school so I throwed a small handful of tobacco in his eyes! He slapped me around quite a bit when he finally caught me.

Eric Anderson lost his finger when he reached into the motor of his car. He later found his finger in a glove. Gus was making wine at the place. While buturing hogs they found a frozen bottle of wine. Gus and Eric worked for Chet Glacier.

John Jenson lived across the Masury River and he would row his boat across to visit the folks.

Tommy Johnsons father was Wally Johnson. He was married to Louise Lingle and her daughter was Terry Lynn Swain. Ted Allie married Buella French. John Ohlson from Westby was a friend of Lorens that were in WW2 together. Johnny Lukin rode for Kris Sorensen and he was of spannish descent. Lou and Dorothy Johnson were the parents of Peggy Nickels. Leroy Vossler, who married Pat Musgrove was from Wolf Point.

When dad took me and the other kids to school it was up hill both ways. Of course that is a lie, but dad was lots of fun and never smacked any of us kids around. He slapped Karen one time as she was fooling with the control nobs on a propane stove. That was when we were moving into Kamrud's basement in Frazer. I was going into the 2nd grade.

We went to school in Frazer for three years. Dad stayed at Zack Bennits and he took care of the cows. He would gather Mom and us kids up on the weekends. He would take us kids and mom over south where we lived in Zacks house.

Dad had 160 acres of land on the Masury River mavbe 7 or 8 miles below Fort Peck Dam. Dad made a verbal agreement with Zack Bennit over a couple of bottles of booze. That partnership lasted 9 years or better with no papers signed.

One night after Zack was purty drunk he headed out from the Nashua Bar to his home in Park Grove with his jeep. He tipped it over on its top in the middle of the road on the highway south of Nashua. He couldn't get out from under the jeep and no one came by to help him out. After an hour or so a couple of guys came by and pushed the jeep over and on its wheels to get Zack out. They found him okay and not hurt much. They found out that Zack had got worried he wouldn't get out till morning so he had gotten out his jackknife and had started to get himself out. They found a small hole in the pavement where he was trying dig himself out!

He was kind of tuff and ornery. I heard that when he was young his folks would put him in a Trunk box. I heard that when he would ride bareback, but he could dam near run down antelope.

One day Zack was in visiting in the Nashua Bar. He had some small square bales in the back of his truck. When he came out of the bar, he noticed that the bales were leaning a little too much for the trip out to the ranch. He got up on the load to straighten up the load and fell off on to the street. He hurt his ribs and figured out that maybe he had some broken ribs. He went back into the bar and he got someone to help wrap his ribs with some opened up beer flats so they would be protected. He had someone tie the flats around his ribs with plastic twine.

A few days later he was up in the rafters of a garage walking on them looking for a roll of canvas to fix the cover for his jeep top with. As he was walking from rafter to rafter he slipped and dropped down between the 16 in spaced rafters and his armpits stopped his fall to the floor. Ouch! This happened a few days after he had cracked his ribs falling from the load of hay!

One evening Zack and I were going out to Zacks in dads old pickup. As we were going up the Powerhouse hill, Ol Zack was trying to down shift the pickup and he kept grinding the gears to get it in a lower gear. He looked over at me and said, "I'm just a poor Ol boy just trying to get along."

Bob Jackson at times when he had too much to drink after leaving the Park Grove Bar, would go over to the Trotter house on the Missouri River to stay for the night. The old Trotter house was only a mile or so north of the bar on the property where Jim Kirklund lives now. When Mick and Tony were younger, Bob would come over after drinking and rough up the boys. A couple years later the boys had driven by the bar and had seen that Bob had been drinking there for a while and figured Bob would be over to the house. This time they would be ready for him. They went out and got some stuff from the calving barn and would play a joke on Bob, for pay back from the past experiences with him. After the bar closed, Bob showed up kind of drunk and started messing with them. The Trotter boys were ready and took Bob down and pulled down his pants and gave him an enema! Dad told me this story that the Trotter boys had told him.

When the Boyums lived by the river in the old days. Larry and I was walking to the Missouri River and Larry's younger brother Terry was following us. We didn't want him along and we told him to go back to the house. He wouldn't go back so we started throwing dirt clods at him. Terry finally said OK but I'll tell a pack of lies on you guys! Then we finally let him come along!!

Thanks to Karen, Dorothy, Karen and Buck for sharing their stories with me so I could share them with you. Hope you enjoy reading them as much as I have.

Loren and Bernice Musgrove, holding grandson Ross taken after
the move to Canada, mid 70's.

The Musgrove kids, taken in front of their home in Montana, from left to right, Buck,
Karl, Karen and Pat. This was probably taken in 1962. I own this property now and this
house is still standing.

This picture is Melvin and Thora Skyberg, taken in 1916 near Elbow Lake, Minnesota.

Photo supplied by Dorothy Skyberg.

This is the Melvin and Thora Skyberg homestead in Montana. This type of home was typical for homesteaders and is even more impressive considering the harsh conditions they lived under, including summer heat and winter cold.

Photo supplied by Dorothy Skyberg.

REDNECKS
(and proud of it)

"If you have ever unloaded your pickup by backing really fast and slamming on the brakes, you might be a redneck.
-Jeff Foxworthy

Find something in life that you love doing. If you make a lot of money, that's a bonus, and if you don't, you still won't hate going to work.
-Jeff Foxworthy

You might be a redneck if... the blue book value of your truck goes up and down depending on how much gas it has in it.
-Jeff Foxworthy

"Is it your drinking arm?"
-Buck Musgrove

Montana Redneck Buried Pipeline

In the summer of 2009, we were on the list to get hooked up to get drinking water from Dry Prairie Water via the Saint Marie water treatment plant north of Glasgow. This was formerly the Glasgow Air Force Base water plant. There was need of a good source of water for the base when it was first built, so they put in an intake in the Pickthorn dredge cuts on the Missouri River just below Fort Peck Dam. This intake was built in about 1957 and a water line was built to supply water to the Glasgow Air Force Base. An agreement was made later between The Dry Prairie Rural Water Authority and Montana Aeronautics Company Organization (owned by Boeing Research who bought part of the Air Force Base) to supply good clean water to the city of Glasgow and later to town of Nashua and the area west of the Milk river and south to the Missouri River. This is rather unique in that it would supply water back to the area that is from where it is pumped out of the Missouri River, via a 40 mile pipeline up and back to the area!

For years we had pretty good water from the sand point well about 25 feet under the surface of the ground for the cattle. We also had water from a well had been drilled years ago by Roy Johnson, approximately 70 feet deep, but it seemed to be running dry. The well water was very hard and contained a high amount of iron in it which made it real corrosive. To make this water usable in the house, I needed many gadgets, including a sand filter, an iron filter, a water softener and a water purifying stem. Honestly, the water still was not really drinkable out of the tap, but we did at times. It used to turn the kids' hair orange from all the iron, discolor much of our clothing in the wash and left a skim that looked like an oil slick on any water surface, especially coffee. We hauled water from the public water tap at Fort Peck which was ten miles away for drinking and coffee.

At that time Dry Prairie came to the farm, my well-pump supplied water underground to the house and was still working, it just was not great quality water. This line was buried six foot under the ground to keep from freezing during the winter. This line had two hydrants between the well and the house. One that could supply water to the lawn and the other was by a tank for the cattle that was outside of the corral. I also had a sand point well and pump that supplied water to the calves in the corral and to the calving barn. So during the winter of 2008-09, I was using the cattle-use hydrant on this line and was letting it run a little all the time to keep the tank full and running so I would not need an electric heater to keep the water tank from freezing.

This system may seem a bit screwy, but works fine if you have a bank of lower ground near the tank so the water can flow away from the full tank so it does not build up ice during the winter. This redneck water system works fine if the power does not go off during extremely cold freezing weather for an extended amount of time. Which is exactly what happened that winter. This very thing happened as my hydrant froze up one night and I could not get the hydrant thawed out the next day to get water to flow through it. It was well below zero degrees. I had forgotten at the time what Harold Miller had told me about such a predicament, that the best way to thaw out a frozen hydrant is to pour hot water on it. However, I think the water line froze under the ground somewhere.

Water was still flowing underneath the hydrant to the house, but the hydrants were not usable. I needed to get water for my cows so I ran a garden hose from my one remaining hydrant in the lawn with about 300 foot of garden hose to a water tank. This garden hose I bought and brought in to fill up the tank for the cows. I could keep it running through the hose a little so it would not freeze. The trouble with these Redneck Watering Systems is that sometimes things go awry!!

That watering system worked for the cows until it froze up one extremely cold night, maybe the power went off in the night long enough that this hydrant froze up too! I still had water pressure in the house even though neither of the hydrants worked as they were frozen and would not close. But we still had water for the house at this time. This worked fine until it got to be about May when the frost went out of the ground and I lost pressure in the house. I tested the water pressure in the well and it was putting out four gallons per minute and in to the house I was only getting about one half gallon per minute, which is not enough for household use. I figured out that one or both of the hydrants had busted the water line under the hydrants so the water pressure was pushing water out into the sand. I did not know which line under the hydrant was broken and it is expensive to get a tractor with a back hoe in to dig up the hydrants and repair them, especially when you do not know where the problem is!! I was still planning on getting Dry Prairie Water in the future, so I did not want to repair the line and then have to abandon it soon after.

Later on that spring I put a new pump in for the cattle which was putting out about 4 gallons a minute and I strung out 500 foot of garden hose to the house and in to the water system through the front lawn faucet and into the house. We supplied the house this way all summer and fall through that garden hose from the cattle well.

I knew Christensen crews were in the area laying water pipe for Dry Prairie Rural Water. They were laying pipe nearby and would eventually bring water to my household and to the neighbors. They thought that maybe we could be hooked up to the line and maybe get water going by late fall if everything worked really well. When they dug the line into the house, I was ready with my plumbing and when they put the empty supply water line in close to the house, I connected it up to the underground line going into the house. I had a shut off valve closed off in my basement and I was ready for them to supply us with good water that late fall! Something happened and they did not get the water flowing until the spring because some pressure relief valves did not come in till the next spring. I had to supply water through the above garden hose to the house all winter. Patty made a statement that if the water froze and we did not have running water to the house plumbing system, then maybe she would move in to Glasgow with her Mother for the winter! I am pretty sure she meant it. I laid small square straw bales on top of the garden hose all the way to the cattle pump well, so it was insulated some from the freezing weather that I knew was coming. It looked like a giant snake with the bales curving all the way to the cattle well.

This was my redneck buried pipeline … buried under sixteen inches of straw! I knew that when we got some snow on the straw bales it would be better insulated from our subzero weather that was coming that winter. I ran a garden hose out the back of the house and kept it running continually, some to water the trees during the winter. This would work if the power did not go off long enough to freeze the hose up or if the pump did not burn out. There were two nights that the temperature got down to twenty-nine degrees below zero but it did not stop the water flow to the house. I just got very lucky! If you can keep water flowing fast enough it will not freeze. I was ready for an emergency if the power went off and I had my Dad's generator covered up near the plug in of the pump. If the power went off and if I could get the generator going in time, I could keep water flowing to the house. We always keep a radio going softly by Patty's side of the bed and one night she woke up and said the power is off!! I got my clothes on and rushed out and started the generator, plugged the pump in and kept the line from freezing up. It was only about fifteen degrees, not very cold, so it did not freeze with the straw on it. I feel that if the hose would not have had the layer of small bales on it would have frozen up. I would have had to gone to town and bought about five hundred more feet up good garden hose to get water supplied to the house.

Another time that same winter the power went off during the day and it was about twenty degrees out, but the sun was shining. I could not get the old generator going so I called my friend Boatride, and I went in to get his generator. It had been a little over an hour without power but when I got his generator started and the water flowing, the line had not frozen up. The Big Guy upstairs was watching over us and I really do thank God for getting us through that winter without any major problems. In the spring, water started flowing down the line from Dry Prairie Rural Water Authority and all I had to do was open the valve into the basement and let water flow into the house. I then closed the faucet valve on the side of the house that had water coming into the house for almost a year, water from the cattle well. I then had to pick up the many straw bales and drain and roll up the hose. One thing is that the trees that I watered on the back side of the house did well being watered all winter long!

Well, I must really be proud to be a Redneck, as this last winter I am doing almost the same thing, but I have the water flowing through the garden hose the opposite direction from the hydrant in the lawn and I am sending water to the cattle tank out by the corrals. I was keeping it flowing about one gallon per minute to keep it from freezing. This did freeze up on me one-time last winter. It was about five degrees below zero when this happened. I could not get it unfrozen with a propane heater so I remembered what Harold Miller, a plumber told me. Just pour hot water on it and it will eventually thaw the frozen hydrant line out. I got a small kettle of hot water and poured it on the frozen hydrant and after about 30 seconds the water started flowing again so I could open and close the hydrant handle. I hooked the new dry hose to the hydrant, opened it up and the cows had water again. This time I put hay bales on the garden hose, so I have my redneck buried pipeline working again!

It is so great to have water supplied to the house and to the cows from Dry Prairie so that when the power goes off, we still have water. When the weather warmed up to about forty degrees above, I drained the extra frozen hose and coiled it up and keep it in the basement ready just in case the hose to the cattle tank froze up again. Dang us Redneck types! Next winter I am going to buy another pump for the cattle well.

Actually, the extra cost for the Dry Prairie extra water that I used was about the same if I had used electricity and a stock tank heater. Hopefully I will have the cattle pump working for next year! I am just getting to old to put me through this stress again for another winter! Well, we'll see!!

Living Off of The Land

I am so fortunate that my grandparents and my parents were farmers and they lived off the land. When I started helping out on the farm, I was very young. Going out with Grandma to get the eggs out of the nests was fun. I also remember helping out in the barn as we always had a milk cow and I remember trying to learn how to milk the cow and take care of her feeding and providing good clear water to her. At that time, we had a few hogs and always had chickens for fresh eggs for the table. I remember attempting to milk the cow with my small hands and trying to get the milk into the bucket. It was fun and I would be with Dad or Grandpa at milking time. I spent at a lot of time sitting in the barn with my Daisy Rider BB gun eliminating as many varmints that I could. It was mostly mice that I shot when they were coming into the barn through holes between the logs in the walls. It was this practice that made me a very good shot. Being a good shot with a rifle helped me during hunting season to help put food on the table. My Dad was also a very good shot and showed me how to thin out the gophers, technically called Richardson ground squirrels. These gophers were taking some of our crops and making dirt mounds that are very hard on our machinery. We also had a lot of magpies that needed to be controlled as they would sit on the backs of cows and peck on the brands which would turn into open wounds that would get cancerous!!

My grandparents worked very hard to make a living just like thousands of others like them that did on their farms or ranches. Some were able to stick it out and make a decent living from the fruits of their labors, but it was never easy for them. Some of the pioneers stuck it out long enough to prove up on their homesteads until it was theirs and then sell out to a good neighbor or to a person that offered to pay more than anyone else could. This is how it was out here in the frontier. Some made it and some did not, and those who did not had to move on to somewhere else. It was a hard life out here, especially on the women who had left homes that were better than the homestead shacks that they moved to. They had to do everything with their hands, packing in water, splitting wood, cooking, cleaning, washing clothes, often with rain water from the roof after a rain or from snow melt, as some homesteads did not have wells with water. If my grandmother did not have snow to melt for washing clothes or rainwater that they saved, then she would go over to the Stevens ranch where there was an artesian well. The Stevens ranch was only about two miles away, but worth it for good water for washing. They were always cutting and splitting wood, gathering kindling and cow pies, when necessary, to keep the stove hot for cooking. There were a lot of other chores to do all the while they were raising and watching over the children in the house.

The men were hard working, and hard drinking at times, and some played instruments for entertainment of themselves or others. If they had a well, they had to draw water for the family and livestock. In cold winter weather they would have to chop holes in the ice to allow the livestock to get to water. When it is winter here in eastern Montana, the temperature often gets below zero degrees for many days in a row, and it is necessary to cut, split and gather wood to keep the house as warm as they can. One of the dangers of wood burning heat in the house is to having a chimney pipe fire. Many a homestead was burned down from dirty creosote buildup on the inside of stovepipes from green wood. They need to be cleaned regularly. Not every home had a properly constructed brick chimney. There were a lot of fires in the old days.

I have spent quite some time out walking our fields looking for arrow heads and other artifacts. I have come on to places that were old home-stead sites. As I am looking around these sites, usually there are artifacts or pieces of steel, brass, copper, rock, brick, concrete, glass, crockery and wood. Sometimes, I know who had lived in the area from my Grandparents, parents and historical papers. I know homes or barns have burned down in the past and I have looked at the remains of the structures that are left on the ground after many years of erosion in the soil. Many of these sites have pieces of beautiful plates, cups and pottery. These are usually homes that were destroyed by fire. It must have been heart breaking for these early day pioneers after a devastating fire. There usually was a loss of many family heirlooms and maybe even some injuries and lost lives in these fires. Some of these people had the means and the fortitude to go on and rebuild. Many had good neighbors and relatives that helped them out in this bad situation.

There were some that were too heartbroken to continue on living here so they let the homestead go or sold it to others to finish out the homestead contract. Some of these abandoned homesteads were never taken over by others and ended up being public land, which is now being administered by the Bureau of Land Management, commonly referred to as the BLM. There is a lot of BLM land in this country that was not fit for farming, so was not settled. Mostly though, the homesteaders found a way to continue on to get their land proved up on and to get a homestead patent that was signed by the United States President who served at that time. Most of these determined people, survived by living off the land and working off the farm to help make ends meet.

As I said earlier, most of these homes did not have brick and masonry chimneys, which is the proper and most safe way of constructing a chimney. Most of them had a stove pipe out of a single wall metal chimney pipe. If this pipe was kept clean with regular scrubbing to eliminate the building up of creosote on the inside of the stove pipe, they could be quite safe. Using green wood and certain types of lumber that has a high concentration of creosote in it, can layer the inside of the pipe and cause fires if not cleaned a few times during the year. If the houses had a brick or rock chimney it was much safer. Even if they had a chimney fire, the wood part next to the brick, would not get hot enough to start the house on fire.

Fires were incredibly dangerous and often were caused by a wood burning stove chimney fire. Fire dangers came in many other forms, as well. Sometime in the 20's, Ed Stevens built a large hip roofed barn on the Stevens Ranch. This barn burned down from a lightning strike. On the Billy Moeker place, a large hip roofed barn burned down from storing hay in it that was too green to dry properly in an enclosed structure. Hay that is baled up on the green side and stored outside can get hot and start burning from internal combustion. But when you put hay up that is way too green in a barn you are taking a real good chance of having a fire.

The Stevens Ranch buildings that are left, are along the hill east of highway 117 four miles south of Nashua. These buildings have survived almost 100 years. This hill is called Molly Stevens Hill and it is on an extremely tight curve of the highway, although in the summer of 2017, the curve was changed slightly, to make it less sharp and the road also moved the highway to the west several hundred feet. The turnoff to our place from Highway 117 was right on this corner and was extremely dangerous when vehicles are going both ways on the highway, although with the road construction that has changed somewhat. This property for the highway was bought from the widow of Ed Stevens, whose name was Molly, when a road was needed to reach Fort Peck when the Corps of Engineers were constructing Fort Peck Dam in the early thirties, and her name has remained connected to the hill and the local area.

The remains of the Stevens Ranch buildings are right along the gravel road that leads to the highway and I drive right by them every time I go to Nashua or Fort Peck. The artesian well on that property had a lot of pressure and flowed out of the ground and Ed Stevens piped it to the log house to have running water in the house in those early years. This artesian well is still flowing out of the rusted pipe some and probably is seven hundred feet deep and provides water and habitat for many varieties of animals, creating a bit of a wet lands area along the road. Ed Stevens died of lung complications after the barn fire at a fairly young age. His young wife Molly was not able to keep up the ranch, so she had to sell off portions of the ranch to start a business in Glasgow to help raise her children with. The ranch at one time went south to the Missouri River. That part of the ranch was bought by Armund Ceruless, who also owned the Park Grove Bar, north of Fort Peck.

Even though the Stevens Ranch buildings and thousands of others in this country like them are considered to look junkie by some and are often burned down. I feel that they a part of our history that has been lost when burned or torn down. I feel these old homestead buildings should be left for future generations to see. They should be photographed, documented and the stories saved for our childrens' children to be able to see and appreciate how our ancestors worked and lived, how they opened up this country, to carve a home out of the prairie, how they established a life is this hard country, and how then and now, farmers try to feed their families, the nation and now the world!!

Using Wood for Heat and Cooking

When my grandparents started farming, the used wood for heat, for cooking and for laundry, and my parents did as well, right up to when electricity came to this countryside. After electricity, mostly wood was used for heating purposes, and cooking and washing made use of electricity and modern appliances.

For many years I used a wood stove in my basement all winter to help heat the house which is something that I had in common with my Dad. There is nothing like coming in when you are cold and warming up by the wood stove. The basement is my main entry way of coming into the house and for cleaning up. We store our potatoes, tomatoes and sometimes apples from the garden in the back of the basement away from the stove. We have a bathroom down there and my son Seth still stays down there. He worked for Town and Country Furniture in Glasgow for years but and now helps me on the farm. My daughter is a Registered Nurse who has her Bachelors degree in Nursing and we are really proud of her accomplishments! She lives in Nashua, owns her home and has a dog and two cats and loves her pets, including the two horses she keeps at our farm! Our other son Shawn lives in Glasgow at TLC and works at Milk River Complex and enjoys his independence. Patty and I are so happy to have three great children.

In 1964 I started college at Montana State College in Bozeman, Montana and I was taking an agriculture short course. I liked the mountains and agriculture courses but after two years of classes, I got into the Montana National Guard. I decided that maybe farming would not be so bad !!! so I went back to the small farm and started farming with Dad and my Grandfather, who was almost retired by that time. I loved the outdoors and hunting which is great in eastern Montana and so farming in the Missouri

River bottomland sounded like the thing to do. I am so happy that I made that decision and I love what I am doing and still living off the land.

I learned many of my habits of living off the land from my father, who learned it from his father before him. For years, my Dad ground his own organic wheat to make flower for his pancakes, using the same recipe that my mother perfected while she was living. He had pancake making down pat and they were great. Right up until his death, he raised a pretty good-sized garden with the help of my sister Diane Forbes and her husband Scott, who lived nearby during the summer and helped watching over Dad. Even after he had retired from farm work, he kept very active and had a routine to get his chores done and it gave him something to do each day. He fed and watered his barn cats twice a day. He would open the barn and shop doors so the cats could go out during the day but would close up before dark so the raccoons could not get in.

Up until his last few years, he would cut his own wood with a chain saw and split the wood with an axe so it would fit in his old coal stove that was in the large addition to his farm house. This addition is notable because it has an old REA pole for a ridge beam. The stove was an old coal stove that was converted to burn wood, but it had a pretty small door. He knew the best way to cut his own wood so it will fit in the small door of his old coal/wood stove. For the wood to fit in the door, it had to be of a particular size and after many years of practice, Dad could eye-ball the correct sized logs with ease. For wood for my Dad's place, either I or Scott Forbes, would bring him logs that were about 6 feet long and he would cut them to smaller pieces that will just fit in the stove door so it will keep a fire all night long! He also had Rick and Silver Tihista bring him firewood, mostly ash and cottonwood, especially in the winter of 2010-2011 when we had 108 inches of snow and you could not find or get near any dry wood. They were bringing him wood in trade for using his car trailer the rest of the year.

He took a lot of pride in keeping his chainsaw sharp and used a small round file for this job. Even though his eyesight was failing he could see well enough to keep the chain sharp on my son Seth's chainsaw. He started using this saw as it was smaller than his older saw, and he could handle it better. I used his larger saw as it is too large for him to handle with ease in his later years. Most of us were concerned about his safety around the house, especially with the saw, but he was still very independent and a little stubborn, and part of his life's drive is to keep his house warm, feed the cats in the barns, help keep his garden, and remain living on the farm as independently as he could. With the help of his family, he was able to live in his farmhouse until his death, which was important to him, and to his family.

He was a perfectionist and kept his house organized so he can find things. His tabletop might not have looked very neat, but it was organized for him. His eyesight had been fading each year so it was important that he put things in the same place so he could find them. He was an amazing man that has done a lot for the limited formal education that he had up until the 8th grade. He fixed and repaired radios and old tube type television sets back in the 60's and 70's. He constructed and set up a lot of towers antennas for people in the area pointing to TV Tower Hill to get reception from Valley County Television.

I still burn dry wood that falls from the cottonwood trees here in the river bottom. Most of these large branches are dead from one reason or another and after a heavy wind they fall to the ground. Most of these branches are large and when you cut them up for the stove, you do not have to split them, which is a nice time saver. During the winter when there is snow on the ground, I have to cut down dead trees that fall in the snow and are off of the frozen ground so I can cut to the proper length for the stove. I have a large wood stove in the basement that we keep going most of the winter except for warm spells. I also have a wood stove in my garage that I use some when I need to do some mechanic work on one my vehicles. I also have a Heatilator fire place on the main level of my house. This fire place has a blower on it to move the air around the room. This is only used for emergencies when the power is off for long periods. I cut a lot of wood for myself from the many dead trees we have on our place. All of the branches that fall off of the trees need to be taken care of, so we utilize them by helping to heat our home. I have two chain saws and my son, Seth has one of his own, which he when used for several years for cutting and selling wood to help make ends meet.

We have clean air here and good water and lots of wood available, so we can sustain ourselves here as long as our health holds up, which my Grandfather did into his 80's, my Father did up until the age of 94, and I hope to do for many years yet to come.

Hunting is in my blood

I still continue to live off the land, but perhaps not as much as in the past. I have always been a hunter-gatherer type. I continue to hunt as hunting is a big part of my life every fall. It is in my blood to go out and hunt deer and elk and I can hardly wait for hunting season to start. By the first of May, I have to have my applications in if I want a chance to draw a permit for moose, bighorn sheep or Rocky Mountain goat. The percentages are not very good to draw one of these tags but if you do not put in for them you sure cannot draw one. I lucked out and drew a bighorn sheep tag in 1972 and I got a good ¾ ram that I have a head mount of. My Dad was hunting with me when I shot the ram in the Augusta area. We started dragging the ram back to the truck but we were damaging the cape so I had to cape out the head and bring the rest out by pack boards. I really enjoyed this hunt with my Dad. It was a very beautiful and rugged country and I have never been back to hunt there since then, although I have been trying to get another permit.

As I mentioned earlier in my tales, early in the season on the first hunt for my ram, my good friend, Dan Williamson and I backpacked into the Bob Marshal Wilderness Area and spent about four days and three nights and all we seen were ewes, young rams and beautiful country. We had the tent set up near a small stream, up fairly high. It had been really nice weather with no snow and it looked like bad weather was coming in so we hiked out before it got dark. It was a fun trip. I remember that we carried in a few beers and put them in a small stream by the tent and we were able to have a cold beer a couple of the nights.

After you get a tag for one of "the big three", meaning a Moose, a Big Horn Sheep and a Rocky Mountain Goat, you have to wait seven years before you can apply again for that species. This meat off this bighorn ram was kind of rubbery, because the rut was going on, but it made burger with the addition of some beef tallow. My Moose was a bit like this as well, and Patty swore you could not even make decent burger out of that critter. Ha! It sure is a nice rack, however! I did draw a tag for a Rocky Mountain Goat once, in the fall of 2017, and made two trips west to the Livingston area, but never came home with the prize.

Hoarder or Collector?

I guess I am kind of a hunter and gatherer type, with a redneck view of things. I am kind of a hoarder, as it is tough for me to throw things away! I come by it honestly as my grandparents and parents were that way from going through the Great Depression. They saved everything that a person might need again to use in the future. You know that when you say to yourself, I might need that sometime! How many times have you gone to throw something in the dumpster and you ask yourself, I might need this sometime in the future? It is a struggle to see something in the dumpster that I need for a project and it is too far away to reach! I wonder if Patty will kick me out of the house if I bring home just one more prize?

I believe that we should have a way in our county to recycle aluminum, steel, plastic, copper or whatever for another person to utilize! Recycling in our area of Montana is quite limited, and that is a shame. This is the year 2012 and who knows what is in store for us. We should prepare some way to survive if we lose our services somehow. I am not a doomsday forecaster, but I am an optimist in the sense that we will be survivors if we prepare for the worst and have the means to survive. Who knows what will happen? We do not want to lose our food services and a clean water source available for our use. If that happened could you survive for a lengthy period of time? Think about it! I think the barter system is still a good way to exchange items with other people. The trouble is most of us have debts that takes money to pay to keep from losing collateral if we could not make our payments!! Let us prepare for anything! And by prepare, I guess I save just about everything I can, because I see the potential for it to be used in the future.

The Winter Doldrums and How to Alleviate Them

We are so blessed to live here in Montana where we have plenty of clean air, good people and an abundance of wildlife. Those of us that are native Montanans have had it pretty good all of our lives. Especially, if we love the outdoors like I do. I have been so fortunate to live on a farm that my Grandparents, Marion and Gertrude Garwood, started when they took over a forty acre homestead in 1920. They proved up on their homestead patent on this property, and after this patent was signed by Woodrow Wilson, it was theirs to do what they wanted with it. This small parcel of land wasn't enough land to make a living on so in 1924 they bought a bordering 120 acre parcel from a neighbor, Grace Schick Graff. My grandparents ran a 10 to 15 cow dairy until the 'dirty thirties' got the best of them in 1936 and they quit the Montana farm for a few years. My grandfather was a hunter and trapper and he got me started in pigs, cows, hunting, farming and trapping. When I showed some interest in trapping he bought me some traps when I was about 12 years old. They were some Oneida Victor, one and a half long spring traps that I still have a few left from the first half dozen that he gave me. I don't have the energy to trap as much as I used to but the desire is still there, it's good exercise and it gets me out of the house. I still do a lot of hunting with both bow and a gun. It's work, but I love it and its great for the body.

Maybe most of the people can't get out and recreate as much as us farmers do in the winter, so I apologize to them for that. Those that have to work forty hour a week can only recreate on weekends or on their days off. Most of the winter the days are so short and the nights are long. Then, it seems like on the weekends the weather is bad and you have to stay inside. Maybe it is cold out or the Montana winds are trying to suck the life out of you. If it's a nice day get out there and do something. Grandpa Marion used to have a saying, "Any winter day that the sun shines and the wind doesn't blow, it's a nice day." So people get out there and have some fun and enjoy our great state. Get out there with binoculars, camera, fishing pole or varmint rifle. When I spend a couple of hours walking around in this crusty snow, I know one thing for sure. It's another day that I don't have to go to the gym!!!

My Montana Redneck Buried Pipeline. In might not look like much, but it worked.

NOTABLE MENTIONS

(everything else)

"You must be the change that you want to see in the world."
-Mahatma Gandhi

The Mail Lady

Many of you may think of my wife Patty as The Mail Lady, but I bet many people do not know how our family got started with the postal service. Back in 1972, Edgar Garwood, who was my father, and Arthur Boyum were the trustees for the Rural Route 1, United States Postal Service out of Nashua, Montana. I was substitute driving the mail route for Arnold Turner, who had the mail route contract at that time. The driver that delivered the mail before him was employed by the US Postal service and he was getting Benefits from the postal service for his time. He took over the job of as Postmaster for the Nashua Post Office, leaving no one to drive the mail route south of Nashua.

The postal service knew that they could save a lot of money by changing up the rural delivery system and to let people that qualified be able to bid for the route. Therefore, the lowest bidder would get the mail route delivery for 4 years, with no benefits. A lot of people did not realize that the costs were a lot higher than they thought to meet the requirements of the route, which included maintaining at least two vehicles to drive, gas and general maintenance on those vehicles and to deliver the mail on these rural (and not very good roads) for six days a week.

Arnold Turner had been driving the mail route, but as he got a bit older and his health started to decline, the stress of delivering the mail six days a week, come rain or shine, snow, sleet or hail, started to wear on him. I started part time driving the mail route for Arnold sometime in the early 1970's. I enjoyed driving the rural mail route because it took me through the Milk and Missouri River bottoms as well as into dry land farming and grazing country. At that time, I was young and had some time to drive the mail route when I was not farming.

Arnold was very particular on the service to the patrons including to be accurate and try not to make mistakes and to keep a good time schedule. Arnold passed away suddenly and left me to drive as I was the only other person that knew the route. Since my Dad and Art Boyum were the trustees, it was up to them to figure out how to finish off the contract, which still was for about two more years. Art did not have time to drive it six days a week, so my mother, Toni Garwood, and I decided to drive it. She would drive when I was farming and I would drive during the winter and during rainy spells when I could not farm. We finished off the contract that Arnold had with the postal service. Then I, my mother and Patty signed a two-year contract with the postal service with me as the primary driver. This worked pretty well for me as I just had a few cows at the time and did not farm as much land at that time. Mom and Patty would drive when I was not able. In 1973, I bought 480 acres of the old Piederbecki ranch south of Tiger Butte and I was running thirty-five more cows over there with my grandfather, Marion Garwood. This took a lot more of my time as the fences were bad shape over there and I had to travel twelve miles one way to get cows back in when they got out into farmers grain fields.

Our mail route was only two miles away from my home and corrals, so I could swing into the farm and check on my calving at my home place. One really nice day when I was calving, I checked on the cows while I was driving by on the mail route and a cow was having a calf and it looked like everything was going well. The weather was warm so I finished delivering the mail and I wanted to keep pretty much on schedule for the patrons. When I got home after finishing the route, I went out to the corral to find this large dead bull Simmental calf dead and the mother cow bawling for it. I was artificial inseminating my cows at that time and this was a good potential bull that could have been worth about $600 in the fall, a very good price for the times. If I would have spent the next twenty minutes or so there, I probably could have saved that calf, but I had a schedule to keep! This was when I decided that I needed to spend more time with the cows during calving time.

It was about this time that I talked Patty into quitting her job fixing hair in Glasgow and running the mail route pretty much all the time and I would drive during the winter and rainy spells. The way Patty tells it, I pretty much told her to start driving the route more and she had to quit fixing hair! I do not quite remember how it all transpired, but she did start driving full time and fixing hair only part time.

Sometime, around thirty years ago now I suppose, I was talking to Gordon Reimche, who had farm land next to us and he said that he had just talked to "The Mail Lady", and had gotten his mail. This term for her has pretty much stuck! She has really been a trooper all these years, carrying the mail, day after day, in some terrible weather conditions, like John and Donna Rorvik, very good friends of our who also drove rural mail routes for many years.

The winter of 2010-2011 started out early in October and we had about six inches of snow and we had more by the end of October. It seemed like it just kept coming and Patty kept hauling the mail. The roads were terrible and the worst part was the wind and grey skies which meant you could not even see where the roads were. By February, we were approaching our "all time" snowfall record. Most mornings I would start the tractor to plow out Seth and Patty so they could get to work. I think there was only two days when Patty did not run the route. There were sections of impassible road where she would have to turn around and go back. We were having a hard time even getting out of our lane road and to the county road and then it was not plowed out. The postmaster in Nashua called the Billings US Postal section center to tell of the problems we were having. Billings was not having near as bad as a winter as we were having and would tell us that all of their routes had been run. When we could not make it in to run the route, this postal employee said he would not pay us for the day. Our contract says all we needed to do is make an attempt and we did. It seems like the contract is two sided and that they can change what they want us to do but we have to abide by our signed contract. After all that we put up with getting the mail delivered with 108 inches of snow on the ground, a record breaker in snow fall for us, and putting up with the US Postal Service. I think this is when we started thinking that it might be time to let the route go. It is just a good part time job with no benefits. After Patty was done on Friday and Saturdays, she would go to work at Vicks Bar! For a little bit of time, several years ago now, she was also working Wednesday nights at the bar too!

John and Donna Rorvik carried the mail three days a week on the old Zack Bennett route south of Fort Peck for many years plus Donna is driving a longer one now out of Glasgow that is six days a week. I know John and Donna have driven that route out south for about 35 years. One June 30th both John and Patty are going to not renew their mail route contracts, quit or maybe retire, and John says they are going to party!! I think we all are going to have a few beers. Patty and I will have been on this route for 40 years with no benefits except for Social Security!! It has been a good part time job, but it has really tied us down and we had not been able to travel like we would have liked. I tell Patty, how are we going to make the payments on our car and other things? She tells me that it is time that I can start taking care of her, this from the mail lady!!

ADDENDUM: At the end of June 2012, Patty and John ended their mail carrying careers. John likes to tell Patty that he retired one day before her, which is technically the truth, as he completed his final route on a Friday and she delivered last on Saturday. That year, at the Rorvik's annual BBQ and firework extravaganza, John and Patty celebrated their postal service retirement with family and friends and a good time was had by all.

The Fire in 1979

I guess this is as good a time as any to tell that story. In the fall of 1979, our family went up to visit the Musgroves in Canada. When we got home it was early November and I planned on trapping some foxes, coons and mink as I knew the fur prices was really up this fall. Trapping helped make ends meet when money was tight and I am thankful for the opportunity to support my family and live off the land at the same time. It was probably a week before I got some traps out but I caught a beautiful red fox and a raccoon the first night out. I wanted to get some more traps out, so I put off skinning the catch and that night it really froze hard. I am the Prince of Procrastination (or so I have been told) so I was busy with some other tasks and I still hadn't done any skinning.

Patty and I had just moved into our new house the year before, and I had not been able to trap that previous fall since we were so busy with the new house. Our new house was all baseboard electric heat so I didn't need the propane in the tank that we used to heat our old trailer house with. Therefore, I decided to hook up the propane tank to the old log house on the property which was plumbed for propane. There was a stove still hooked up to the line and I decided to turn this old house into a workshop with heat. I tried but I couldn't get the stove lit so I went out and got my portable heater and a small tank to heat the room. My daughter Stacy, who was about six at the time, went back to the main house and told Patty that I was having trouble starting the stove. It was just after dark and Patty was getting supper cooked. I had the small heater going and I opened the door into the next room that I had some supplies in that I needed. This door really drug hard on the floor when I opened it.

Thinking back on it years later, I had forgotten to turn off the main valve on the large propane tank after I could not get the first stove lit. I guess I was in too much of a hurry to heat the room. Anyway, I forgot that there was open copper propane line in this room that I walked in to get something. All the time that I was trying to get the first stove lit propane was flowing on the floor in another room. When I walked into this other room, I couldn't smell the propane as I had worked with it so much that evening. Apparently, the propane flowed the few feet out to my lit camp stove and ignited the whole room while I was in there.

I had just gone to a Jaycee meeting a few days before and they were giving a class on fire safety and I remembered I had to stop breathing to keep from burning my lungs, and this knowledge probably saved my life. The explosion spun me around but I didn't lose my feet and I headed to open the door that I had just gone through. The pressure of the fire closed the door before I got to it. There was fire going up the walls on three sides of the room but I thought opening the door was the quickest way out. I grabbed a hold of the doorknob with my right hand and then with the left hand over it to try to get the stuck door open. It was only a couple seconds and I had to let go of the doorknob because of the heat. And I still didn't have the door open. I found out then that my hands wouldn't open or close any more. I was still holding my breath and I looked out the door to a back room and I ran in there and kicked out a low window and crawled out into the cool of the night.

There was just a skiff of snow on the ground and I found out later that if I would had put snow on my face and hands I maybe would not have had as many third degree burns. I don't know but I heard that the cold snow would have maybe stopped the burning feeling. It was freezing out and I was well dressed, wearing a down filled coat, which is a natural fire retardant, so I was pretty well protected except for my hands and face. I had a cap on, but it blew off and I burned most of my hair off with extreme burns on the top of my head and I have a small bald spot ever since. As I walked back to the house, I remember that the cold air felt good and it was then that I was very thankful to God that Stacy had gone back to the house when she did and wasn't in the fire. I kicked on the door until Patty came to the door. I can only imagine her shock when she saw me!

I waited out in the cool air until Patty called my mother to come over to watch our three young kids and to also inform the hospital that she was bringing me in. As it turned out I went into the Glasgow Deaconess Hospital and they put me in to an isolated room that was kept free of germs as the doctors were worried about my burned areas getting infected. My father was gone to a meeting in Miles City that day but returned to help out later in the evening. It was very fortunate that Dave Anderson and a friend were driving nearby. They turned off the main valve of the propane tank and got my Jennings compound bow and some other articles out of the old house and started putting water from a hose on the building until the Nashua Fire Department arrived and put the fire out. The firemen had to pull the logs apart on the end of building to get the fire out. It was a solid cottonwood log cabin covered with stucco and it was quite sturdy. I am still able to use the end of the log house for storage, as the fire never damaged that end of the building.

I spent 45 days in the intensive care room but I was thankful to be close to home so friends and relatives could come and visit with me. It was my decision to stay in Glasgow and not to go to Salt Lake City. I am really thankful for everyone who helped us from feeding cows, and John Rorvik and others to getting my calves to Glasgow Livestock so I would have some cash flow during this tough time. The Nashua Jaycees had a dance at the Civic Center where they raised money to also help Patty and I, and I am so thankful about the support from our wonderful small community. The hardest part for me might have been that I missed a whole hunting season while I was healing up. My family was very helpful during this time with the farm and home, especially Patty as she was up to see me every day in the hospital after she had delivered the mail and she always brought the children in so see me, which helped me get through that difficult time. After I was out of the hospital, she drove me to Great Falls for numerous trips for hand and face plastic surgery. My hands have healed up very well as far as I am concerned and I am able to do most of the things necessary to be able to run a farm and ranch. My left hand was damaged worse as it was closer to the open line which was the hottest part of the fire even though the flames were all around on the walls and floor. I am a very positive person and it has helped for my full recovery and I am very thankful to be alive and still be able to function as a father and husband!

Fort Peck Interpretive Center

One of the largest Tyrannosaurus Rex skeletons, nicknamed Pecks Rex, was found in the badlands in the area south of the Missouri River in 1997 and a cast of this massive dinosaur is still located in the Fort Peck Interpretive Center. This includes the dinosaur replica cast of the "full size" skeleton, the head and also the replica of the skin on skeleton version of Peck's Rex full size. There are many exhibits of the Fort Peck Dam construction from 1933 to 1940 plus many other interesting exhibits of early day history and of the native wildlife and fish species of the area, including live viewing tanks that display Walleye and Northern Pike. There are also many other smaller dinosaurs exhibited there. This center is a must if you visit the area. It is located along the Missouri River and the just west of the power houses below Fort Peck dam. There are many public meetings held in the Interpretive Center and I always walk around and view the exhibit's every time I am in the building. There is always something new on display or I find an exhibit that I have missed.

In the last couple of years, they have added a movie of the construction of the making of the Fort Peck Dam. You can sit on a bench and watch it as many times that you want. There are exhibits of many mounted larger size animals, which is a particular favorite activity of mine, as well as small mammals and reptiles from this area. As far as I am concerned, it is a real must see!!

Alan Moum: Vintage Beer Guy, Chef and Kayaker with Whales

My first cousin Alan, who is my Mom's brother Al's son, is a beer drinker like me! The difference between us is that he only drinks vintage beer, and I will drink any kind of beer! When he drinks beer, it is only the best of vintage beers from all over the world and fancy micro-brew's. I also love beer, but I drink the good old American macro-brew's, like Busch Light, Bud Light and Pabst, most of the time. I have tipped a few beers with him and most of them are great beers with lots of flavor and gusto! I do thank him for helping me to acquire some tasting skills for more flavored beer. When he comes to visit, he usually has several brands of vintage beer and even some beer that he has made himself. I think he has been making beer for twenty years now, maybe longer. I have always thought of making my own beer, but I guess I did not think I had the patience to have to wait 30 to 60 days for it to age. He did finally give me the encouragement to brew my first batch and it did turn out fairly good, if I do say so myself. I think there is only one bottle left in the fridge.

Basically, I am just a regular beer guy! I do not drink hard liquor and wine is a little too sweet for my taste buds. I just like beer, and most of the time it is the light variety. Remember the Tom T. Hall song, I Like Beer? "I like beer, it makes me a jolly good fellow, I like beer" etc, etc. That is me. I prefer Busch Light anymore and it has been my beer for several years. Certainly, that does not mean that I will not drink another beer if it is offered to me, especially if it is Cold, Wet and Free! The key word here is free! I guess over the years I have turned a bit into a "Tightwad Redneck" type of a person. I started drinking Schlitz beer back in the 1960's just because most of the people that I ran with also drank the brew. If we went to a branding before I was legal, it seemed most of the people also drank this brand. Just maybe it was about the only beer that was left after all of the adults had a few and went home? Just maybe this was the reason that it was the beer that us kids snuck out to have? Anyway, I kind of got hooked on that brand. I drank it steady for about three years or more, I can remember when we got a buyer to get us some beer, we usually asked for Schlitz by name, but we did not ask the buyer to take the beer back and get something else if he brought the wrong brand to us!! During 1969, while Patty and I were dating each other, Patty, Gary and Marilynn were drinking Olympia and I was drinking Schlitz beer. Actually, Olympia was not too bad of a beer, and it was always easier to order all of the same beer so I started drinking it too. Maybe it had something to do with Oly beer label, since when we were drinking bottles us guys had to see how many dots were under the Olympia bottle label!!

At times I like to try other beers when I order in a bar, especially when I am with friends. I like to order Schlitz because I still like it, but also to see the look on the bartenders face and from my buddies! Not every bar around here has Schlitz on stock, but I do know the bars that do!

I think that it was the fall of 2005 that I went to Seattle for my second cousins, Erika's wedding. This was when I got to know Alan a little better, as he is about 15 years or so younger than me. We had a few vintage beers at his folks place, Uncle Al and Aunt Joyce Moum. Alan is a great chef and cook, and he fixed some oysters that we picked from the seashore right next to their house! What a great meal he had cooked for me and then we had a few vintage beers! I was kind of hooked on some of these vintage beers. I was talking about maybe making some hefeweizen, a wheat beer, because at the time I had a bin full of low protein wheat that is great for making wheat beer. I never got around to doing that because I did not get a beer making kit. Then, in the winter of 2005, I got a computer so I was able to e-mail Alan and we could visit a little more about things! He has been back to the farm a few times since 2005 and we have always got along great and I enjoy having a few with him. He has some great home brews that he made himself. I finally saw a cheap homebrew kit when Patty and I were Christmas shopping and I bought one. I waited until the holidays were over and I brewed up a batch and about 20 days later I bottled it. My son Seth had said that he was not going to take a chance of getting poisoned!!! Can you believe that? Well, a few weeks later I tried one bottle by myself, and it did not seem half bad! A week later I pulled out a another bottle and Seth, Patty and I ended up drinking that one and a couple more bottles. I kind of think that maybe Seth was even kind of impressed. Maybe! Anyway, none of us were worse off because of it. I was kind of proud of the beer for my first try, even though it was a little flat, and it did not have a ton of flavor. I think that I liked it, but I think I should have let it age a little more!!

Several years ago now, Vern and Dan, two friends of Seth's, whom I had become acquainted with over the years and who had been home brewing for some time, let me watch as they cooked up a batch of beer, so I could see how it is done. I drank one of their pale ales and I was impressed with the taste of the beer. I did get over to the house to watch the bottling of their beer in glass bottles. You need to have a bottle capper machine for glass bottles. You also need to save all the bottles that you can. I had bottled mine the day before and I had used the special plastic bottles with special twist on and off plastic caps. Every one that hears that this kit has plastic bottles and they give me that look! It has worked well for this batch so we will see how they work for future batches. Time will tell.

Alan has been writing articles about vintage beer for the *Northwest Brewing News* from Welches, Oregon, since 2001. I have read several of his articles and he does know his beer! I do not know if he still does write for this publication but it is a great paper that tells about home brewing and all of the beer tasting festivals. It also has all the recent vintage beer releases that have come out recently. One article that Alan wrote in the Oct and Nov, 2003 edition of the *Northwest Brewing News*, is very interesting to me. The Bottle in Front of Me: Vintage Beer News-Home brewing Memories by Alan J. Moum. Alan starts out by remembering the smells that came from his grandparents' home, after they were brewing a batch of beer. Since that day, he has brewed many batches and the sweet smell of the brewing beer is still the same as it was from his youth in his grandparents' house as it is now these days when he gets a batch going. Another memorable moment is from going to a homebrew club meeting where a lot of tasting of different beers went on. He learned quite a lot from tasting a pale ale beer that a friend Tom had brewed. Then they drank a beer of the same vintage from the year earlier than the other one. Then they drank one from a couple of years before the last. Alan said and I quote him, "We had never thought much about aged beer before. I knew immediately that I would never think of beer the same way again." In the past, Alan has gone to a lot of the brewery tours and tastings, and I am sure he still does. One thing that I know from his articles and visiting with him is that he does know his beer.

Alan and Andrew Ericson, Jim and Becky Ericson's son, went to Germany several years ago for a visit. Alan got to try many of the different beers that Germany has to offer. They said that it was quite an experience and I think that they would go there again sometime.

I know that Alan loves to photograph animals and when he is in Maui visiting the Ericson's he always gets in a kayak to do some ocean paddling. He has paddled out to visit with the whales and he has gotten extremely close to them. He has gotten some great pictures of them. A few years ago, he had a calf come so close to him he could have reached out and touched it. He decided he did not have the right to touch the calf with the mother so close. He sent me a couple pictures of whales that he has taken of them when he has been near in the kayak. He sometimes paddles out two miles from shore to visit them. He spends enough time with them that they accept him and do not get scared. If the weather is good and the wind does not come up, it is the best kind of experience.

Several years ago, he was visiting my folks on the farm. He walked out right at daylight above the hill behind the house. He mistakenly forgot to take a camera along and he walked very near a pronghorn antelope buck. He had the wind right and the antelope did not know what he was. He was just standing still and the antelope was snorting, trying to figure him out. It finally walked around him to smell him and then it took off. This was a great experience and he really enjoyed the encounter and talks about it to this day.

I had a Busch light after supper and now, while I am writing this, I decided to have one of my home brewed beers. This one had a head and was quite tasty! I am going to have to brew another batch before too long. I just wish that I would have started doing this a long time ago. I still have about sixty bushels of low protein wheat and I am going to have to save some for some hefeweizen wheat beer for future batches!! Thanks Alan, Skaal!!

The Missouri River Conservation District Council, MRCDC of Montana

The MRCDC was formed in around the year 2000, based on a need to address and to help with problems that are happening yearly on and along the Missouri River in Montana. The members on the board are comprised of the following:

- One member from each of the Montana County Conservation districts that encompass the Missouri River system in Montana. Each of these persons are an elected Supervisor or appointed Supervisor from their own county conservation districts encompassing the Missouri River.

- One employee of the DNRC, Department of Natural Resources Council from Montana

- One employee from the NRCS, Natural Resources Council Service from Montana

- One employee from the MACD, Montana Association of Conservation Districts

- One paid secretary to take minutes of all meetings, including minutes of CMR (Charles M. Russell) Community Working Group and to help keep us members organized.

- One paid Coordinator who attends many public meetings and who keeps an office in Great Falls for the MRCDC.

- If interested, please contact the MRCDC @ mrcd@missouririvercouncil.info

The state of Montana is the first state of the 15 states encompassing the Missouri River system to organize and fund a true grassroots entity/organization focused solely on conservation efforts along the Missouri River. Through this council, the conservation districts and their constituents (you, if you are a registered voter within the district boundaries) are given a unified front and collective voice when addressing natural resource issues, opportunities and challenges associated with the Missouri River. Conservation Districts, through public elections, which represent local residents' views and concerns regarding natural resources. I feel this gives this council a true grassroots perspective of Missouri River issues.

The Mission Statement is as follows, "Our mission is to represent natural resource and environmental interests on the Missouri River and the associated uplands. The council believes the conservation of the river and the sustainability of its various uses can be accomplished through grassroots collaboration, education, incentives, and voluntary action."

I have been a supervisor on the Valley County Conservation District for at least seventeen years and in 2017, I ran for and was elected for another three-year term, which will carry into 2020. I was an Associate Supervisor for three years before that, with my primary function being that I was to watch over concerns of the Missouri River in Valley County. I became the one member on our Valley county board to represent us at the quarterly Missouri River Conservation Districts Council. I met Buzz Mattelin, whose real name is Milo but no one calls him that, from the Roosevelt County Conservation District and he encouraged me to start going to the Lower Missouri River meetings as well, since our mission statements for both organizations were very similar.

The first Coordinator of the MRCDC was Gayla Wortman. The next Coordinator was Vicki Marquis and she did an excellent job for five or six years. She is now going to college in Missoula for a law degree. After that our coordinator was Laurie Riley and our present coordinator is Rachael Frost and she has been our coordinator for five or six years and also is doing a great job for the council. She goes to a great number of meetings with the MRCDC and the Charles M Russell Local Working Group, CMR Comprehensive Conservation Plan and a lot of other meetings as well.

Some of the early representatives on the MRCDC (Missouri River Conservation Districts Council) past board were:

- Jeanne Rae Kirkegard: Lower Reach, McCone CD
- Buzz Mattelin: Lower Reach, Roosevelt CD
- Dick Iverson: Lower Reach, Richland CD
- Nick Schultz: Reservoir Reach, Petroleum CD
- Dean Rogge: Reservoir Reach, Garfield CD
- Bill French: Reservoir Reach, Phillips CD
- Ron Garwood: Reservoir Reach, Valley CD
- Rick Anderson: Middle Reach, Choteau CD
- Dana Darlington: Middle Reach, Big Sandy CD
- Paul Geis: Middle Reach, Fergus CD
- Dennis Mitchell: Middle Reach, Blaine CD
- John Venhusen: Upper Reach, Gallatin CD
- Jim Beck: Upper Reach, Broadwater CD
- Scott Blackman: Upper Reach, Lewis and Clark CD
- John Chase: Upper Reach, Cascade CD
- Karl Christians: DNRC, Helena
- Jeff Teberi: MACD, Helena
- Tim Bregeman: NRCS, Bozeman

- Laurie Riley: Coordinator, Great Falls
- Carie Hess: Secretary, Winnett

I have been very fortunate to have been on this council all these years. I have met many great people and I consider many of these as good friends. We have a lot of goals in common for the betterment of the Missouri River and the State of Montana. Some of the past members that have been on the council that I would like to recognize are: Curt Blaine CD; Gayla Wortman, Coordinator, Cascade CD; Vicki Marquis, Coordinator; Bob Anderson and Buzz Mattelin, Roosevelt CD; Tom, Iverson Richland CD; Monty Billing Garfield CD and Lauri Riley.

Karl Christians has been on the MRCD Council from its inception, which was before I got on the council in 2001. He works for the Department of Natural Resources (DNRC) for the state of Montana and has been very active and helpful for the council. I have gotten to know him very well as he is a rancher and also a bow hunter, like me. During the dry years in Helena, he shipped his cattle to Valley County and he ran cows with Jack and Andrea Billingsley and also with Will Lauckner. These are people I know very well and I was quite surprised when I found out he had run cows with them. Karl and I have a lot in common as we are both bow and rifle hunters and I get along with him very well. He has been very helpful in getting the Garfield County pilot grazing project going for some of the ranchers that have graz-ing permits on the Charles M. Russell (CMR) National Wildlife Refuge.

Charles M Russell Local Working Group

After about three years of going to meetings and working with the staff of the Charles M. Russell (CMR) National Wildlife Refuge's Comprehensive Conservation Plan (CCP) and Environmental Impact Statement (EIS) for the CMR, the MRCD council decided that a CMR Local Working Stakeholder Group needed to be organized from all the stakeholders from the six county area surrounding the Fort Peck Lake and the CMR. This stakeholder group is comprised of many groups and individuals of diverse opinions. I was at the first meeting of the CMR Stakeholder meeting in Jordan, Montana. The first decision was to call the stakeholder group the CMR National Wildlife Refuge (NWR) Local Working Group. We are an informal group of interested organizations, agencies, community leaders, landowners, CMR staff and others who gather to discuss important happenings that affect our area. The meetings are held every other month in rotating locations around the lake within the six county areas. The six counties surrounding the lake are Garfield, Petroleum, Fergus, Phillips, Valley and McCone. The towns where the meetings are held are Jordan, Winnett, Lewistown, Malta, Fort Peck, Circle and then back to Jordan and continuing to rotate around the Fort Peck Lake in that order. I have been to a lot of these meetings but have missed some too, and most of those misses are related to when I am busy farming and ranching or for bad road conditions. Even though I did not want to or need to go to any more meetings (because it does take time away from my farm and family), I feel these CMR Local Working Group meetings are important to me and my constituents, and I will continue to attend them if my farming business lets me.

I have met a lot of nice people at these meetings and I guess I am surprised that with our diverse interests, that we have gotten along quite well. Bill Milton has done a great job keeping the meetings fair and allowing everyone a chance to talk and express their own personal point of view or concerns. The interests that the majority of us have agreed on for the time being is to concentrate on the sage grouse and the noxious weed issue. I am not very patient with these kinds of issues dealing with the CMR and I was hoping that things would happen a little faster, but because we are such a diverse group of people with many areas of interest, changes seem to happen slowly.

I have been hunting on the land surrounding the lake which is now known as the Charles M. Russel Wildlife Refuge, that was once originally known as the Fort Peck Game Range, since the fifties. The fall of 1957 was when I got my first big game license to hunt deer. We did not have many deer around our place or in the hills near our farm, so we went out to the beautiful and rugged country near what is known locally as The Pines cabin area. We did hunt some near the Pines Cabin Area but we had more luck finding game further west near the Stone House area and over to Timber Creek. I remember going in and talking to Don Burke and his mother Myrtle to ask about going hunting in the early years.

I have gotten to love the Missouri breaks country. It is really beautiful out there with its pine trees, sagebrush, juniper and sandstone outcroppings. This is the same area that I still hunt for elk and mule deer during the archery season when I get an either sex elk permit in the drawings. You have to apply for an elk permit in the drawings and get lucky enough to draw a permit. You have to buy an elk tag first and if you are not lucky on the archery drawing, a person can still go out west in any area that has general season hunting allowed in the rifle or archery season and still be able to hunt elk. I have been hunting in that country for over fifty years now and I feel that the countryside looks almost the same as it used too. I feel the country around the lake is fully protected even without any more proposed wilderness designation areas. It would be nice if the hunters and sightseers could have a little more access to the back country to photograph and watch wildlife as more trails would be open to vehicle use. Instead, a lot of the roads we used to hunt and retrieve game have been closed off. I know that some of these roads were closed off after the US Fish and Wildlife Service took over the control of the area, somewhere between 1974 and 1976, around the Fort Peck Lake. Before these dates, there was a joint effort with the Bureau of Land Management (BLM) and the US Fish and Wildlife Service in managing the CMR. Rancher permit holders, hunters, fisherman, hunting enthusiasts and the wildlife were all doing well. One reason that the Fish and Wildlife Service can close off previously used numbered trails is if the area in question is in or near a Proposed Wilderness Area. We already have too many proposed wilderness areas in the CMR that have had numbered trails closed off, and I believe some of these areas should be taken off the wilderness designation list. At least some of these trails could be opened to vehicle use for a few hours in the middle of the day for game retrieval.

A diverse group of people interested in this area put in comments about our concerns or recommendations for the CMR, and all of the comments are supposedly in for the CCP and the EIS for the next fifteen years or so for the Charles M Russell National Wildlife Refuge. We, as stakeholders for the CMR, are all hopeful that the comments that we sent in to the CCP to process will be looked at fairly, especially from those of us in the six counties that are surrounding the Fort Peck Lake. Those of us that live around the lake want to be good neighbors with the CMR. We just hope that the CMR wants to be good neighbors with us!!

Neighboring ranchers and their cattle depend on grazing the grass on the CMR. Controlled grazing reduces the risk for fires. Long, thick grass is fuel for fires, and once they get started, the fires burn so hot that it destroys the trees, junipers and sagebrush habitat that the wildlife need for protection. The cows that are grazing on the CMR, as they always have in the past, keep the grass grazed down in a managed way so that there is not as much fuel for uncontrolled fires. We also need cows in the CMR to help provide tax money for the counties which provide the services to the residents of the counties. An example of the benefit of this tax money is the upkeep of our roads and the funding local firefighting services. The cattle on the CMR would also provide income to the United States with grazing fees.

In the time I have spent going to these meetings, I have met a lot of nice people that really care for their communities. Two men that I meet from attending these meetings are from the Jordan area are Monty Billing and Dean Rogge. Both of these men are Garfield County Conservation District Supervisors. I have been to many meetings with these men and I really respect them. They are both cattle ranchers and Monty also has a herd of sheep. One statement that Monty has said that really hits home is, "Every time we leave home to go to a meeting our place suffers". When we go to these meetings and conferences, we do so because we are trying to make our communities better places to live in, to benefit how the public has access and use of government lands and for our farms and ranches to be profitable and sustainable. We do not get paid to go to meetings though we are sometimes reimbursed for our mileage. We just want our communities to be thriving, want to make good use of public lands and for people not to feel as they have no options but to move away from the area because of inability to access the grazing on the CMR which can poorly affect farm and ranching possibilities.

The Garfield County Conservation Boys

Monty Billing and Dean Rogge, whom I mentioned briefly earlier, are two supervisors from the Garfield County Conservation District that I have known for a few years. They are both great guys that I have had a few beers with them after meetings in Jordan, Lewistown, Glasgow and Fort Peck. They both care for their communities and county and the land that borders the Fort Peck Lake. That is why they are active in their conservation district and the CMR Stakeholder Local Working Group. We have been going to the meetings every other month that are held in the counties that surrounds Fort Peck Lake.

There are many different groups that have been going to these meetings, along with local farmers and ranchers. Also, at these stakeholder meetings there are some local people from the surrounding areas where the meetings are held and that also includes CMR staff. In the early 2010's, the CMR manager, Rick Potts, and Deputy CMR manager, Bill Berg, and former CMR manager, Barron Crawford, attended most of the meetings. Most of these people really cared about the CMR, the counties surrounding the CMR or both. Those of us that come to these CMR Stakeholder meetings have gotten to know each other and we have really gotten along well even though we have very diverse interests and ideas about the management of the CMR.

In about 1976 the US Fish and Wildlife Service took over complete management of the CMR and that is when wildlife became number one priority there. People and cows became two and three and I am not really sure what order they fall in. We all have worked hard on our comments to the CMR Comprehensive Conservation Plan and the Environmental Impact Statement. I feel in the end the people in the surrounding six county area will get the short end of the stick. I hope not as this area is very important for the economy of the area. The final decision based on our comments was published in a large manual in 2012 and it used the Missouri River Conservation District Councils input and comments in implementing a plan for the CMR, which seems to be an improvement on what we had in the past. There is still room for improvement, as far I can see, and that is why I continue to attend meetings and take part in councils. Of the many people who have gone to these meetings for the betterment of the CMR and its bordering counties, I think Monty and Dean had only missed one or two meeting at the time the impact statement was released.

Dean Rogge is from Sand Springs and has a fairly large cow herd and he raises dry land wheat and does custom combining also. I have known him for many years and he is very active in helping to keep bison out of the CMR and the surrounding countryside. We have great concerns that if free ranging bison are put on the CMR, it will have a negative effect on the local communities. Free ranging bison are bison that are not contained within a high wire fence. Free ranging bison could go anywhere they want to. In the winter when Fort Peck Lake freezes over, need for grazing or a bad storm could push bison across the lake and allow them to onto private farms and ranches and damage personal property and resources.

I have had a few beers with him after meetings and he has become a friend and I enjoy visiting with him. We have shared those beers at the Hell Creek Bar, Park Grove Bar and other watering holes around the lake. One night after the bison meeting in Glasgow a few winters back, Dean, Monty, Jeanne Kirkegard and I decided to have a beer at the Gateway Bar near Wheeler, but it was closed. The Gateway Bar burned down a couple weeks after this meeting in Glasgow and it was really missed by the Fort Peck residents and many local people. After our attempted stop at the Gateway, we then decided to go down to the Park Grove Bar. When we got to Park Grove, the bar was closed too. It was not our lucky night!! Dean said that we should have gotten an eighteen pack somewhere in Glasgow, but we thought we could get some in Fort Peck. I told Dean and Jeanne that if I had driven my farm pickup that I had a cooler with some beer in it. Anyway, we went our separate ways home without a drink for the road. Dean is a great guy and cares a lot for his family, ranch and the community.

Monty Billing lives east of Jordan and north of highway 200, west of Flowing Wells. He raises beef cows and has a herd of sheep west of the Dry Arm of Fort Peck Lake. He served for years as the chairman of the Garfield County Conservation District in Jordan, although Dean Rogge is currently the chairman. I met his youngest son and his wife at the Hell Creek Bar after the CMR meeting in April 2012. His oldest son Lane lived in Glasgow and worked for Fossum Ready Mix in Glasgow for years, but is now back on the ranch. Monty has told me that he has an orange Oldsmobile 442 Judge. I finally got to see that car and boy is it a beautiful muscle car!

Monty is another great guy that likes to have a beer with friends. I have really been able to get to know him well and after a meeting in Circle we had a few at the Brockway Bar. When we decided to go home, I found out he only had about 30 miles to go and I had about 75. The trip to Fort Peck from Flowing Wells is crooked, up and down, and you really have to watch for deer along that roadway. That night there were not many of them along the road after the winter of 2010-2011, which took a toll on the deer population. Dean and Monty are good friends, I like them both and they have been on the Garfield County Conservation District together for some time.

Ken and April Alto

I met Ken Alto the fall of 2010 when he was driving down a county road near my farm. We met on the road and visited about coyotes and whitetail deer. It was rifle season for deer and he had recently moved here from Minnesota and he was not a Montana resident at the time, so he could only hunt whitetail does and coyotes. I told him that my place was in the Block Management for the state of Montana and he could hunt both on my place. To do that all he had to do was sign up at the Block Management sign up box and go hunting. While we were visiting, I found out that he was an avid bow hunter and he had hunted and taken deer, black bear, elk and Rocky Mountain Goat with either bow or rifle in several states. He was also on the Hoyt pro staff for several years. We visited about hunting and hit it off really well. I learned that his wife April had taken a mule deer doe with a bow and arrow that fall. I was impressed as there are very few women around here that bow hunt. I have since learned that more and more women are becoming dedicated bow hunters. I think that is a great thing and it is good for our sport. I have been bow hunting since 1966 and I had only met one other woman who was out archery hunting for deer.

Both Ken and April had archery elk permits and hunted out south for elk and deer in the fall of 2011. I had run into them twice out at the Carney coulee gate while bow hunting that fall. Ken got a nice bull elk opening morning that fall and April had two close encounters with bull elk too. Ken spent quite a bit of time guiding April when she had time off from her work. They both took large mule deer bucks during the rifle season. She worked at Pamida, which has since become a Shopko, and later accepted the manager position of the Alco store, which was newly opened just before Christmas in Wolf Point. She now works for All Seasons Home Center and Lumber in Glasgow. Ken and I have hunted elk, gophers and coyotes and I enjoy his expertise at bow hunting as he has taken many whitetail bucks, bull elk and black bears with a bow. I am sure I will have many experiences hunting and visiting with them in the future.

Ken had hunted with Jim Ward last winter calling coyotes and maybe doing some trapping. They ended up the season killing 53 coyotes and some other fur for the winter. This was really impressive for them. When Jim was driving the bus for Valley County Transit, in the winter of 2003-04, he had seen a wolverine cross the road about a mile from my house. A week before that, I had seen some large bounding tracks and I wondered if they could have been wolverine or river otter. Jim told me that he had seen the wolverine about a week after he seen it, and about two weeks after I had seen the mystery tracks by the river.

Verlin (Smutz) Borgen

I have known Verlin Borgen for many years and we have hunted together for deer and elk with a bow and rifle for at least thirty years or so. Verlin and I both had our archery elk tags for area 631 north of Fort Peck Lake, which is from Timber Creek East to the Murray Road. Verlin's nickname has always been Smutz and that is what I call him most of the time and most people that know him do too. His brother is Dale Borgen, another good friend and hunting partner of mine.

I first met Verlin and Dale Borgen when we had a Jaycee Chapter in Nashua. I also met Mike Buchman, and Leroy Novak and the four of them lived close together north of Nashua. They have always hunted together. Kendall Vaughn hunted with us a few years until he moved to Glasgow. We got to talking about hunting and they let me get into their hunting club and I have enjoyed their companionship over the years. We have hunted out south in the Missouri breaks, West of Timber Creek, North of White Sulphur Springs with Otto Ohlson and North of Big Mountain by Whitefish. All of these hunting trips we stayed in the big blue tent these guys had made before I hunted with them. It was a huge spacious tent where we could sleep on one end and on the other end we had the stoves and the cooking supplies. We had a lot of fun and parties in this tent after the hunting was over for the day. One year we came back from White Sulphur Springs with three elk. Most of the time we came back with a lot of hunting stories and we always had a good time. I hunted with Dale quite a bit in 1993 when he had his either sex elk permit but I wasn't with him when he bagged a nice six-point bull later in the season.

Most of us started bow hunting and applying for either sex elk permits in the drawings held by Montana Fish Wildlife and Parks. I had started bow hunting in 1966 so I tried to get them interested in the sport. All of them but Mike took the bow hunting course and became proficient bow hunters. Dale is probably the best bow hunter of us all and has taken two spikes and a six point bull.

Smutz was married to Danette Miller and they have three lovely daughters, Whitney, Blair and Darby. The girls are all hunters just like Verlin is. Smutz and I have been hunting for many years together, so I have got to spend some time with his daughters, too. Whitney got a nice four point white tail buck when she was in high school on my place.

Smutz and I have hunted the most together with many close encounters with elk. Even though we haven't been real successful we hunt alike and we enjoy each others company. We have had many shots at elk and I have missed a lot of bulls and have wounded a few that got away. Verlin has taken a cow with his bow and I am a horn hunter and I haven't taken a shot at a cow. I don't know what it is about elk but I get bull fever just about the time I draw on one with my bow and something goes wrong. It seems like elk just have my number but I have taken a cow and a calf with a rifle. Dale has been too busy with his custom harvesting and hasn't been able to hunt during the early bow season the last few years. As long as we still get our elk archery permits we will still hunt together and have fun!

A Louisiana Man Called Boatride

I first met Keith Meche, commonly known to the locals as Boatride, when he started working for the Agland Co-op Cenex station in Nashua. He has a CDL and delivers bulk gas and spread fertilizer for the Cenex customers and he also worked in the station. He now works for Wilbur Ellis in Wolf Point, spreading fertilizer and delivering chemicals. Boatride is from Louisiana and used to have a southern brogue that was extremely hard to understand. Especially when Keith was drinking, he would talk so fast and I would have to ask him to repeat his words. I have gotten to know him over the years and really like him as a friend. I can understand him a lot better, too, although I do not know if it is because he has lost some of his accent or I have just gotten used to it. Probably a bit of both!!

Boatride and I have a lot of things in common, such as our interest in hunting and fishing. We both bow hunt and rifle hunt, and sometimes I tag along in the winter when Boat is ice fishing. He's become a good friend over the years that he has lived here and I am happy to call him my friend.

Around ten years ago, Smutz told me that we need to take Keith Meche (Boatride) along bow hunting as he had drawn the either sex elk tag for our area and he was hunting the area for the first time and did not know his way around. I agreed, as Keith is fun to be around and it sounded like fun to take him out. The only problem is he had not hunted with a bow much before that hunting year and it would be a real learning experience. Bow hunting is a sport of patience and a person needs to practice a lot to be proficient at it. I have been archery hunting for deer since 1967 and I am still learning!

We pulled Verlin's old camper trailer out to the cottonwood campground on the Page-Whitham Block Management area in Carpenter Creek. The Montana Fish Wildlife and Parks have a hunter access program that pays landowners that give access to their property for hunters. The hunters have to sign up daily in the designated boxes and then they can hunt in those locations. This is a great program for the hunters and also for the landowners. You can stay in this campground by signing up each day. I have had my property here in the Missouri River in Block Management for seven years and I plan on doing so for some time in the future, as I think it is a great program.

One of the first hunts that the three of us were on in fall of 2009, was when we went east of camp toward the Harpers Ridge area. We spotted a herd of elk grazing near the road and they were not aware of us. We were up on a little ridge watching them and they grazed out of sight. They had gone behind a hill into a valley and the acted like they were about to bed down. There was a nice six-point bull in the herd, so we made a plan to get the wind right and try to locate them again. We grabbed our bows, all the necessary equipment to hunt with and our daypacks. These always have water, snacks and survival equipment. When you head out after elk you might have to trail them for miles. It might be after dark when you get back to the truck, so you have to be prepared.

We walked a little closer to the elk and we decided to split up and surround the area where the elk were last sighted. I circled a little farther around and started to a little ridge to do some glassing and find the elk again. Before I got to the top, I saw some of the elk moving around the hill and I knew that they had been alerted and were moving out. I got down but they acted like they had seen me and there was no chance of getting close enough for a shot with an arrow. I went up to the ridge and I saw Boatride walking down in the creek bottom and he was trying to get up on some elk but they were spooky, since as I had mentioned, they had sensed us. I got the wind right and started hunting again towards where the small herd had gone, but after a couple of miles, I knew they had left the area. I got back to the pickup a couple of hours after I had seen Keith down in the coulee. When I got back to the pickup the boys were already into the beer and as it was getting hot, I needed one too!

I asked them what had happened to the elk. Keith said that he seen a spike bull and a cow that were moving away and he decided to go after them. He was walking towards them when he came to the edge of a bank. All of a sudden, a bull stood up right under the bank, just below and within ten feet of him, and then took off running. Of course, there is no chance of making a shot at a running elk when you have a bow in your hands and do not have an arrow nocked. Keith was concentrating on the spike and was in a hurry, and missed seeing the bigger prize. We have learned from experience that when you come over an edge of a bank, a hunter needs to look for antlers. Boatride had not seen the large bull until the elk stood up. He said that if he would have been about four feet closer to the elk, his antlers would have hit him as the bull jumped up and his head came back. I think it almost scared him to be that close to a bull and not know he was there. If he would have paid a little more attention, and to look over these hills slower, things might have been different. But those things come with experience. We as bow hunters have had this happen if we have hunted enough, but I have never been that close to a live elk and this must have been pretty exciting to him on his first bow hunt elk stalk!

Bernard "Ben" and Myrtle (Berg) Stenbakken

Ben Stenbakken was my mother's Uncle. Ben's father and elder brother both homesteaded west of the Porcupine Creek and about eight miles Northwest of Nashua. His father passed away in 1933 shortly after filing on the homestead. Ben took over the farming responsibilities of his fathers' land when he was 23 years old, and he eventually took over his brother's homestead, as well. He married Myrtle Berg and they lived on the Stenbakken homestead until the mid 1930's. These were tough years for farmers because of the extended drought. In 1934 the Stenbakken's moved into the house in Nashua that Ben had built for them.

Ben accepted the managership of the Farmers Union Oil Company in 1935. Three sons and four daughters were born to the Stenbakkens. They include: Ardis (Mrs. Harry House), Bernard Jr., Raymond Leroy, Donald Ray, Eulane Mae (Mrs. Howard Quiring), Darlene Joan (Mrs. William Durell), and Marlys Ann (Mrs. Albert Urdahl). All three of Ben's sons died young. Myrtle also died at a very young age of 34 from cardiac arrest. Ben worked hard to keep his family together following Myrtle's death. He was a skilled carpenter and built many houses in the area, one of them being the Martin Anderson house. Ben's sister Inga (Mrs. Adolph Moum) was my grandmother on my mothers' side of the family.

Jim and Becky Ericson

My cousin Jim was very close to our Grandpa Moum and lived next to him in a trailer park when Grandpa was older; Jim really watched over him. Jim had worked in Alaska at a cannery somewhere in the Aleutian Islands for a few summers. It was pretty good money and he helped work his way through college to become a tax preparer. He had one failed marriage but then he met Becky and they have been good for each other. They have two children, Tara and Andrew. Now they live on Maui in the Hawaiian Islands; it is the real paradise. They have lived there for thirty or more years.

Patty and I were fortunate to have visited them in about 2000. We really thank them for giving us a room to stay for several days and showing us around the beautiful island. We had such a great time that Patty did not want to come back to cold and snowy Montana in January. January is notoriously cold in eastern Montana. While we were in Hawaii, we did not get to surf but Jim took us on a small submarine trip, which was really unbelievable. The fish that we saw from this submarine were really beautiful. He also took us on a ship to watch whales coming out of the water, breaching and rolling.

When we were on our trip to Maui, we took a couple days off to give Jim and Becky a rest and flew over to Oahu to visit Honolulu, and also to see Pearl Harbor and the sunken ship, the USS Arizona, and the USS Arizona Memorial. What an experience!! I think everyone should go through the memorial and believe me when I say that you probably will not come out with dry eyes. There is a lot to see, including a wall where the names of all the sailors that perished there have been inscribed! I bought a cap there with the Arizona Memorial on it and I still wear it to special events!

Patty and I really enjoyed walking around Honolulu, and near Waikiki Beach at night to shop and see the sights. We walked around for hours, partly because we got a little lost. We blame that on the streets not being all parallel. After we walked back to where we knew we had been, there was no problem finding our way back to the room just off the beach. We went out shopping one more night and with all the shops open late at night, it kind of reminded us of the shops in Banff, Canada.

As an aside, Patty and I had our honeymooned in Banff, Alberta. We spent time walking around town, and really enjoyed the night shopping that was available. September of 1969 was when we spent a few days there, which was the first of several trips we have made to Banff. The next morning after the first day in Banff we had to brush about four inches of snow off the 1965 red and white Ford Galaxy we drove on that trip. This car was a hardtop and had a 390 engine in it. I sure wish we still had that car! Why is it that those old cars that we had then, would be so neat to have now? We went back to Banff twenty-five years later and it had not changed much, except that it was bigger!

Back in Maui we visited much of the island with Jim and Becky's help. We would like to go back and see more of the island, but I am afraid that Patty might really stay!! Becky was busy at work, but Jim took some time away from his tax work to spend with us and show us some of the beaches, and we sure did enjoy ourselves. I was taping surfers on the North Beach and in the background, I got to film a whale coming out of the water and breaching. I was able to get several whales breaching on the trip on my movie camera. My cousin Jim said I was extremely lucky to get this footage done in one visit to the islands. We went up to the top of 10,000 foot Mount Haleakala, where there is an information center and some observatories. Haleakala, which is also known as East Maui Volcano, means "House of the Sun" and is considered a sacred place to the gods of the islands.

We stayed with Jim and Becky so it saved us quite a bit of money from not having to stay in a hotel, which we really appreciated. We also got to visit and old friend, Eric Nelson and his wife. Eric was a year younger than I was in high school at NHS. He is an eye doctor on Maui.

Jim, Becky and their son Andrew came to visit us in the fall of 2007, I believe. I was moving the combine to a field about two miles from the house and I met them on the gravel road. We talked for a little while and they wanted to take Patty and I out to eat. I finished moving the combine and we picked up Patty and we went to the Park Grove Bar to eat. The Park Grove Bar and Cafe has been around for years, and my daughter Stacy worked there for many years, both during and after college. It has great food! Larry DuBeau owned it for over thirty years and Harold and Erma Brown owned it before that. Larry passed away this last year, but it is still owned by his family and his daughter Kim and her children are still running the place. It is a long time favorite gathering place of locals and is known for its great food!!!

Park Grove is one of the many dam towns that popped up to service the 15,000 to 20,000 people that were in the area of Fort Peck when the dam was built in the 1930's. Park Grove still has a grove of cottonwood trees next to the Dredge Cuts and it is a great little recreation and fishing place. This was the location of the Swing Bridge that allowed large dredge boats to go back and forth in the bridge channel. The bridge would swing out of the way for the dredge boats to pass. Then it would swing back into position for the trains and cars to cross to provide access to Fort Peck from Nashua on Highway 117.

We had a great couple of days visiting with the Ericson's. While they were here, they also spent time visiting my Dad, Edgar Garwood. My mother Theona, known as Toni to many, had passed away the fall before. Jim's mother Ellie was my mothers' older sister by about four years but she had passed away many years ago. Jim was not able to make it to Moms funeral because they live in Hawaii. Mom was eighty-one and had had diabetes pretty bad and suffered from dizzy spells. She had fallen a few months before and torn her shoulder. Then she fell and broke her hip; a couple of weeks after leaving the hospital she passed away. My father was heartbroken for many years. But he learned how to cook, clean and do laundry and into his 90's he was still very independent. His favorite meal to cook, as well as eat, is Mom's homemade whole-wheat pancakes, and he was very good at it. Some days when he got up real early in the morning he would end up having two breakfasts!

Andrew at the time of that visit was kind of sick and did not get to see much of the farm. A year later when he was working in the Seattle area he drove out to Montana for a visit and because he had missed so much the year before. He had tire problems and had to leave his car and catch a ride to the farm. Later that evening we got his tires fixed. We had a great visit and we were able to go out to the Fort Peck Interpretive Center which had been closed for the weekend when he had visited the year before. There is a tremendous amount of local history there about homesteading, animal mounts and dinosaur replicas; there is also a lot of information about the building of Fort Peck Dam and the Power Houses. In the Interpretive Center there is a bone cast replica of Peck's Rex, which is a large Tyrannosaurus Rex, which was famously found southeast of the Fort Peck Dam. I have a great picture of Andrew admiring the skull of this large dinosaur.

Dave and Sue Renner

Dave Renner has been a classmate of mine in the Nashua school system since about the 3rd grade and then graduating with me in 1964. He lived about 35 north of Nashua on the Porcupine creek which runs only about 100 feet from the house. His stepfather, Adlore Bouchard, was a farmer and had a herd of cows that he ran during the summer on his private and Bureau of Indian Affairs land. Adlore married Dave's mother, Irene and she had three children Dave, Larry and Donna. Adlore, Irene and the kids lived and worked the ranch until his death. All of the Renner kids graduated from Nashua High School. The Renner ranch is located within the Fort Peck Indian Reservation on the East Fork of The Porcupine Creek. Dave and Sue still live on the ranch in the same house that Adlore and Irene lived in. They had bought the land from old William Trebas. His son Bill Trebas was in my class in Nashua until he was an eighth grader and then they moved to the Flathead Valley. About a year ago Bill showed up in this area and we hadn't seen him since 1960.

When Dave and I graduated from Nashua we decided to go to Montana State College in Bozeman, Montana. We put in for a room together and we stayed in Hedges 2 dormitory. I can remember Mom and Dad taking me to Bozeman to go to college and what an exciting time it was to be in the mountains. We drove around the town and college some and then they took me to the Montana State College campus and we looked around some. It was later that we moved my stuff up to the fourth floor. Dave had already moved into our room and was waiting there for me. It seems like so long ago as there was no such thing as cell phones then, so we didn't know of each other's plans except we were rooming together. I remember that I just couldn't wait to be on my own! It was a busy and crazy first year there and I don't remember studying much, but we did some. I was taking agriculture courses and I had an interest in farming, even back then. Except I took Econ 101 and I was lost in it. It was almost a month in class before I figured out it was about economics. I think I ended up with a D in this class as I could care less about it! I got C's for most of the other courses. Dave was taking all general courses which were tougher.

It was quite an experience for two redneck farmer types to be in this environment. Dave had a cousin, Harry Stannebein who was also in his first year at Bozeman, but he was in a different dorm. We met a lot of nice people in our floor in the dorm. I remember meeting Gary Mercer back then and then about 10 years later, we got reacquainted when I got active in the Montana Jaycees. I later got to know Dirty Harry Stannebein and his wife Marlys when Patty and I were active in Jaycees and Jayceens.

I remember that MSC (as it was known at that time) had a really good football team and Jan Stenerud from Norway was the field goal and extra point kicker on the team and he just didn't miss. At the time we never would have suspected but he later would be drafted into the NFL and ended up playing for the Kansas City Chiefs for the majority of his career. Stenerud was one of the first players to be used as a dedicated kicker because of his accuracy and early in his career he set records for his accuracy. He was the first place kicker to be inducted into the NFL hall of fame and it's pretty neat to have been able to see some of his college games in person.

In 1964 MSC would become the Small College Champions in the country. That particular year Dave and I made the trip to Missoula on a train for the game against the Grizzlies. We lost the game to them and it was the only loss for the year but we still ended up as the champions!

In Dave and I's second year, we could have a car at college so my dad and I bought a 1959 Pontiac Starchief and this was the only car that the boys from Nashua had that year. The four of us were Dan Williamson, Dennis Meland, Dave and I. Gas was fairly cheap, about 36 cents per gallon and we always found enough money for gas and beer. That year was a lot of fun time but I think we all flunked out so maybe it wasn't so good! I remember a couple of trips to go back for the holidays. One time we had eight boys and girls in it for the trip to Glasgow. There was five from Glasgow, Ron, Don, Sharon, Linda, Nina, Dave, Dan and I. That car was a big boat but it was great for traveling back and forth with a crowd.

After the second year at college, Dave went into the Navy and I joined the Montana National Guard. I think Dave had two tours in Nam and he was a mechanic on a river boat on the Mekong Delta. He told me many stories about taking some gunfire from the riverbanks. A few years ago, the four of us from Nashua, that were together that second year of college, we got together in Glasgow for a couple of beers. We met at Dennis's sisters home, Janice and Steve Lawrence, in Glasgow. We had a great visit for a couple of hours and that was the first time we had all been together since 1966. Dennis went into the Navy and retired after 20 plus years. Dan went into construction and has a business with his brother Jim. Dan and Judy moved from Glasgow to western Montana several years ago.

Dave took over and bought the ranch after his dad passed away. Dave had been welding in Malta and married Sue there. I stood up for them at their wedding. He built up the cow herd to about 70 mother cows. For a lot of years he, Sue and the kids would come down to help with our branding and in return we would help with his branding. Both Dave and I artificially inseminated our cows for a few years. I quit doing that as it took quite a bit of my time and I was farming more later so I went back to using bulls. Dave inseminated longer so he built his cow herd up with better genes. I started buying bulls from Dave and he was buying hay from me when he didn't have enough off of his place in dry years. He didn't have any irrigation access, so in dry years he didn't have much hay production. There were times when I would get a half a beef from Dave as he always had some beef on feed for butchering. Sue has been working at Valley View Nursing Home for maybe 20 years, so in a year or so she is going to retire. She has to drive 50 miles to work so she stays with one of her daughters in Glasgow some nights and when the roads are bad.

Adlore and Irene Bouchard bought the place that Dave lives on from Bill Trebas, Sr. Dave and Sue bought the place from Irene and they have the place paid off. In the last two years Dave and Sue sold off the cows last year and are leasing the grazing to neighbor Mark Bengochea. Dave has had Diabetes and it has affected his eyesight in one eye. He has to get shots in the eye every couple of months to renew the eyesight so he can see to drive. Dave and Sue still bowl in Nashua in the mixed league along with their daughters Melissa, Diane and other daughter Darla and her husband Kurt Shipman. Leroy Novak and I substitute bowl with them. They also have two sons Scott and James. Kurt and Darla have three children, Anthony, Jake and Darci. James and Kristi have three children, Brooke, David and Alexis. Scott and Melissa have three children Emily, Matt and Peyton. Diane and her husband Jared have a daughter, Kellan. Melissa has a son Liam. I am a substitute bowler for their team in the Tuesday night league at Vicks lanes in Nashua. Van and Linda Warren Dostert run the Vicks Lanes for many years. They were both a year younger than me at Nashua High School and I have been friends with them for years. They live at a beautiful house on Fort Peck Lake.

One day at the branding at my place we had quite a few people over to help. Dave, Sue and the kids were here at my branding. We were catching the calves by hand and Dave reached down to grab a back leg of a calf and it kicked right at that time. The sharp hoof caught Dave right between the thumb and pointer finger and the sharp hoof cut his hand open. It had to be stitched up by a doctor. So Sue took him to Glasgow to the doctor's office or maybe to emergency. By the time they got back we were done branding and the party had started. Somehow Dave missed out on the major party as we were drinking along the road and Dave and Sue ended up at the house with Patty and a few others. His hand healed up fine and I found out that my liability insurance was good as it paid the doctor bill.

Lois Lonnquist- "Fifty Cents an Hour"

If you have an interest in the Fort Peck Dam project, great information can be found on the "boom towns" and life for the people that worked on and near the project in 50 Cents an Hour by Lois Lonnquist. I recommend it to persons who are interested in local history, and even if you are not, you still might find the stories of the dam and the people who built it to be very interesting.

Betty Daniels Arneson- "Richland Dryland"

Another book that people might find interesting was written by my friend Jim Arneson's mother Betty. Betty lived in a beautiful old house on Pleasant Street in Miles City and Patty and I were guests there and were impressed with the beautiful old home. We didn't realize it at the time, but this house was right next to the apartment that Stacy lived in while going to Nursing School in Miles City. Betty's book is about family history and local lore in the pioneering days of Richland County.

A Moonshiner Friend

Grandpa had a friend, "Rawhide" Johnson, who lived just across the Missouri on the site where the Fort Peck Dam spillway is now. His real name was Louis Johnson. Jack Nickels Sr. told me there were two Louis Johnsons in the area! The other Louis Johnson was Jack's father-in-law. Before the dam days and the spillway construction had been started, Rawhide had a rowboat and would come over to the north side of the river to go to Nashua to get provisions. The road came through Grandpa's yard, up the hill near the house and then was five miles to town. There were times that Grandpa would take him into town as he did not have a horse on this side of the river. I am sure they always had a good time because Grandpa liked to drink, and so did Rawhide. We heard later from reputable sources that old Rawhide had a still hidden out in a coulee over in McCone County somewhere. I also had heard this same information from another man that had been known in the past to himself distill spirits from grain.

A story my dad tells about Rawhide is that one time he came up to the house on his way to Nashua. Dad really like Rawhide. Dad had a candy bar and sliced it into small slices, except about a third of the bar that he was going to save for later. He told Rawhide to take a piece, and Rawhide took the largest piece and ate it! Dad said he was almost devastated that most of his bar was gone. Rawhide sure chuckled at Dad's reaction! On the return trip back from Nashua, Rawhide had a whole bag of chocolate candy for Dad. By the time he had finished that bag of candy, Dad was so sick of chocolate that he did not eat any for a long time.

One year, Rawhide had an excess of potatoes from his garden. My Grandparents and Rawhide went over to his garden and dug a large amount of potatoes. They put the potatoes in the rowboat and they all started over to the north side of the river. Dad was fairly young and the river was smooth but the boat was overloaded with all of them and the potatoes. While Rawhide was rowing, Dad put his fingers on the edge of the boat, and he could feel the water with his extended fingers. Rawhide told Dad that if they did not rock the boat that they would be okay. It was almost dark when they got to the Valley county side of the river. He visually lined up to trees from the other side of the river, to guide him to a downed tree that he used to tie up the boat. He rowed alongside this tree and he said "Marion to reach out and grab the rope". In the darkness, Grandpa could not see it, but the rope was there and easy to reach. Grandpa had his team and a wagon nearby to put their spuds in and go home. Rawhide rowed himself back to his house across the river in the darkness.

Loren Musgrove's story (with some help from Harold Brown) about Bob Jackson and the Trotter boys

Loren had told me this story many years ago about a situation that had happened at the Park Grove Bar back in the early 60's when he was at the bar having a beverage. I could not quite remember the details of the story that Loren told, but I had some help with the details. Years later, I was talking to Harold Brown at the bar, since he had come back for the party that Larry DuBeau had thrown celebrating thirty years of his owning the Park Grove Bar and Cafe, which was in May of 2012. Larry and his wife Fritzie (Bondy) had purchased the bar from Harold and Erma Brown. I asked Harold if he remembered the story about when Mick Trotter was taking the railroad ties out of Bob Jacksons pickup for a joke. Harold looked kind of sheepish at me and said, "I was involved in it".

This is how Harold told the story.

Tony Trotter was always was a jokester. He and his brother Mick pulled up to the bar and seen a lot of posts in the back of Bob Jackson's pickup. Many people will use rail road ties as fence posts, as they last quite a while the soil. He told Mick that they should unload the posts from the pickup and hide them in the borrow pit across from the bar to pull a joke on Bob. They figured that Bob might not even know that they were gone until morning. They went into the bar where Harold, Loren and Bob were having a drink and I think Erma Brown was bartending at the time all this was going down. The Trotter boys had a drink with them and then Mick and Harold went outside to take the posts. Tony was supposed to have another beer with Bob and keep him occupied. After a while, Tony walked over to the window and exclaimed "Bob, someone is taking your posts!" Bob jumped up and went outside and grabbed his 30-30 rifle not knowing who was stealing the posts as it was dark out. Harold said that Bob held the gun on them and made them carry all the posts that were across the road and put them back in his pickup. All this time Tony was chuckling and having another drink at the bar. Harold shook his head and said about Bob Jackson, "that damned Bob!!"

The best part of the joke was that Tony convinced his brother Mick to steal the posts, and then ratted him out to Bob Jackson. Those Trotter boys were always playing practical jokes on each other as well as many others.

Janice and Denny Shanks

I have already mentioned Billy, Bill Nicol, who has been a good friend for many years, and was part of my "rattlesnake taming" operation, but Punk and Maxine's daughter Janice and I have been classmates since first grade. Janice and her husband Dennis Shanks have been active in the community for many years and they pretty much started and ran the Nashua Winter fest that was sponsored by The Nashua Sleighers, which was a local snowmobile club and who promoted other winter activities. In the 70's the Nashua Jaycees and Jayceens took over the Winter Fest and it was always successful! There always was a huge turnout in Nashua for the two days of the fest and it helped out the local business quite a bit.

Janice and I were classmates and we graduated from Nashua in 1964. Janice and I were on the Nashua School Board together for the seven years. I was the board chairman for five years, but Janice continued on the board for several more years. We have always had a close class and have had a good turnout at reunions and mini reunions. I really appreciate the work Janice has done over the years for our class get-togethers, also have to thank Isabelle Hill Collins, another classmate and friend, for all the help for all the help organizing past reunions from where she now lives in Minnesota (but had lived in Branson Missouri for several years). Janice and Maxine have always helped by being on the Nashua Reunion Committee for the All-School Reunions every five years. We just had another fun and successful reunion in the summer of 2016 and our next one will be in 2021.

Dennis retired after about 43 years from the Montana State Roads Department. They had a retirement party for him and I wrote a poem for him in about two days and planned on reading it at the party but we arrived late and I chickened out and just gave it to Janice. The party was at the Ridge Runners Club in Glasgow. This is a beautiful, huge log building where many functions are held from the roping and ranching community, and also other local community events, such as wedding receptions and fundraisers. I do not see them as much as I used too but we are still good friends and they keep busy visiting their children and grandchildren in the Dakotas.

Here is the poem I wrote for Denny's Retirement …

An Ode to Dennis and His Retirement Blues

Denny and Janice are friends of mine,
    I've known them for a while
And thinking of retirement
    Even makes me pause and smile

But Denny, now that your works all done
    There's nothing you can do
I can't even imagine now
    What's in store for you

And even though you've lost that list
    I'm sorry, but it's true
The women, they never forget
    The list of the honey-doooo!

Back in the old days'

Together we drank a few
It was January and cold
And the Winter-Fest was new

You and Jan helped start it
For all of us kids
Some were young and some were old
And some of us were on the skids

It was a great time for all
And the sleds were really loud
With the sleighers, businesses, Jaycees and friends
Winter-Fest really made us proud

And forgetting Poland on the track
After the sleds were done racing
We'd thought he was in the bar
But we found him on Pete's, cold and a pacing

And now that you're retired
And just don't know what to do!
You will have to find something right away
Or go back to the lost list of the honey-doooo!

To the shop or Bergies
Or have a can of brew
Or coffee it up with the bunch
And gossip it up with the crew

Maybe riding, fishing, haying or hunting
This has happened to a few
That's a whole lot better
Then the Hell of the honey-doooo!

Or you can go and get some cows

It only takes a few
And then you can fence till dark
As if you were on the crew

Gosh! Maybe it doesn't sound so bad!
To find that lost list of the honey-doooo!

One afternoon I was talking to Dennis and Janice Shanks when they were out at our place for a visit and some hunting. We were talking while they were watching their two grandsons while their daughter Janelle, who is my son Seth's classmate, was hunting deer with her husband Troy, who was guiding her. The boys were climbing up into the playhouse fort at our place, while Dennis and Janice took turns watching the boys and visiting with me. Dennis was walking around the other side of the fort and Janice reminded me of how much of a redneck Dennis could be. Janice asked me if I had heard the "coon huntin'" story about Dennis. I said yes but could she tell it again. Janice started telling me the yarn!

One night during a past summer they were in bed and Dennis could hear a raccoon rattling the pet dishes out on the front porch. He jumped out of bed and grabbed the shotgun and headed out the front door to shoot it. Janice followed him out the door with her camera (she almost always has a camera) and was about to take his picture when she noticed that he was standing out there in "the buff". She said she could not take a picture of him like *that,* although I think she was tempted to! Anyway, he could not see enough to shoot accurately as it was dark out. To solve that problem, the next day he taped a flashlight on the barrel of the gun just in case the coon came back!! A couple of days later, the critter came back in the middle of the night and Dennis jumped out of bed and made the mad dash to the front door with gun in hand and the flashlight on. Janice was following in his footsteps with her trusty camera and beings Dennis had his shorts on this time, she snapped a picture of his backside as he was trying to get a shot off. I am a redneck too and I can only imagine in my mind what this whole scenario looked like!

A few minutes later, back at our place after Jan had told the story on Dennis, Janice went to look over the old riverbank to see if the hunters were in sight and Dennis told me a story about Janice. I kind of think Dennis sensed that Jan had told the "coon huntin'" story about him and so it was payback time. Anyway, he told the story about Janice at a dance in Nashua at the civic center. I guess Janice was trying to take a picture of someone and she had to get the shot just right and she was backing up and tripped over a chair leg and fell flat on her back. She was just sitting up and trying to get everything back in place when Johnny Bellon rushed over and started to help her up. She exclaimed to him to "wait", as she was more concerned with trying to get her wig turned around and back on the right place on her head than getting up off the floor. I think Johnny had seen her predicament and was trying to get her up with her hair all tousled up. Wow!

Oh, by the way, Janice said Dennis got the raccoon and since Janice was following Dennis around with her camera in the middle of the night, they both may have caught a cold!

John Bellon

Johnny is about as close to a real character as you will ever find! When you talk to him, you will end up laughing. He is about like his dad, Henry who had a nickname, "ol' bellering Bellon". He was an old irrigated and dryland farmer and retained a German accent so that when he wanted help he would holler, "Yonneeee". You could hear him hollering a long way away while trying to get Ingrahm and Johnny to help him. Ingraham was Johnny's brother and he was quite a character, too! John is two years older than me and I remember him at school functions as he was always goofing off!

John and I were in the Army National Guard together even though he joined up a year or so before me. Wayne Hill was also a national guardsman and he and John were good friends. They had left for basic training and tank training at Fort Knox, Kentucky a few months before I had to go! At the time, when Ron Kalinski, another guy from Glasgow, and I were sent to Fort Knox, I had forgotten that they were also at training somewhere in Kentucky.

After about 4 weeks of tough training at the basic training camp the company had a Physical Training (PT) contest between companies at Fort Knox. I and a few others did well on our PT test and were rewarded with a weekend off to go to Louisville. A friend of mine, Ace Danes, who was from Billings and I took the bus to town. We had gone to a couple of bars and I heard a raucous voice that sounded familiar. I looked over and there was Bellon and Hill! We went over to see them, and I could not believe how much weight they had lost since the last time I had seen them in Nashua. They both looked like they were wrestlers, like on television. John's shoulders were twice as wide as his hips. I bet Wayne had lost 50 pounds. We had a couple of beers and then I found out from them that this was their last day in Kentucky and they were getting on the train for Montana in the morning. I was so down because I had three more months of training before I could go home! I was happy for them, kinda, and maybe a little jealous!

Timber Creek Bill Anderson, Ron and Rose Stoneberg, Jason and Sierra Holt, Bob and Sylvan Walden

Along time local rancher in the south Hinsdale countryside was Bill Anderson, known to many locals as Timber Creek Bill. He lived his whole life about 50 miles south of Hinsdale/Saco area, and this ranch is known both as the Anderson Ranch and as The Horse Ranch. He passed away on the ranch several years ago from an accident trying to heat the house with a small generator during a bad snowstorm in a tough winter. He was a real cowboy and lived his whole life without electricity. I remember meeting him while going to his ranch house to get permission to hunt with my Father and Grandfather, maybe fifty years ago. He was a real horseman and spent a lot of time on a horse. I also remember seeing him in Glasgow when Loren Musgrove was with me, as they were old friends, and I got reintroduced to Bill at that time. In the old days he and Loren rode together for the Etchart

Ranch, I believe. One day about 20 years ago, I remember seeing him on the Timber Creek Road. Smutz and I had found some elk sheds and we tied them on the handlebars of my four-wheeler in the back of my pickup for a joke. We had put a tarp over the ATV with the antlers sticking out. We were stopped glassing for game off the side of the road. Bill happened to be near by and he drove up to look at the elk. After looking and seeing the ATV under the tarp he said to us, "So that's the deal." I always enjoyed visiting with him as he was a real cowboy character.

I have known Timber Creek Bill's daughter Rose and her brother McKey (or McKee?) Anderson since we met at 4H camp at the Pines Youth Camp when we were younger. I am not sure how to spell his name, but it's pronounced Muh-Key. He, Rose and another sister are still part owners in the ranch.

I got to know Rose, and her husband Ron Stoneberg, better when we started the Valley Resource council back in the 1970's. At that time, we helped stop a Corps of Engineer project which would have put a reregulation dam on the Missouri River and would have taken some of our property. I got to meet Ron when he was a biologist with Montana Fish, Wildlife and Parks. Rose is a veterinarian and they raise cattle on Timber Creek south of Hinsdale on The Horse Ranch. They have been very active trying to keep free ranging bison from being turned loose on the CMR and neighboring BLM lands. They also have been active trying to keep their water rights and other neighbors water rights from being taken by the CMR water compact. Ron is originally from Canada but moved to Missoula for college. He jokes that got two Master's and a Mrs!!! The ranch they live on gets its electric power from wind or solar sources and one day when I was out to their place to visit, Rose joked that the wind was blowing that day, so she could make some coffee! Ha!

Ron and Rose have two daughters, Sierra and Sylvan, and both of them are involved in the ranching industry.

Jason Holt is also an active member of the CMR NWS local working group who I met a couple of years ago. He has a doctorate in mathematics. He is now a cattleman on The Horse Ranch, which is 50 miles south of Hinsdale, along with Ron and Rose Stoneberg, and his wife, Sierra. Sierra Stoneberg Holt is now an associate supervisor with the Valley County Conservation District and is very helpful to the district for her work on the water rights Compact on the CMR and the free roaming bison issue. She has a doctorate in Botany and she majored in range management. She is the daughter of Ron and Rose Stoneberg and they all live on the Anderson ranch, which could be affected by a large neighboring ranch which has been sold to the American Prairie Foundation (APF) for possible bison grazing in the near future. I believe in the last year or two, Jason and Sierra have moved into Hinsdale to make it easier for their children to attend school in Hinsdale.

Bob Walden and Sylvan live on a ranch out south of the Fort Peck Dam spillway in McCone County. They are currently ranching on the Walt Collins place. Sylvan is the daughter of Ron and Rose Stoneberg and was featured on the cover of Montana Woman magazine and was featured in an article Western Horseman magazine. Sylvan has degrees in range science and animal science. Bob is a Montana brand inspector and is stationed at the Glasgow Livestock Sales Company in Glasgow. They run cattle and train horses for their ranch work and their children are currently going to school in Nashua.

Timber Creek Bill and his brother Jack attended the Lone Pine School, which was about 11 miles, by horseback, away from the ranch. The Lone Pine School had a dormitory so the children could stay there from Monday until Friday.

Larry Potter

Several years ago, I was driving into Nashua to the Ag-land gas station and I seen a guy walking down the sidewalk toward the B&B grocery store. He was wearing a cowboy hat and I am pretty sure he had cowboy boots on! I waved like I do to most people I know, and he waved back. I kind of stared thinking he maybe was someone that I had met before. I took care of business in town and I went home. The next time I went to Nashua, I seen the same gentleman and he went into The Vicks Bar. After I picked up my supplies and put diesel fuel in my tank in the back of my pickup, I stopped at Vicks to have a beer and I ordered a beer and I went over to the cowboy and introduced myself. He said that he was new in town and his name was Larry Potter! I told him I knew a man by that name who had passed away a couple of years ago. He said he had heard that before and then he said, "I guess I am the live Larry Potter". I chuckled to myself. I have all found out that he has quite a sense of humor! My wife Patty works Friday and Saturday afternoons at Vicks as a bartender and she said that Larry and Robyn had been in during her shift and she really liked them! Robyn's daughter wanted some sagebrush, so the four of us went down by the river near my irrigation pump to cut down some fragrant sagebrush. It was a beautiful day and we barbecued some burgers and had a great time!

They had moved here from Colorado to be closer to her daughter that was living in the area. Larry was remodeling a small house that they had bought in Nashua. He has since become the maintenance man for the town of Nashua, and he has done an excellent job. One day while I was visiting with him, I had mentioned that when we go out archery elk hunting, we go by The Pines! He said that he didn't know that there were any pine trees in this area. Patty and I said we could take them out to The Pines Recreation Area. Larry said that he missed the smell of the pine trees! That fall, sadly, we didn't get a chance to take them out there. During this last winter Robyn got sick and suddenly passed away! She was well liked by the community and with her BLM workers in the Glasgow office. Everyone that knew her misses her very much. That next spring, I stopped into Larry's house and said, you want to go to the pines? While driving out there he said the area we were driving through looked like an area in Nebraska which had rolling hills and sagebrush. Later on down the road he said it looked like Eastern Colorado. When we drove into the Pines, Larry had a big grin on his face.

We had a great time and we had a beer by the Fort Peck Lake and talked about Robyn and the pine smells. Larry said if she had come out here, she probably would have wanted to go back to her home state of Colorado!

On the way back, I took Larry through the Pines Cabin area to see some of the houses. On the way in a homeowner had waved and he looked familiar. On the way out I seen that it was Bruce Riggin whom I had hunted with from the South Country archery elk camp from several years ago. He invited us in and showed us his very nice cabin. His very best room is his bedroom where he can glass, with his binoculars, across a finger of the lake to watch the elk. We had a beer and enjoyed the view that he had!

When Patty comes back from working at the bar, she will say that Larry says to tell me, "Hey". He is a good friend of mine and many others too!

Some stories written down and given to me from Ken Bales:

- Kirk Stanley was a neighbor of the Bales. He lived about three miles above Fort Peck Dam.

- Dave Francis had a place where the Fort Peck Dam is located now.

- John Ferguson owned and operated a ferry by Old Fort Peck.

- Ken used to look around for artifacts at the old Fort Peck Trading Post.

- The Bales went to school at third point and their teacher was Ruth Putz. In later years this short red-haired lady would become the Valley County Superintendent of Schools and hold the position for many years. She was a writer and authored some published articles. Ken was good friends with Ruth and they wrote back and forth some after the Bales went to Indiana.

- Later on Ken worked construction in California and later returned to Western Montana to retire.

- D Stockton was a rodeo rider and Ken thought he was a nephew of Bert Delay.

- Leo Hatcher had a ferry below Fort Peck and he got in a fight with a person that owned another river ferry. Leo lost an eye in the fight and his ferry burned up later!

- The Lismus Ferry was north of Duck creek and went over to the Haxby Point area.

- It was also reported by Ken Bales that a man by the name of Potts had a lot of land around Fort Peck.

- Ed Helland had a place and lived near the Bales.

- Joe Frazer owned Wheeler and Ken picked rocks and worked some for Joe at Wheeler.

- The McLeans, Gladys Aiken and Vern Booth lived close to the Bales farmstead.

- Pleas Pointer drowned while crossing the river.

Most of the Bales family returned back to Indiana in 1935 after they lost their large log house to the Fort Peck Dam project. This is where they had come from before they homesteaded in Montana. My father, Edgar Garwood, remembers meeting the Bales family on the new Fort Peck to Nashua road, now Highway 117, and visited with them as they were leaving their farm and going back to Indiana. This meeting took place at the Molly Stevens Hill and Dad being fourteen at the time does not know how his parents knew to meet them there or if it was just a lucky circumstance! There were no phones in this country in those days. Dad remembered later that Ken had ridden ahead to tell the Garwood family that the Bales family was moving away from eastern Montana because of the dam project!

The Fort Peck Game Range

I know that I dwell quite a bit on the subject about The Fort Peck Game Range and how I think the management of the area has gone astray! I have gone to a lot of meetings to discuss the future of The Charles M Russell Wildlife National Refuge (which is what the Fort Peck Game Range is now called) and how it is being managed by US Fish and Wildlife Service. I, and many other landowners, hunters and concerned citizens, helped with impact statements included in the Comprehensive Conservation Plan (CCP) and the Environmental Impact Statement (EIS). What bothers me a little, or maybe a lot, is the in the final draft of the CCP/EIS statement, is the history section of the CMR. While Lewis and Clark's journey is mentioned as being important to the area, there seems to be very little credit given to the many pioneers and homesteaders who had to give up their livelihoods and homes and ranches when the Federal government bought out their ranches at cut rate prices, or about the people who did not sell their land and lost everything when the reservoir filled up and covered their livelihoods with water. I know that the lake and dam has prevented flooding in later years and has provided a great recreation area for many, but I think that the names of these many people like George Nicol, Myron Brown and Ken Bales, and the many others that had to give up their places should have been mentioned by name. I personally knew each of these men and their fathers had to give up their homesteads and homesteading rights for Fort Peck Dam Project.

Each time that US Fish and Wildlife service completes a CCP/EIS and it seems like they have an agenda in mind. It seems to me like each new plan has questionable promotion and betterment of the locals, at least as far as access to the area is concerned. The ranchers, farmers and local citizens in the six county area around the Fort Peck Lake seem to lose more than they gain. Who knows what the true agenda is for the CMR: The Big Open, Buffalo Commons, or a large Wilderness area with no roads. Possibly even a National Park designation. I once asked Barron Crawford, the former CMR Manager, why we cannot just leave the CMR as it has been managed for the last 15 years? He answered! "So we can move on" but I am honestly not sure what he meant when he said that. Move on from what?

Every 15 or 20 years, a new impact statement is released, which effects management of these public access lands. It seems like each time there is a new statement, people lose a little more ease of access to these lands, and at many meetings it seems obvious that the wildlife of the focus of the management program, and people and cows are further down on the list. I am not sure when the next statement will come out, there was one in the early 80's and one in 2012. It might be years before there are more changes made, or it might happen more quickly. I worry what those changes might mean for the locals around the lake.

James B. Kurz and Daisy from Wisconsin

It was in about August of 2005 when I was checking out my border fences along the Missouri River and I looked over toward my irrigation pump and I saw some movement near it. I could see that it was some sort of boat or canoe and I thought that it probably was a river floater or a fisherman. We get a lot of canoe floaters that put in near Fort Peck and they canoe down to the School Trust Fishing Access Site which I maintain as a caretaker for Montana Fish, Wildlife and Parks. I am used to people canoeing down river. But this canoe was coming upriver, as opposed to down river, with a black dog running alongside. I was just amazed, and I decided to wait until he came closer to visit a moment with this energetic individual. It is easy to float down river, but quite a bit of work to fight the current and push upriver. I figured this was possibly someone from a few miles down the river or from the Fishing Access Site, which is just down river from where my pump site. He came to the shore and we started visiting. When I found out that Jim was from Wisconsin and had paddled all the way up to here, I really was flabbergasted! We visited for a half an hour or so talking about adventures he already had on this canoe trip, about the Lewis and Clark Expedition and some about the history of this area. He told me about climbing up Signal Hill the evening before and how a thunderstorm had caught him and he got wet. This was the same hill Clark climbed up on in 1805 to get a birds-eye view the area, including the Milk River and the Missouri River, which was up ahead of them. From this observation point you can see the curvaceous Milk River and Porcupine Creek that flows from the North Country into the Milk. This is how Nashua was named, the meeting of the waters. The Lewis and Clark leaders had thought that this creek was possibly a river that came all the way from the Canadian country, which England had control of at the time.

While we sat on the riverbank and visited, Daisy, Jim's dog, and my dog Maxine, or Max as we usually call her, ran and played in the pasture. The dogs were both black and about the same size and they had a great time running together. Interestingly enough, Lewis had a large black dog, a Newfoundland, named Seaman who traveled with them on their expedition and I always thought it was pretty neat that Jim was making the same journey with his own black dog, while I had my faithful black dog/companion at myside when we met.

I asked Jim if he had thought about writing a book about the adventure and he said something about how he just did not know. He asked me how far it was to Fort Peck and I told him and also told him to stay on the North bank of the river because somewhere along the north side of the river was a possible campsite of the Lewis and Clark Expedition. We had a great visit, but eventually Jim had to move on and I had work to do. A few hours later I started baling hay and the next morning I stacked the bales and started the irrigation pump to water the fields that I had just hayed.

Two days later, I got a call from Ron Bondy, a man who lived in Park Grove, who told me that he had met Jim and that he was staying at a campground near Fort Peck. I had some free time and I checked some of the campgrounds out to see if I could find him and visit some more. He had visited the newly opened Interpretive Center, which was where Ron had met him. I did not find him at any of the campgrounds and he probably had left our area already as his plan had been to cross the lake and visit the Hell Creek State Park, which is on the south side of the lake. If you ask me, it is pretty darn impressive to cross that big water in a small canoe, although Jim's canoe was modified with an outrigger to help with stability of the vessel, but the water can still get really rough in only a little bit of wind. Jim had given me a postcard with his address, phone and e-mail. He had gotten some of these printed up in Wolf Point a couple of days before I met him. He had also written down my address and phone number although I did not have an e-mail address then. I did not hear anything more about him until I got a call from him later during the winter.

Late in the fall of 2005, with my daughter Stacy's encouragement, I purchased a computer. At first about all I could do on it was to reply to some e-mails. I am a redneck history lover and I never paid much attention to English and I never took any writing courses. I am not sure if I was as crazy about local and Montana history then, but I sure am now. About December of that year I got a call from Jim and he told me about the rest of his trip up to the Three Forks area and then he had met up his son and they paddled down the Yellowstone River, finishing the canoe trip at Williston, North Dakota. It was November and freezing weather, so they decided to end the canoe trip. He decided that a book was in his future and he asked me, and several of the people he came across on his journey, to write a chapter about our own sections of the river. He wanted to hear about some of our history and about the Lewis and Clark expedition as they traveled through our area.

I had just gotten my computer and I did not know if I could write anything, but I decided to give it a try. Stacy helped me to get started and I fumbled through my story. I was lucky that my spelling has always been good and thank God, for spelling and punctuation check, which I cannot seem to get to work right now!! Stacy!! Help!! I guess I should have paid a little more attention in English class! I know that maybe my classmates will say that I should have paid *a lot* more attention in English class. I learned most of my English in my freshman year from Erma Badt, and I thank my Montana History teacher, Loren O'Connor. The stories were a bit of a struggle to get down on the 'puter and I jumped around a lot but in a disorganized and redneck way, I got it finished. As a matter of fact, I almost got carried away! I am Norwegian, you know! And did I mention that I am a red neck? There are things that I do or say, that are just the way that I am, and I brag about them to people, to make a joke! Stacy one time said to me, "Dad, we know that you are a Redneck, but do you need to be so proud of it!!!"

Jim Kurz had finished his book, *We Were on the Missouri 2005*, and it came out in about 2006. I have had a lot of enjoyment, sense of accomplishment and pride after I wrote a chapter in his book. One of my classmates, Isabelle Hill Collins, said to me, "you are in print now". I have purchased several of Jim's books, thirty or so, from Jim and I sell some or give some to my friends and relatives. I do not know about my being in print, but the process has gotten me started writing a little more, and I really enjoy it! Izze has been very supportive of me in my writing and I thank her very much for her confidence in me.

About my redneck way of writing, she says, "that's just your writing style". Whatever that means! It seems that I have been writing on this book for about three years total time and due to a delay in editing, working on it for about seven years now.

Jim Kurz authored another book on this amazing canoe trip called *Out My Backdoor*, and I wish him the best on it. This book has been written by him about the trip and it has many pictures of the trip in it. He has a CD of pictures in each of these two books that have many color pictures of the trip that I think is worth the cost of each book. I have talked to Jim in the past and he has been helpful to me in my own writings and authoring my own book.

Jim had taken another canoe trip up into Canada a couple of years ago and the following spring he wrote another book on this trip and had just sent it off to the printer. I do not know what the name of this most recent book that he has written, but I will be sure to read it when I get a chance. It is called *Navigating North* and it is about a canoe trip from Wisconsin and into Ontario.

I have to thank Jim Kurz for asking me to write a few stories for his book and getting me into writing. I really have enjoyed the Redneck writing way that I do, and I apologize to those who can really write!! All I can say is that I call it "Ron's Ramblings", or maybe "Ramblings of a Redneck!"

Verlin Borgen, with his Bronco at the Murray Camp, one of our bases when hunting. We have spent many a fall hunting season at this location, which was made available to hunters by the Wittmayer Grazing Association District.

The postcard that I received from Jim Kurtz that was the reason I ever started writing stories down. The first was for his book and that interest evolved into this book of stories that I am happy to share with anyone who is interested.

CONCLUSION

(the end, for now)

"It's not the years in your life that counts. It's the life in your years."
- Abraham Lincoln

"Courage is what it takes to stand up and speak, it's also what it takes to sit down and listen."
-Sir Winston Churchill

The Fort Peck Dam on the Missouri River

There is no perfect answer for the best management of a reservoir that was created by man, that nature never meant to exist. There will never be a perfect answer, because man cannot completely control mother nature, and to some extent the people that depend of the waters of the Missouri for survival, the people that use the river and lake for recreation, and the people that are charged with managing the waterway, will always be slightly at odds.

The 2011 Missouri River High Water Event

I feel that the lake was probably too high the spring of 2011 for a lot of reasons that I will not get into now. But I do feel that some of the later flooding could have been avoided if the lake would have been as low as it was a couple of years before, which was during a major drought in eastern Montana. Of course, it is unrealistic for the lake to be incredibly low without a drought, but perhaps there needs to be some middle ground, so there is room for the lake to fill up in times of need. Anyway, in 2011, the lake was already quite high and so there was very little or anything the Corps of Engineers could do with all the water flooding the streams and rivers in the spring, upriver of Fort Peck Dam. The water level in the dams downriver on the Missouri River were also high, which impacted those areas and eventually, when the spring melt came, they lost their flood control protection, just like Fort Peck did.

What complicated the highwater event near my farm was that the Milk River was also at near record flood levels, and being it was only one mile below the spillway and my farm, these high water flows also impacted the Missouri River. Between the high flow from the power houses, the spillway being open, and the back up from the Milk River, it caused the Missouri to rise at least ten feet in elevation at my pump sites. A lot of people had their farms and houses flooded down river from the confluence of the Milk and Missouri rivers, and that was a shame! Honestly, we were lucky that only our pump sites and erosion to the river banks were the worst damage that we personally received. But can you imagine what it would have been like if Fort Peck Dam would not have been there? We would have had a major flood event on our property, and no control at all, and hundreds of others in addition to the people who were already affected! I am so thankful that we have the dam here to help with flood protection!

I think if it was not for the dam, the flooding on the river would have been much, much worse, both here at my place and at my Dads' farm. An interesting fact is that, after the dam was built and the reservoir started to fill, the water of Fort Peck Lake is at least two-hundred feet over our heads here. My Dad never liked it when the reservoir was full, but people who use the reservoir for recreation prefer the water high. I think that it is good thing that the Corps of Engineers is lowering the waters of the lake some, that way, when we have years of high water run-off from the mountains, the reservoir has some room to fill up before we get into such a high water predicament again.

The Flooding of the 2011 Milk, Musselshell and Missouri Rivers in Montana (in greater detail)

In the Spring of 2011, flooding was the theme for Valley County, as it was for many other areas of Montana. Record snow falls, both in the plains and the mountains, and high rain events inevitably lead to record run off of both minor and major waterways. This run off created flooding of small creeks, including the Porcupine Creek, Cherry Creek, Antelope Creek, Beaver Creek and many more that flow into the Milk River and then into the Missouri River.

The events that led to the eventual flooding of the Missouri are many. Part of the problem stems from the period of time when we had a 10 year long drought in Montana, which caused a decrease in water flow that impacted the lake water levels, which were very low for many years. Prior to this drought, the last time the Fort Peck Spillway gates had to be opened to allow high water out the lake was in 1997. Since then the combination of a 10 year long drought in the above stream areas of Fort Peck lake and too high of water releases through the turbines to generate power had caused the lake levels to go down. In about 2007 the level of the water on Fort Peck Lake was at an all-time low since the Fort Peck Dam was completed in 1940.

These low levels of water on the lake caused problems for many. These included problems for fisherman, who struggled to even get boats in the water, since the water had receded so far from boat ramps that access to the water was very difficult, and for Montana Fish, Wildlife and Parks, who needed access to the lake to do their annual walleye and northern pike egg retrieval from female fish that try to spawn in Fort Peck Lake (yes, I know it is a reservoir!).

The low water levels affected FWP management of the lake fisheries because the lake does not have very good areas that allow certain fish to spawn in, even if they spawn well in rivers. This is in part to the manmade lake itself, and to the nature of the fish, notably Walleye and Chinook Salmon, which are not native species, therefore Fort Peck is an unsatisfactory place to spawn. The survival rate for spawning is very poor in the lake without assistance. Therefore, Montana Fish, Wildlife and Parks have fish hatcheries in Miles City and Fort Peck that provide young hatchery fingerlings to other water bodies in Montana and other states. Therefore, they needed access to conduct their spring netting operations to collect eggs for spawning.

As mentioned, fisherman also had trouble getting access to the waters of Fort Peck Lake to put in their boats since the water had receded so far from the majority of the boat ramps on the lake. In some places, the boat docks were hundreds of feet from the actual water. There are only so many numbered roads in the Charles M Russell National Wildlife Refuge, which entirely encompasses the Fort Peck Lake. You can only access the waters for your boats on numbered roads that go to the lake, so the low waters of the lake from about 2006 to 2009 put many boat ramps so low that they were not usable. Of course, this lack of access increased the demand for change. There were many recreationalists and businessmen in the area wanted the lake full, or at least high enough to be accessible, which of course makes sense. This helps fishing and recreation and the local economy, which everyone can support, as we all wish to thrive in this country side we love.

The waters of Fort Peck had been low for so long that the mud flats above the water level all around the lake ended up providing the perfect place for grass, weeds, and other vegetation to expand. A juniper looking weed which was an ornamental plant that was brought in for yards started taking over some of the lake shore. This plant is called Salt Cedar and in the years of low lake levels, it took over quite a bit of the lake shore and was becoming a real problem and was difficult for the Corps to control. Each year as the shoreline got lower, the Salt Cedar would have new seed being germinated and the weed was expanding. It was reported that inundation (flooding or high water) for a couple of months would kill the plant. Of course, the high water helped kill the Salt Cedar, so this might have been another reason for the Corps to keep the water level quite high. Other reasons to keep the water levels high, after being low for so long, is the grass and vegetation that grew when the water was low, now provided an excellent habitat for young fish to spawn, survive and grow, which was a benefit to recreation on the lake.

In the years prior to 2010-11, which was a record snowfall year, there had been several years of favorable high snowpack in the mountains above Fort Peck Dam, the level of the lake started to rise. Then in then in years from 2008 to 2010 the water level in the lake had come up about 12 feet per year. Because of the rising water levels most people were able to recreate on Fort Peck Lake as access had been restored to boat ramps and marina's all around the lake. However, a full lake leaves little room for increased water flow and limits the Corps ability for flood management, which became a problem in 2011.

Then in the spring of 2011 much of Montana had record snowfall which melted fast, combined with heavy rainfalls that came fast and hard and suddenly the lake, which was high to start with, was on the rise. The Musselshell and most all of rivers that flowed into the Missouri River above the Fort Peck were at record high levels and the lake got so high that the Corps of Engineers had to start releasing water through the spillway gates. At that same time the Milk River was flooding and reached a record high at several places, including at Saco, Hinsdale, Vandalia, Glasgow and Nashua. This flooding caused flooded farm and ranch land that adversely affected many people along the Milk River. The dike system that was built by the Corps of Engineers at Glasgow and Nashua and other towns along the Milk River proved their integrity, for the most part, and allowed these towns to escape major flooding, although the Corps worked very hard to build up and strengthen some areas of this dike system. The flooding from the Milk River along with the high levels of releases from Fort Peck Dam put the

Missouri River below the spillway at flood stage. Most of the dams below Fort Peck had above average water flowing into them as well, so there was a problem with how to let the water out of Fort Peck as safely as they could. It felt like a domino effect, with water being released, filling another reservoir, which caused the need to release water, etc, and effected every dam and reservoir along the Missouri River.

The Musselshell River was flooding its banks and twice flooded parts of the town of Roundup and all of this record high water flows were headed into the Missouri and therefore Fort Peck Lake. When the Corps decided to start releasing water from the spillway, they did it in stages to allow the residents that lived along the river time to prepare for the high water. They had releases from the spillway, first at 10,000 cubic feet per second (CFS) and notified the downstream residents that they would release another 10,000 CFS at a certain time and date so people could prepare the best that they could. These scheduled releases, which were well communicated to the pubic by the Corp of Engineers, were effective and really helped the people below the dam make a plan on how to best manage and protect their properties.

Every stream and river downstream of the spillway was flooding, so the river elevation was really an unknown and possibly under-estimated because of the flooding that was going on. The unknown was how these record releases, even in stages, would affect the elevation of the river or the erosion of the banks. At the highest release from the spillway, the flow was at 65,000 CFS, which was a record high for Fort Peck spillway gates. This was the highest amount of water flowing down the river since the completion of the dam in 1940.

Because the flooding Milk River was only a mile down river from the spillway, this caused the Missouri River to raise even more and back upriver. I have a pump site about two and a half miles upstream of the spillway. The Corps of Engineers had reported that when they had to start releasing water from the spillway, that the level in the river could raise about 10 feet above the then river level. I had checked out my pump and I figured that a 10 feet rise would put the water level a little under my electric motor and pump. I kind of figured that my pump site would be okay. As the spillway was opened a little every few days this gave us time to watch over our property. I kept watching the pump site every day to monitor the river level. The river was coming up about one and a half feet for every 10,000 CFS release.

Finally, the water level was up to only about a foot below my electric motor one evening and the next day was scheduled for another release of water. I decided to not take any more chances and I went and got my loader tractor and pulled the motor and left the pump as it was still hooked to the pipe that goes up to the elevated ditch. I did hook the chain from the pump to the pole just in case. The next day the water level was touching the pump and a few days later it would have been up to the middle of the motor and I would not have been able to have got it out. I lucked out and got the motor out in time. I would like to thank the Corps of Engineers for keeping us informed of the releases from the spillway.

Terry Kincannon, who has a house on the river at Idlewild, (another place name left over from the Fort Peck Dam Boom towns) said that at his place he could see a line in the river where he figured the river had backed up to. I figure the combined water from the spillway and Milk River flow backed water up the river at least 6 miles. It is just amazing that it could back over three rapids and six miles to do that.

I have lived all of my life below the Fort Peck Dam, with probably an average of 200 feet of water over my head where we live on my farm. From my Dad's farm, which is a mile further away from the dam, you can see the spillway and the vehicles driving across the top of the road on Highway 24. The concrete spillway, which lies below the spillway gates, is one mile long down to the river and my house is about two miles (as the crow flies) from the lower end of it. Though I am unable to see the spillway from my home, it is very noisy when the spillway gates are open and flowing water is coming down. This high lake water and the flooding event has opened a lot of eyes and even though we thought we were protected from flooding, we have to realize that we still live in a flood plain, and I have not even started building my Ark yet! The Fort Peck dam has proved to us living below the it that it is very stable. It is very sobering however to realize that even with the dam, we still need to be aware that the river can affect us!!

Many people in Valley County were affected by the high water of the flood year of 2011, along the Milk River, the Missouri River and the many creeks that feed them. Many people lost homes and livestock. There were people stranded either away from their homes for several months or some stranded in them. Many families lost crop and pasture land to the water, and with all of this, they lost income, their livelihood, and are still trying to recover. The flooding along the Missouri might have been of a different nature than the Milk, but still affected the people that live along it, with pasture land and fields being lost for a time, pump sites out of commission, damaging erosion of the river banks, and much property threatened and some lost.

When the water was high against the face of the Dam, many rumors abounded in the area. Many people said they heard "the Dam is cracking" or "shifting", or "it is going to give out" or "it is starting to slide" and many other such things. Of course, this did not happen!! The Corps of Engineers had their 75th anniversary of the Fort Peck Dam the summer of 2012. The year prior, with the lake level at a record high for about three months total proved the integrity and the safety of Fort Peck Dam.

We learned a lot from that flood season. We learned that the dam held up, as it had in the past when the lake has been high, we learned that the bottom of the spillway needs a little more shoring up, where all of the water was crashing down, it had a greater impact on the concrete and the river bed than many had though it would. We learned that all of the turmoil on the river created some darn good fishing! We learned that ultimately, as much as we feel protected in this day and age, Mother Nature is still in control and is going to give us a run for our money, and we just need to do the best we can.

Now, the summer of 2018 and the spring of 2019...

Last year in 2018 there was an abundance of snowpack in the mountains above the Missouri River. The Fort Peck Lake was fairy full and there was an abundance of water coming down the Missouri River into the lake. The Corps decided to open some of the spillway gates to lower the lake as the powerhouse tunnels were at maximum capacity and the water in the lake was rising and the elevation of the water was nearing full capacity. The spillway gates remained open, with small flows most of the summer, to relieve the pressure of a full lake. The Corps does not like an almost full lake, (and neither do I as I live below the lake), as they lose flood control if there is a major rain or snow event in the upstream area. The spillway gates being open did not seem to hurt much except for a small area river bank erosion, which is near my father's pump site. The event caused a lot of fish to migrate up the Missouri River to the spillway area as there was an abundance of forage fish coming down into the river from the lake. From our farm it was really neat, as it sounded like a waterfall at times when the wind was right or there was no wind. It was really kind of soothing sitting on the deck and listening to it. They spilled water until about December so there was a build up of ice in the low areas along to river. The Corps needed to get rid of the excess water in the lake to have room for the spring runoff. The flood year in 2011 taught us all lessons in how to best try manage the Mighty Mo!

The winter of 2018-19 there was above normal snowpack in the plains and the mountains so there was an abundance of water coming into the lake. If the lake would not have been lowered during the 2018 year, there probably would have been much more flooding in the Missouri River basin than there is going on now in April of 2019. Time will tell about the impact on the Missouri with the rest of the spring and summer, as much of the mountain snowpack has not melted yet.

Already this spring, the Milk River, which flows into the Missouri River below the dam, has been flooding in many areas along the river, along with many streams flowing in to it. Roads are covered in water and some people are fording some of those crossings with tractors, just to get access to food and medical attention and to go to work. One local Glasgow boy even took a kayak to get to prom this last weekend!! The weather service had not predicted flooding in the spring of 2019, perhaps because there was an underestimate about the moisture amounts in our local snowpack as well as the frozen ground had not been considered. Anyway, there was more runoff from warmer weather than normal and the above normal snowpack from the plains and mountains, and it is early in the season. Time will tell how bad this flood season might be. Mother nature still is in control!!

CREDITS AND COMPLIMENTS

Compliments of The US Army Corps of Engineers, Draft AOP, Courtesy of the Corps of Engineers

We Were On The Missouri 2005, by James B. Kurz

Out my Backdoor, by James B. Kurz

Nashua Community History 1897-1977 The Way it Was, A Bridge Between Then and Now

Footprints in the Valley Volumes One, Two and Three

Richland Dryland by Betty Daniels Arneson

Fifty Cents an Hour by Lois Lonnquist

ABOUT THE AUTHOR

Ron Garwood was born on a cold winter night, or so his mother told him. He was raised on a farm south Nashua, Montana, near the confluence of the Milk and Missouri Rivers in rural Valley County. The farm started with a homestead in 1920 and the next year his grandparents migrated from Ohio and placed roots in northeastern Montana. The farm was added onto many times over the years, and the operation was continued by his own parents and still remains an active family operation. Along with his own farmland which he has acquired over the years, Ron is active in local conservation groups. Besides a love of farming and ranching, he has an interest in wildlife, being an outdoorsman and exploring the countryside right out his back door. He has an interest in the history of the area and the characters that have called this area of rural northeastern Montana home.

This picture was taken of me by my daughter a couple years ago when we went to Slippery Ann Wildlife Viewing Area to watch and listen to the elk bugle in the fall. It is a pretty amazing experience and I would recommend that people take the opportunity if they ever have the chance.